Engineering Your WRITING Success

How Engineers Can Master Effective On-The-Job Communication Skills

James E. Vincler & Nancy Horlick Vincler

Professional Publications, Inc. • Belmont, CA

Production Manager: Aline M. Sullivan
Project Editor: Jessica R. Whitney
Copy Editor: Jessica R. Whitney
Book Designer: Charles P. Oey
Typesetter: Cathy Schrott
Illustrator: Charles P. Oey
Proofreader: Kate Hayes
Cover Designer: Charles P. Oey

ENGINEERING YOUR WRITING SUCCESS

Printed in the United States of America

Professional Publications, Inc.
1250 Fifth Avenue, Belmont, CA 94002
(415) 593-9119

Current printing of this edition: **1**

Library of Congress Cataloging-in-Publication Data
Vincler, James E. (James Edward), 1941–
    Engineering your writing success: how engineers can master effective on-the-job communication skills / James E. Vincler & Nancy Horlick Vincler.
        p.   cm.
    Includes bibliographical references and index.
    ISBN 0-912045-90-6 (perfect bound)
    1. Technical writing.   2. Communication of technical information.
    I. Vincler, Nancy Horlick, 1943–   .   II. Title.
    T11.V55   1996
     808'.0666--dc20   95-47941
                                                                            CIP

Dedication

We dedicate this book to the thousands of engineers who have attended our writing workshops. We learned a lot from you.

Table of Contents

Acknowledgments

Lots of people helped us with this book by contributing ideas, knowledge, and information. Our only fear is that we may have forgotten to mention one of you. Thanks for your help.

Dan Amey, E. I. duPont de Nemours & Co.

Steven Ashley, *Mechanical Engineering Magazine*

Susan Stewart Baldwin, The Hoffman Agency

Gene Bella, Westinghouse Electric Corp.

Avery and Judy Blake, Media Merchants

Linda Jay Brandt, Editorial Services

Ronald W. Budd, Hughes Space & Communications

Joseph Clark, Walter Mathews, and Rose Eufinger, Mathews & Clark
    Communications

Julie Clarke, Scitor Corporation

Mary C. Currie, Golden Gate Bridge, Highway and Transportation District

Joe Fowler, Cirrus Logic Inc.

Rick Gilbert, Frederick Gilbert Associates

William W. Hague, Media Sales Associates

Bob Hanz, Altera Corporation

Warren Hausman, Stanford University

Penny Hill, Hill Associates

Ned Himmel (and Kit Wilson and other reference-desk staff), Redwood City (CA)
    Public Library

Marian Hirsch, Consulting Writer

Richard L. Horlick, Armco Inc. (retired)

Sarah Lahey, Vincler Communications, Inc.

Phil Lenihan, Cahners Publishing Co.

Mike Lyons, Potrero Management Partners

Billie Markim, Sun Microsystems, Inc.

Antje McNaughton, Altera Corporation
John Prendergast, *Civil Engineering Magazine*
Beverly Principal, Bernard Hodes Advertising
Mark Rosensweig, *Chemical Engineering Progress*
Jeffrey C. Smith, Integrated Device Technology, Inc.
Ernie Swanson, IBM Corporation
Roy Twitty, Twitty Associates
Phil Venuti, Hewlett-Packard Company
Claudia Winters, Sun Microsystems, Inc.
Janet Woodworth, Intel Corporation
Richard Zanetti, *Chemical Engineering Magazine*

Of course, we also thank the expert and warm-hearted team at Professional Publications, Inc. Project Editor Jessica R. Whitney and Proofreader/Composition Associate Kate Hayes took Post-It™ notes to new diplomatic heights. Senior Marketing Coordinator Catherine Bayer, Design/Composition Leader Chuck Oey, Composition Associate Cathy Schrott, and other production staff helped to round out PPI's capable "can-do" crew that brought this book to you.

Unless otherwise noted, quotations used in this book are in the public domain.

Preface

This book is for the working engineer whose rude awakening in life was learning that writing and presenting are part of an engineer's job.

We understand the problem, and we're here to help.

Of all the jobs you do as an engineer, creating written and oral presentations is probably your least favorite. On-the-job writing consumes more time than you care to take. It's the one job you'd most like to jettison. After all, you studied engineering to engineer, not to write about it. In college, you may have avoided all communication classes except the absolutely required, if-you-don't-take-this-course-you-won't-graduate-and-may-face-a-firing-squad writing classes.

We understand. We felt the same about math.

Perhaps, though, you *enjoy* writing and presenting ideas for the world to see. You may view your document as the physical evidence of your efforts and results. You may like thinking through a problem, reviewing the project, recording your progress, or seeing your accomplishments down on paper.

Whatever your outlook, you realize that you can't escape on-the-job communication. A thriving business is lubricated by written and oral presentations. The greatest idea in the world is useless until it is communicated clearly.

This book will make your communication projects easier by slashing your writing time and simplifying your writing process so that you can better control your communication time and allow more time for your other priorities.

We based this book on our enjoyable and successful experience in helping thousands of engineers, through our workshops and individual coaching sessions, to ease the writing burden.

Before designing our writing training, we asked ourselves and some of our engineering friends, "Who, more than anyone else, shies away from writing?" You guessed it. So we decided to build courses for engineers. Our structural approach appealed immediately to the engineers' sense of logic.

Today, though we work with other business people as well, engineers are still among our favorite groups to train. Engineers usually come in with a positive, open-minded attitude. Once they see the logic of writing, they quickly become more confident communicators.

Logic is a key word in this book. You will learn how you can apply your analytical skills to the logic of writing and presenting. You'll learn time-tested methods for trouble-shooting any writing job. You will then have the tools to write quickly, clearly, and concisely—for faster results.

This book shows you how to plan and produce a professional-looking document or stand-up presentation without procrastinating. You'll also learn fast ways to decide which information is relevant or irrelevant, thus saving yourself a lot of valuable time.

Would you like to reduce your rewrites, have readers understand your message the first time, and receive fewer questions from your readers? This book will show you how. The techniques described in these pages will help you to:

▶ Slash your writing time.

▶ Explain your brilliant ideas lucidly and logically.

▶ Produce reports and proposals that bring results.

▶ Build confidence in your communication skills.

▶ Persuasively present your ideas to customers and top management.

In short, using the skills learned in this book, you'll become a better writer, a more confident presenter, and, in turn, a more productive engineer. You will find yourself using these new skills throughout your career.

Read This Introduction

Engineering Writing Versus Academic Writing

Engineering writing differs dramatically from academic writing.

In the engineering/business environment, you are not writing novels to entertain people; nor are you writing compositions to prove that you did your homework. If, like many engineers, you are having difficulty writing in a business environment, perhaps you're trying to apply your academic writing experience to your engineering writing. The problem is that your *readers* and your *purpose* have changed.

Readers of your engineering documents and readers of your academic papers differ in their knowledge of your subject. In college, your academic reports were written for a professor who (we hope) knew more about the subject than you did. Thus, your purpose in academic writing was to demonstrate knowledge of the subject.

Now that you are in the real world of engineering, your engineering activities are dedicated to commerce; your purpose for writing has changed because your readers have changed. Your readers, whether they have more or less education than you do, know less about your subject than you do. That's why you're writing to them—to tell them about something they don't know. Your purpose is not to *demonstrate* your knowledge, but rather to *share* your knowledge in a way that your readers can use it. This is a critical difference. *You want to share knowledge, not demonstrate knowledge.* If you don't recognize this difference when you move from academia to business, you'll still be writing college compositions, not engineering documentation. However, once you realize this difference between engineering and academic writing, you've taken the first step toward becoming a successful engineering writer.

The overall purpose of engineering writing is to *communicate information efficiently* to a reader who in some way will use that information. An executive uses a report to make a decision. A fellow engineer uses a report to design a circuit or a bridge or to understand a problem. A technician uses a procedure to operate some equipment.

Everything we tell you in this book is aimed toward helping you to communicate information efficiently. This book will help you realize, too, that writing and engineering are alike in many ways. That's why you can engineer a writing or speaking project successfully.

How This Book is Organized

The first chapter explains how you can use your innate sense of logic to become a good engineering writer. The second chapter shows you how to decide on your message. The next few chapters introduce the writing process, explain how to work *with* the process, and show you how to organize your writing projects quickly to reduce writing time.

Part Two moves logically through topics of words, sentences, and paragraphs.

Since sentences are the most intricate part of writing, we have divided their discussion into three distinct chapters. In the first two, you will learn the components of a sentence and how to build those components into meaningful patterns, including the powerful active-voice pattern. In the third, you will see how to use four different sentence structures for different logical purposes.

The chapter on paragraphs introduces you to multiple writing strategies to use for various writing goals. Part Two wraps up with tips for troubleshooting the common editing problems that plague engineering writers.

Part Three explains specific types of engineering documents, such as memos, letters, reports, proposals, procedures, data sheets, and articles.

Part Four tells you how to prepare and give a successful presentation by building on the skills you learn in Parts One, Two, and Three. The final chapter, on meetings, adds tips for producing better results in fewer meetings.

Having already worked with thousands of engineers in our writing seminars, we know that the guidelines in this book will help you, the professional engineer who probably doesn't like writing but knows that writing is a crucial part of the engineering job.

We enjoyed writing this book for you, and we sincerely believe that it will make all your writing projects a lot easier to handle.

Good luck and good writing.

PART ONE

Engineering Your Writing Success

I Discovering Your Natural Writing Talent

Ernie, an engineer, smiled as he tallied the final test results on his fuel-filter project. Most of the news was good. The test results had confirmed his theory. His idea was sound; it would work. Granted, he needed a bit more funding to verify his findings, but he figured he could justify his request for the added funds.

Slowly his smile faded. Ernie now had to write a report about his project and its results. He dreaded writing. To him, a report was merely a mopping-up operation. He would rather move on immediately to the follow-up project. But to get approval for the follow-up, Ernie had to document the results of the initial project. Aargh!

Where to start? Ernie stared at the ceiling, then out the window, then down at his test-results tally. He fiddled and fussed around and finally plunged into the job, feeling little confidence and a lot of trepidation. A week later, he emerged from his work cubicle with his report. Two days later, he was refused funding.

If you, like Ernie, dread writing your reports or you receive disappointing responses to them, here's help. Part One of this book will help you drain the dread, apply your logic to writing, and get the desired results from your readers. You will learn how to plan, write, enhance, format, and edit your messages to grab and persuade your readers.

How Better Writing Will Benefit You

When you design a product, system, or structure, you expect certain results. You want your product to function right, you want the system to run smoothly, or you want the structure to stand safely as enduring testimony to your talents. In other words, you want your efforts to succeed.

A well-engineered, successful design brings desired benefits. It may bring your company a contract win; may improve your team's chances for another contract from the same customer; or may earn you credibility, visibility, respect, a raise, or a promotion.

A writing project has to be engineered just like any other project. You have to plan, design, and construct a proposal or report. In short, you have to engineer. If your writing project is well engineered, it, too, can bring you many benefits. So let's talk about how to engineer a writing project, even when you dread starting it.

How to Approach a Dreaded Writing Job

You can approach writing one of two ways: haphazardly or logically. You can jump right in, without planning or forethought, and plow your way through a document—stumbling here, going off on a tangent there, getting bogged down in another direction, pulling yourself up and starting off on a new path, running into obstacles, bouncing off and careening down another trail, and eventually reaching the end. That's the haphazard approach.

Or you can plan ahead, put your thoughts in order, head toward a specific purpose with a specific reader in mind, and quickly finish the job. That's the logical approach. That's the engineering approach.

Perhaps you take the haphazard approach or one that's somewhere between haphazard and logical. Or maybe you start the job logically but still don't finish quickly. Whatever the case, these first few chapters will show you how to engineer your writing jobs logically—with less dread, more efficiency, and better results.

Your Logical Advantage

Since the logical approach is the most effective, you, as an engineer, already have an advantage: You understand logic. Perhaps an inherent sense of logic led you to choose engineering as your career. You took courses that were mainly technical, scientific, or math oriented; thus, you fine-tuned your logical thought process.

Meanwhile, you probably avoided writing classes in college because you'd had your fill of compositions in grade school and high school. Math and science seemed to offer more black-and-white answers to problems, whereas language and social-science courses tended toward more gray areas.

Clear engineering writing has a logical structure. To be a good writer, you must have a logical mind. *People who have the most trouble with writing are those who have trouble thinking through a problem logically.*

Since you have already survived all those engineering and math courses, you have the potential to become a very skilled engineering writer. We're going to show you the components of a good writing project. If you apply your inherent sense of logic to a writing project, you should have few problems organizing a sentence, paragraph, or report.

Engineering and Writing Are Alike

Engineering and writing activities have several parallels. Engineering is, in part, the practice of applying logic and knowledge to the design and building of structures for practical, efficient uses. So is writing.

Engineered structures are buildings, bridges, dams, roads, airplanes, machines, systems, circuitry, chemical products, or computers. Written structures are documents.

Both disciplines require that you know the purpose, user/reader, and intended use of the product. To create a cohesive, appealing, and useful structure in either discipline, you must keep the purpose, user, and uses in mind. You must also consider what unexpected uses, stresses, resistance, or environments your structure might need to withstand.

San Francisco's famed Golden Gate Bridge is a perfect example of engineering for unexpected stresses. Its builder, Joseph B. Strauss, was an engineering-safety-standards advocate and, interestingly, a poet.

The experts designing that picturesque structure over the San Francisco Bay purposely engineered the weight tolerances to keep the bridge safe for traffic far heavier than the traffic of 1937, when the bridge was built. Five decades later those tolerances were tested in an unusual way.

On May 24, 1987, during its 50th-anniversary celebration, the Golden Gate Bridge was closed to vehicles to let people walk across the famous structure. Unexpectedly, 300,000 people squeezed onto the span, literally flattening the natural arch of the bridge for the first time in the structure's history. The bridge held the load. Golden Gate Bridge, Highway and Transportation District engineers said that only limited space—not weight-bearing concerns—prevented thousands more people from getting on the bridge deck.

Previously, in 1951, the bridge withstood record 69-mph winds that set up a torsional motion, causing one side of the deck to rear about 12 feet above the other. After that, the engineers reinforced the deck with cross-bracing beneath the roadway. After the 7.1-magnitude Loma Prieta earthquake in 1989, engineers continued seismic retrofitting to ensure that the bridge would withstand an earthquake of 8.0 magnitude or greater.

So, although you might not predict all the specific resistances your engineered structure may have to withstand, you know that if you build a sound structure, it will stand. The same holds true for a well-designed report.

Just as you might resist writing a report, your readers might resist the points you present in it. You may not know how many different readers will read your message—or with what resistance they might interpret it. Such resistance may be in the form of misinterpretation, objections, or political forces. Yet you must design the report (the overall structure) to overcome resistance even beyond what you expect. Then you must put it out there for the world to see.

Just as the current engineering staff of the Golden Gate Bridge must reinforce the past brilliant engineering that created the famous span, you may have to reinforce your report's key points by following up with supporting memos about project results and enhancements.

Yet here's good news about writing: The more solidly you design and build your original structure (the report), the less redesign and follow-up repair (rewriting or later explanation) you will have to do.

How to Structure Writing Successfully

Using a builder's point of view, let's visualize the structures within the report.

The foundation of a clear report is a well-defined key point. In other words, you must have something to say. The construction of your report rises from that foundation. Just as a house built on a weak foundation can fall, a report built on a weak key point can fall short of its purpose. The success of your report depends on the validity of your key point.

A house is like a box that contains rooms (inner boxes) created by walls, some supporting the entire structure, some adding interest. These rooms, in turn, contain smaller boxes such as closets and cabinets. These smaller boxes can either support or add interest. In a report, the progressively smaller boxes are the sections, which are created by the paragraphs and sentences, some supporting the overall structure and others adding interest. Even smaller boxes, such as clauses, phrases, or words, can also either support or add interest to the document.

Within both engineered and written structures, the internal supporting structures of the original design must provide stability. The building blocks of the main structure (report) are the facts, observations, and ideas that you stack up to prove your key point. Beams and braces prevent a house from buckling; facts, figures, reasons, and examples prevent a document from buckling under a reader's resistance. For example, if you are writing a request to buy expensive equipment, your request will be approved only if it contains supporting information proving that the savings will exceed the expenditure.

To be functional, the house also depends on some systems—heating, plumbing, electrical—that are governed by logical laws: Heat rises. Water seeks its own level. Electricity rises and seeks out the person with the steel-handled screwdriver. Knowing these laws helps one prevent chaos or peril in the house.

The competent electrician must wire a house according to standards of a logical system already determined by other electrical experts. If he doesn't, and if he connects the white wire to the black wire, he puts in peril the next person who will work with the wiring. If the electrician follows the predetermined system, the next person to work on the system will *understand* the electrician's work.

The logical system that makes writing functional and prevents chaotic expression is *grammar*. It consists of laws that help us understand one another through our language. A writing project has a logical structure and a logical system to make the structure work. If you can think logically, you will easily understand the writing process.

How to Approach Writing Rationally

Just as there is a logical approach to building a bridge or highway or designing a circuit, there is a time-tested approach to writing engineering documents. You will actually save time for yourself by walking through all three steps of the writing process:

1. Planning

2. Drafting

3. Editing

If writing is not the most appealing part of your job, you may often try to accomplish all three steps of that process at once, hoping that your first draft will be the final draft. That's understandable, because you want to get on to your other, more appealing engineering tasks. Yet a one-step approach to the writing job rarely produces a usable final draft.

Would you try to design, test, and refine a tool, machine, computer program, building, or manufacturing system in one sitting? No, you first need time to plan the product. You ask about the product's purpose ("Why does the world need it?"), form ("What is it?"), function ("What does it do?"), markets ("Who will use it, and who else might use it?"), benefits ("Why will people buy it?"), applications ("How else might people use it?"), and resource requirements ("What facilities, people, and money do we need to make it?").

If you try to achieve the final draft of your *written* product before taking time to think about what you want to say and why, your one-step process will actually take you much more time than the three-step process would.

For example, one engineer who has designed sanitation systems in several countries said that writing is a painful process for him. When asked what makes the task painful, he replied, "I always want to perfect the first paragraph before moving on to the second. Sometimes I spend two hours just on that first paragraph. I do the same for the second paragraph, and so on. By the fifth or sixth paragraph, I often realize that my opening paragraphs still aren't right, and I want to say something else instead. I have a hard time tossing out all the work that I did up front. I waste a lot of time trying to get the perfect draft done in the first attempt."

Does that scenario sound familiar? Learn from that engineer's experience. Resist the temptation to delve right into the first draft. Remember the rational way to write; you'll thank yourself later. By allowing yourself time—even if only a few minutes—to analyze and plan the writing job, you will face fewer revisions.

Then, when writing the first draft, remember that it's a *rough* draft, your first "data dump." Don't stop to edit. Just get your ideas down on paper or into the computer, without losing your train of thought.

The third step, editing, is still a critical one. That's when you polish the rough ideas and correct the mechanical errors that can distract readers from the content.

Engineering your writing projects with this rational 1-2-3 process will greatly enhance your ability to produce successful written documents.

In the next chapter, we'll start showing you how to drain the dread of writing, as we walk you through the planning process.

Summary of This Chapter's Main Points

▶ The writing process is logical.

▶ Apply your sense of logic to each writing job.

▶ Engineering and writing are alike in that both disciplines must produce structures for practical, efficient uses.

▶ Consider what unexpected uses and resistance your document might have to withstand.

▶ A clear key point is a document's foundation.

▶ Design and build your document solidly to reduce the need for redesign (rewriting) and repair (follow-up explanations).

▶ View grammar as a logical system that helps you turn your thoughts into sensible sentences to produce logical documents.

▶ Use a three-part pattern to organize and write your document: planning, drafting, and editing.

2 Designing a Message That Reaches Your Reader

"Writing comes more easily if you have something to say."

—Sholem Asch
Yiddish novelist
and playwright
(1880–1957)

If you abide by the following simple principle of engineering writing, it will guide you through some of the toughest writing projects. Don't be fooled by the apparent simplicity of this principle. Beneath the surface are complications that can get a writer into a world of trouble.

Essentially, the principle is that your *reader* and your *purpose* determine your *message*. So before you begin a writing project, you will have to determine to whom you are writing and why you are writing. With this knowledge, you can quickly head in the right direction. You can focus your research, determine your document's level of detail, and weed out unnecessary information before you start writing.

The next point—a crucial point to remember—is that although you may have several secondary readers and possibly some secondary purposes, each document you write can have only one *primary* reader and only one *primary* purpose. And you always write to the primary reader and toward the primary purpose.

If you have more than one reader or more than one purpose, then you will have more than one message and, therefore, more than one document to write. Let's express this principle as a literary equation.

One Reader + One Purpose = One Message

Two Readers + One Purpose = Two Messages

One Reader + Two Purposes = Two Messages

How to Focus on Your Reader

By one reader we mean one *type* or *category* of reader. As you write, keep in mind the picture of a single reader. A professional writer views the reader in the singular, to help focus his or her writing.

A friend of ours who writes an insider newsletter for the high-tech industry named a particular company president as his primary reader. Whenever he sits down to write, he imagines he is writing directly to that person. His rationale is that if he writes to answer that president's questions, he'll answer most company presidents' questions.

If you're writing specifications for maintenance technicians (a category), your primary reader is a maintenance technician. Your purpose is to explain how to maintain assembly equipment. As you write, think of a maintenance technician you know. Write to him or her. If you don't know a maintenance technician personally, you probably know enough about maintenance technicians in general to conjure up an image to keep in mind while writing.

Similarly, an electrical engineer writing a journal article on a new computer chip has as his primary audience the design engineers who, he hopes, will use the chip in designing their computers. So his primary reader is a design engineer. The electrical engineer's purpose is to explain the benefits of using the new chip. As he writes, he envisions a design engineer he talked to at the last trade show, and he writes to that person.

Even though you obviously can't go around and shake hands with all your readers and get to know them beforehand, you have to know your readers' needs. That is why being a writer carries a large burden. It's up to you to communicate your idea clearly to your reader. If a reader doesn't understand what's written, it is not the reader's fault—it's the writer's fault. As the writer, you must explain so your reader will understand. That's why we say you have to know your reader *before you start writing*. Imagining your reader as you write helps you subconsciously select and delete bits of information and also helps you decide how to say something.

Even before planning your writing job, take a moment to profile your reader and determine his or her needs. Then consider the best way to approach this reader. Asking yourself the following questions will help you form a picture in your mind, even if you don't know the reader personally.

Picture Your Reader

Imagine a very busy executive. She's standing at her desk, phone cradled on her shoulder. She's signing some papers while her secretary puts a stack of reports on her desk. You have to get through to her. How? Your best bet would be to write a very short memo, preferably in a list format that will grab her attention. She can quickly read it, digest it, and act on it. She'll probably ignore anything that's over one page.

Now imagine a fellow dressed in a dark-colored, three-piece business suit, with vest and suit jacket buttoned. He's standing up, legs slightly apart, arms folded in front of him. Here's a reader you have to sell your idea to. This guy is going to be a tough sell. How do you approach him? Tell him what's in it for him. Explain how your idea will benefit him, his department, his team.

▶ Is your reader a manager, a peer, a vendor, a customer, or someone who works under your supervision?

▶ What is this person's interest in your subject—high, medium, or low?

▶ What is this person's attitude toward you and your subject—friendly, hostile, indifferent, or skeptical?

▶ Finally, what is your reader's educational level and (more importantly) his or her knowledge of your subject?

Thinking about your reader's needs will also save you from including a lot of unnecessary information. For example, let's say that you have to write a routine report on a system breakdown. You will write your report from the following facts:

The system in one of your departments crashed. No one could determine the cause, so no one could repair the system. You remembered, though, that Jeff in a nearby department had a similar breakdown last month, so you asked him for advice. Jeff looked at your system and, after two hours of investigation, determined that an internal switch had malfunctioned. He replaced the switch. As a result of the breakdown, your production run fell behind one day.

Your reader is the production manager. Of all the information above, which is the most important to the production manager?

Most important is the fact that production is one day behind. This delay means the production manager has to add an extra shift and inform the Marketing Department about the delayed production so that Marketing can warn customers.

Important to the production manager, but only *secondarily* important at this point, is the cause of the breakdown: the malfunctioning switch.

Least important to the production manager now is who fixed the system. Therefore, in your report to the production manager, you will first mention the production slowdown and then the cause. Depending on your reader's needs, that may be all the information your report contains.

Now let's change readers. Your reader now is the maintenance supervisor. What will be most important to this person? The obvious answer is the *cause* of the breakdown: the malfunctioning switch. In fact, the maintenance supervisor will probably want more details so he can determine whether breakdowns will be a recurring problem. The maintenance supervisor isn't as concerned about the production slowdown and Jeff's role in fixing the system.

Let's switch readers one more time. This time you, as Jeff's manager, are writing Jeff's performance review, and your reader is your manager. Which information is important now? How about the fact that Jeff unselfishly took two hours from his busy schedule to help your department?

By profiling your reader before you write, you'll better understand your reader's needs. You'll have a better feel for when—and when not—to focus on the details.

How to Write for Nontechnical Readers

One engineering-writing aspect that many authors find frustrating is the conveying of technical information to nontechnical readers. The problem is not difficult to solve if you remember that your message will be determined by your reader and your purpose.

To what extent does your reader understand the technology? The understanding could be a lot or a little. What does the reader want to do with that information? Does a marketing vice president want to go out and design a circuit? Not likely. Well, what does she want? She wants to sell the circuit. Therefore, instead of telling her how to build the circuit, tell her what the circuit does or, more specifically, how it will make the customer's life easier.

Does a salesman explain the internal workings of a car to a mother who needs a van to haul the neighborhood kids to Little League practice and ballet classes? No. He talks about room, safety, fuel economy, and easy maneuvering. He knows his audience (a non-technical person) and his purpose (to convince her that this van will meet her needs).

The nontechnical person just learning how to drive doesn't care how a stick shift works mechanically. He's satisfied that the car moves when he lets out the clutch and steps on the accelerator. More importantly, he doesn't need such detailed information to be a good driver.

You are writing to people with different educational levels and a spectrum of technical expertise that goes from none to even-more-than-you-care-to-know. Your writing goal is to communicate information clearly to these various readers. As long as you keep your reader and your reader's needs in mind as you write, you shouldn't have difficulty writing to these various levels of education.

One puckish force, however, can prevent you from communicating clearly to those having different levels of knowledge or different areas of expertise. That force is the ego. The ego is that self-loving center in the mind that says, "I know more about this subject than he does, and he's probably not smart enough to understand this subject anyway, because he's only a salesman. I'm not going to waste my precious time trying to explain it clearly to him. So there."

This ego problem crops up in many professions. Physicians are often chided for bandying about medical terms when conversing with patients. The average patient doesn't know what an aneurysm (widening of an artery) or a fasciculation (muscle twitch) is, but many doctors glibly use such terms while quickly describing a patient's condition, thereby causing the patient to suffer hypertension (high blood pressure). If a physician uses terms without explaining them to his or her patient, that physician is guilty of poor communication.

Don't let your ego be your communication downfall. You have every right to be proud of your engineering degree and any advanced degrees you have earned. But now's the time to apply that knowledge and describe that application through clear communication. Technical ideas and projects are rarely so complex that they can't be explained to a layman. Albert Einstein said that the theory of relativity could be explained to virtually anyone. He also explained relativity very succinctly:

> When a man sits with a pretty girl for an hour, it seems like a minute.
> But let him sit on a hot stove for a minute, and it's longer than an hour.
> That's relativity.
> (Source: Barbara Rowes, *The Book of Quotes*. E.P. Dutton, New York, 1979.)

To communicate to various levels of education and technical expertise, you may have to practice some introspection. Remember, your purpose is to *communicate*, not to *impress*. You're *sharing* knowledge, not *demonstrating* it. Simply stated, don't let your ego prevent you from communicating to those who have less education or who have different technical expertise than you do.

Recently, one of our high-tech clients called us in to discuss a communication problem one of his departments was having. A team of technicians was trying to adjust equipment for electronic-circuit assembly by using specifications written by engineers in another department. Work in the technicians' department was moving slowly because the technicians had to keep asking the engineers to interpret the specifications. The engineers, in turn, became annoyed at the constant questions. Their annoyance soon grew into anger aimed at the technicians, whom they now regarded as brain-dead dolts incapable of understanding technical writing of any kind. The technicians, on the other hand, found the engineers to be a pain in the lower extremity. Meanwhile, production was slowing and upper management was unhappy. What should have been a simple business process was becoming a team-culture clash that was eroding the company's bottom line.

We read several examples of the specs, and we agreed with the technicians. The specs were unreadable. But we weren't sure why, because we also had read some reports and memos written by the same engineers who had written the specs. The reports and memos, except for the usual wordiness and occasional grammatical error, were fairly easy to read. Compared to the specs, the engineers' reports and memos read like great literature, and we wondered why the writing style in the specs was so different from that in the reports and memos.

Our assignment was simple enough: Teach the engineers how to write clear specs. So we developed a workshop based on the principles of clear, concise writing. Once we began working with the writers, we found the reason for the discrepancy.

The root cause, as it turns out, was much deeper and more Machiavellian than we suspected. The root cause stemmed from that persistent villain: the ego. The writers' stated (and failed) purpose in writing the specs had been to explain to the technicians how to adjust the equipment. However, their unstated (and accomplished) subconscious purpose was to prove that the technicians couldn't possibly understand the specifications. Why? Attitude. The writers all had at least an undergraduate college degree, and most had post-graduate degrees. The technicians had no more than high-school educations. Here was a chance to show off the master's degrees. The writers' egos wouldn't allow them to explain the specifications clearly to someone with less education. Instead, the writers deliberately included obscurities that few intelligent people could decipher.

> *"No one can write decently who is distrustful of the reader's intelligence, or whose attitude is patronizing."*
>
> —E. B. White
> American writer
> and humorist
> (1899–1985)

The writers in this case made two mistakes. First, they tried to impress their readers instead of communicating information to them. The writers didn't realize that the primary purpose of *all* engineering writing is to convey information quickly and efficiently to the reader, who can act on the information, either now or in the future.

The second mistake the writers made stemmed from a lack of respect for their readers. The writers did consider, as *you* should, the readers' education and background. But instead of writing without condescension, to accommodate that background, the engineers purposely wrote so that their readers could not possibly understand the specs. A haughty attitude prevented the engineers from respecting their readers and then writing to those respected readers.

The engineers were equating education with intelligence. The fact that a person lacks a college education does not mean that the person is stupid. Mensa International, whose members claim IQs in the top two percent of the population, is filled with nondegreed people who work in a variety of nonintellectual fields *by choice*.

The engineers' approach to writing was flawed because their attitude was negative. They lacked the one thing that helps to give all engineering writing a professional tone: respect for the reader.

They forgot, or perhaps didn't know, one of the main tenets of engineering writing: If a reader does not understand what a writer has written, it is the writer's fault. As a writer, you must ensure that your reader will understand what you have written. Otherwise, you are wasting everyone's precious time.

How to Deal with Multiple Readers

Now let's assume you are writing a technical report on your latest project. The report will be distributed to fellow engineers in your company to inform them of your work. Thus, your primary reader is a fellow engineer.

But this report, like many reports, is also going to top management. To add to your quandary, top management is not as technically astute or up to date on this technology as your fellow engineers are. That means you now have two primary readers—fellow engineers and top management—and each of these readers has different needs, so you now have two purposes. But we just said you can write to only one primary reader and have one primary purpose in a single document.

The easiest way out of this dilemma is to divide the report into two sections and treat each section as a separate document. The main section is the full technical report that goes to your fellow engineers, and the second section is an executive summary for top management. The executive summary gives an overview of the project without including all the technical details the engineers need. Your primary reader for the executive summary is a top-management executive. The main body of the report, which includes all the technical information, is for the engineers.

The trick is to treat the executive summary and the main body of the report as separate documents as you write them, but treat them as one two-part document when you send the report out. Doing so will let you follow the principle of one reader per document. Following that principle will make your writing job easier.

For example, as you write the main document, think of a colleague who will be receiving the report. Imagine you are sitting with her at lunch, explaining your ideas. Since she understands the technology, you confidently use the technical terms and include the details she needs. Your purpose is to explain how other engineers can implement the knowledge you gained from your project.

However, when you write the executive summary, you may envision the vice president whose background is in marketing or finance. You automatically refrain from using technical terms that this person doesn't understand. The vice president, you realize, wants only an overview of your project so that he may view its relationship to the company as a whole. So you delete the details. Instead of describing the trees, you describe the forest. Your purpose is to give this executive reader an overview of your project.

By viewing the two main sections of your report as separate documents, you can concentrate on and write to the primary reader of each section. You can use that technique in any document that appears to have several primary readers. Many company reports are distributed to several departments. In such cases, determine which of the departments are primary readers and which are only secondary readers who will receive the document on a for-your-information (FYI) basis. Don't waste time writing mainly to secondary readers.

If a report has specific sections meant for specific departments, each of which is a primary reader, treat those sections as separate documents. As you write each section, keep in mind the types of readers who will read that section. Envision each type of reader—a purchasing agent, an accountant, a sales representative, a top executive, a mechanical engineer, a civil engineer, or a chemist.

Avoid Switching Readers

Writing to one reader is not always as easy as it may seem. Sometimes subtle changes, like a switch in person or point of view, can throw the reader off. Such a switch usually indicates a lack of concentration on one primary reader.

For example, let's assume for a moment that we're writing instructions on how to operate a piece of equipment. The primary reader is the equipment operator. A possible secondary reader is the operator's supervisor. To write clear instructions, we must write to the operator in the second person, using imperative (command) sentences, which take the "you" point of view and are the easiest for readers to understand. We want to avoid switching back and forth between the primary reader and secondary reader.

As we begin writing, we keep the operator in mind and write instructions such as:

> To start the equipment, pull the red lever forward until it is horizontal. Next, push the green button and hold it in for about two seconds, until you hear a click. Release the green button and push the blue button for three seconds. Doing so will activate the equipment.
>
> Now the operator should carefully check the surrounding work area for clearance.

Do you see the mistake in that last sentence? We suddenly switched readers. Instead of writing directly to our primary reader, the operator, we started writing to our secondary reader, the supervisor. We switched from writing in the second person (*you*) to writing in the third person (*the operator*). If we were to constantly switch back and forth between readers of our instructions, we could do an excellent job of confusing all readers—primary and secondary.

Pinpointing Your Purpose

All writing jobs must have a definite purpose. Roman philosopher Seneca said that if you don't know which harbor you are heading for, no wind is the right wind. Yankee baseball player Yogi Berra said that people who don't know where they are going usually wind up somewhere else. Before you write, it's best to know where you're headed. If you don't know, you'll waste too much time on rewrites.

The overall purpose of any engineering document—be it a memo, technical report, or whatever—is to *communicate information efficiently* to a reader who in some way will use that information. Your reader will make a decision, design a circuit, request capital equipment, learn how to use a software program, or build a better bridge after reading your document.

Purposes in your engineering writing tasks fall into a hierarchy, usually distinguished by short- or long-term goals. Your overall purpose—to communicate information efficiently—is a constant. This purpose is also an *unstated* purpose, because you wouldn't sit down and write, "The purpose of this report is to convey information to my reader efficiently." Another often-unstated purpose is problem solving, especially if your report is part of a larger whole.

For example, you may write a report on constituents of fiber-reinforced composites, while another engineer reports on binder material. Several other people may also produce reports on composite materials. Together, these reports will help the company solve a material-cracking problem. Yet when you wrote your report, your primary purpose was just to inform your reader of the differences between chopped fibers and continuous fibers. Though unstated, your long-term purpose was to help solve the material-cracking problem.

You may also have an unstated purpose when your report is meant to stand alone. For example, your instruction manual may have as its stated purpose "to teach new employees how to use the water fountain," but your long-term, unstated purpose is to keep the hallway from being flooded.

Because of these unstated purposes, you should consider how your document fits into the company's big picture. Your report on the best method for applying epoxy grout during hot weather may be just another piece to the puzzle of building precast bridge sections. Knowing how your report fits into the big picture may influence the way you write your report. For example, assume you have little experience working with epoxy grout and you have just investigated the methods for applying epoxy grout during hot weather to determine which method is best. Your report must discuss the various methods. Your purpose is to *inform* your reader, who will make the final decision. If, on the other hand, you're a veteran grouter who knows from experience the best method for applying epoxy grout during hot weather, your report may take the form of a *procedure* to be followed out in the field. In this case, your purpose is to instruct, and you write your document a lot differently.

So knowing your short- and long-term purposes is mandatory. Remember, every writing job has one *primary* purpose (usually the short-term purpose) and often has one or more *secondary* purposes (usually the long-term purpose). When you write, you write to fulfill your short-term purpose. If you think of one reader and one purpose, your writing will stay focused.

Choosing from Five Short-Term Purposes

Generally speaking, engineering writing has five short-term purposes:

► to inform
► to instruct
► to persuade
► to request
► to promote goodwill

The following table shows various types of engineering writing and their short-term purposes.

Type of Document	Purpose
announcement	informs
article (magazine/journal)	informs, persuades
complaint letter	persuades
conference paper	informs, persuades
congratulation	promotes goodwill
data sheet	informs
instruction	instructs
manual	instructs
memo	informs, instructs, persuades, requests
performance review	informs
presentation	informs, persuades, instructs
procedure	instructs
proposal	persuades
query letter	requests, persuades
recommendation letter	informs
requisition	requests
response letter	informs, persuades
report	
activity report	informs
failure analysis	informs
incident report	informs
technical report	informs
trip report	informs
specification	informs, instructs
speech	informs, persuades
thank-you note	promotes goodwill

Notice that several of those business documents can fall into more than one "purpose" category. The purpose of a journal article is usually to inform. But if you are writing about a new microchip that your company would like to see designed into the next generation of computers, you may want to change your purpose from informing to persuading. It's crucial to know which route you are taking, because writing to inform is a lot different from writing to persuade.

How Much Detail and Data?

The level of detail you put into a document depends on—you guessed it—reader and purpose. Let's go back to our system crash that Jeff repaired by replacing a malfunctioning switch.

If you are Jeff's manager and you are writing to the production manager about the situation, your purpose is probably to inform. But let's change the scenario and say that this is the third time in two weeks that the system has crashed because of a malfunctioning switch. Maybe your purpose now is to persuade the production manager to replace all the switches. With the same reader but a different purpose, your message has changed. You're no longer just informing; now you want your report to bring action. You want to persuade. As situations change, purposes change and messages change.

What Managers Say

Most managers tell us that they receive too much detail in the reports they read. And they don't have time for all that detail. The best thing you can do before writing any report is to ask your manager how much detail he or she wants to see. You may be pleasantly surprised at how often you expect to spend days or weeks on a report when your readers might be expecting only a one-page summary of your project to date.

The best approach to take with these mandatory routine reports is to summarize your activities succinctly in one sentence or paragraph, leaving out all the details. Then ask yourself, "Does my reader need any more information?" If the answer is "yes," you can easily expand a sentence into a paragraph or expand a paragraph into several paragraphs. If, on the other hand, the answer to your question is "No, my reader doesn't need more information," then you are through writing. Think of the time you just saved.

Bigger Isn't Always Better

As you design your report, picture yourself designing a house. In house design, bigger isn't always better. A family with a home office and many hobbies may need a two-story, five-bedroom home with a large family room and a triple-car garage. In contrast, a single resident may want only a one-story, smaller house with a panoramic view of the ocean.

The same is true for report design. A bigger report isn't always better. When assigned a report-writing task, you may first think that you have to include all the details you have researched. However, your readers may not need all the details.

The details that you're thinking of using or researching for your report fall into two types: the "need-to-know" items and the "nice-to-know" trivia.

▶ The need-to-know details are what your reader needs to know about the topic in order to understand and accept the main points of your message.

▶ The nice-to-know details are those that you may savor but that your reader doesn't necessarily need to fully understand and accept your main points.

The Ups and Downs of the Analytical Approach

As a technical thinker, you're probably analytical by nature. That quality makes you a valued member of a technical team. The downside of being analytical is that you may go overboard with details, in the process burying or forgetting to mention the main point. You have to remind yourself that excessive use of details only works against you, unless your readers have requested all the specifics.

The excessive detail can also annoy readers. What you view as a fascinating failure analysis may be only a jumble of numbers to a reader who doesn't know how to read the numbers. That reader relies on you to interpret the numbers in terms of a revealed problem, a minor glitch, or an explosive danger. On the other hand, many readers respect your expertise on the technical details and just want you to interpret the details.

Who Needs What?

What you have to discern is which readers do need the details and which don't. Generally speaking, the higher up the corporate ladder a person is, the fewer details that person wants in a report. Top executives want to know that you moved from Point A to Point B and are now on your way to Point C. What they don't all care about is how you got to Point B, or how you plan to get to Point C. They just want to know the bottom line. Mid-level managers want more detail on the hows and whys. A peer or subordinate who may have to handle a similar project may want all the details from you.

If you are unsure about whether your reader will need the details, consider what your reader plans to do with the information you are providing. A fellow engineer who is working on a similar problem wants all the how-to details. On the other hand, a manager or executive probably needs just the results to make a decision.

Review the data that you've gathered. To decide which data you need and which you don't, ask yourself the following questions when you're considering the importance of specific details:

▶ Are the details needed to support my main point?

▶ Do the details support my solution to a problem?

▶ Do the details support a questionable or controversial point in my report?

▶ Has my reader asked for such details?

If you answer "yes" to any of the above questions, include the necessary details. If you answer "no" to all four questions, delete those unneeded details. Your reader will thank you.

Because your profession requires you to focus on details, you still may have difficulty learning when and when not to include a lot of detail in your writing projects. The following story may help you to remember that focusing on the details can sometimes demand great sacrifice.

> A priest, a doctor, and an engineer are awaiting their death by guillotine. When the executioner asks who will volunteer to be the first, the priest replies, "I shall go first. My soul is ready to meet God."
>
> The executioner places the priest's head on the block and pulls the cord. The blade drops swiftly and stops just one inch above the priest's neck.
>
> "Mon Dieu!" cries the executioner. "It is a miracle. Father, you are free to go." Then he asks who will be next. The doctor volunteers, saying, "I have no fear of death. I see it all the time. I am ready."
>
> The executioner places the doctor's head on the block, pulls the cord, and again the blade falls and stops just an inch from its target.
>
> "Sacré bleu!" shouts the executioner. "Another miracle. Please, monsieur, you may go." And he sends the doctor off.
>
> He looks at the engineer, and says, "Well, monsieur, you are next."
>
> Looking up at the guillotine's superstructure, the engineer replies, "You know, I think I see your problem."

Don't lose your head in the details. Keep your eye on the big picture: your purpose at hand. Doing so will help you design a message that reaches your reader.

Summary of This Chapter's Main Points

▶ One Reader + One Purpose = One Message

▶ Write to the primary reader and toward the primary purpose.

▶ Know your reader's needs before writing.

▶ Don't bog down nontechnical readers with technical details they don't need.

▶ For multiple readers, divide the document into sections and consider each section as a separate document as you write.

▶ Avoid switching readers.

▶ Remember that the overall purpose of engineering writing is to *communicate information efficiently* to a reader who needs the information to make a decision or perform a task.

▶ Select your details carefully. Different readers and different purposes require different details, even though you may be writing about the same subject or situation.

3 Organizing and Reducing Your Writing Time

Too many engineers equate writing a report with writing the great American novel, because the main writing models we studied in school were those of the famous writers of fiction. Then we read those famous writers' quotes about the agony of writing. With all this hyperbole about sweating blood and slashing veins, no wonder we're intimidated when we have to write a simple report. Few, if any, schools taught us how to approach real-life, on-the-job writing assignments. As a result, many people approach a technical report with all the apprehension of someone who has been asked to write the next *Gone with the Wind*.

Good Reports Are Not Written in Blood

You don't have to be a Hemingway to be a good engineering writer; you don't have to open a vein to produce a persuasive proposal. True, writing—especially creative writing—can be an arduous task. Sometimes writing does require a lot of hard work. But the job is probably not nearly as difficult as some of the professional writers would like you to think, especially if you view all the hyperbole from a different angle. Consider the following perspective:

A human trait shared by both professional writers and professional engineers is pride in hard-won accomplishments. Let's assume for a moment that you are an electrical engineer. To become an electrical engineer, you went through several years of specialized schooling. You no doubt had to learn Maxwell's equations. In doing so, you entered the fraternity of people who learned some really difficult equations that would completely baffle the guy on the street—"Maxwell? Maxwell who? What equations? What are you talking about? I didn't see any equations."

"Writing is easy; all you do is sit staring at a blank sheet of paper until the drops of blood form on your forehead."

—Gene Fowler
American writer
(1890–1960)

"There's nothing to writing. All you do is sit down at a typewriter and open a vein."

—Walter W. ("Red") Smith
American sportswriter
(1905–1982)

You have paid your dues, and you are now a member of an elite profession. And what do members of an elite profession do? Some of them look slightly askance at those outside the group who have not paid their dues. This attitude is displayed across a broad spectrum: At one end is a helpful person willingly offering advice and encouragement to a questioner; at the other end is the condescending elitist purposely trying to confuse a questioner.

Many professionals like to create the impression that their profession is elite because of the special knowledge they must have to attain membership. As an electrical engineer, for example, how do you feel when your accountant starts talking about his spreadsheet intricacies, as though implying that what you do can't really be all that difficult? Does that bother you? Do you feel somewhat put down? Yet don't you feel that the knowledge *you* have should somehow be reserved for only the members of your elite group?

A manager once asked an engineer why he had written such a turgid, dense, incomprehensible explanation of a certain technical problem that could have been explained much more clearly.

"Because," the engineer replied, "I had to plow through all those dense textbooks to learn this stuff. Why should I make it any easier for the next guy?" He had purposely built a jargon wall for the reader to climb.

Granted, that engineer was an extremist, but don't you even slightly harbor similar feelings about your hard-earned knowledge? We all do. We all have egos. Lawyers talk in legal jargon and doctors talk in medical jargon, perhaps not wanting us to understand what they understand.

Professional writers are no different. That's why you hear all that wailing and weeping about how difficult it is to write. Now let's look at how we can make writing a less arduous task by revealing what the professional writers understand. To begin with, let's examine the differences and similarities of entertainment writing versus engineering writing.

Entertainment writing (novels, stories, magazine articles, film scripts) and engineering writing differ from one another and require different writing methods. Granted, both you and the novelist face the blank piece of paper with trepidation, but for different reasons: The novelist is creating characters, events, situations, plots, and themes mostly from her own imagination. So sitting and staring at the blank piece of paper is part of the novelist's creative process. Thus, the novelist really isn't procrastinating; her imagination is creating the information she wants to communicate to her reader.

As an engineering writer, though, you are not creating events or situations; you're reporting them. Your information already exists—coming not from your imagination, but from hard facts. When you stare at and ponder that blank page, you aren't creating situations from your imagination. You're just trying to figure out how to get started.

The Procrastination Pitfall

If you don't know how to get started, you procrastinate and soon begin the downward spiral toward increased anxiety, greater frustration, and diminished chances of success.

When you finally do rush in to beat the deadline, the "final" report comes bouncing back, bleeding with red pencil marks. Soon you feel like Sisyphus, the mythical king of Corinth who was doomed forever in Hades to roll a heavy stone uphill, only to have it always roll down again. No wonder you and other engineering writers may dread the thought of writing.

But writing a report does not have to be a Sisyphaen task. Overcoming this initial writer's block is easy if you understand the writing process and work *with* it instead of against it. Instead of pushing the stone uphill, walk with it as it rolls downhill.

Remember that writing is a three-step process—no more, no less.

Step One: Planning

Step Two: Drafting

Step Three: Editing

If you complete the steps in order, you'll perform your task quickly and efficiently. If you try to skip a step, combine two steps, combine all three steps, or complete the steps in the wrong order, you'll roll back into the pit of procrastination, frustration, and fear of failure.

The Secret to Writing Fast

The three steps look simple enough—and they *can* be simple, if you follow each in order. Most engineering writers run into trouble because they simply don't plan well. They either skip the planning stage or try to combine it with the second and third steps. Doing so is usually a recipe for disaster. Would you try to build a highway or design a circuit without a blueprint? Don't build a document without a blueprint, either.

The secret to efficient engineering writing is *time allocation*. To write efficiently, you have to allocate your limited time wisely. Start by spending time on Step One, planning. By spending sufficient time on Step One, you will considerably shorten the entire writing process. That's the truth. That's the bottom line. That's the secret to slashing your writing time. Follow the steps in order and you will spend less time writing. Period.

The Planning Solution

Planning solves two underlying problems: lack of direction and lack of organization.

First, planning will aim you in the right direction, because the planning stage forces you to focus on your reader and purpose, both of which determine your document's content (message). Heading in the right direction means that you will not have to backtrack and do a lot of rewriting after you've discovered halfway through the project that you were either writing to the wrong reader or trying to accomplish the wrong purpose. Planning forces you to think before you write.

Second, planning helps you organize your content before you even begin writing. By the time you get to the drafting stage (Step Two), your document will be about 80 percent organized already. Step Two then becomes a quick information dump; and Step

Three, editing, becomes a fairly easy polishing job. In fact, you shouldn't have to revise your first draft more than once or twice. That's it.

How to Use a Quick-Plan System

To plan a successful writing project, you'll need some information on your reader and your purpose. Some of the information is already in your head, some is in your data-collecting notes, some is available from other people, and some you'll have to dig up from various sources. Take out a tablet or open a fresh document on your computer and set up a planning sheet with the following headings:

Topic
Primary Reader
Secondary Readers
Purpose
Problem
Main Points
Design
One-Sentence Summary

Beside each of those headings you will fill in some information. To speed up your planning, though, fill in just key words (not full sentences) for now. Here are brief guidelines as to what type of information to jot down for each heading:

Topic

Identify your topic, such as "Vendor Qualifications," "Activated Sludge Aeration Methods," "PC Board Problems," or "West Coast Trip Summary." This identification may or may not serve as a title, too. State your topic as clearly as you can. Make sure that you fully understand what you're writing about.

Primary Reader

Of all the readers of this document, who is the primary reader? Take your time here. Remember, the primary reader is the person you will address in this document. Naming a secondary reader as the primary reader at this point would send you writing in the wrong direction. Your primary reader will determine your message and your tone.

Your primary reader will also determine whether you will write in the first person ("I," "we"), second person ("you"), or third person ("he," "she," "it," "they"). For example, a procedure is written for the user, not the user's supervisor, and is written in the second person. A lot of reports have to be rewritten because the writer didn't write to the real primary reader.

Remember, if you have more than one primary reader (or more than one *type* of primary reader), you may have more than one document to write, or you may have to separate your document into sections, each aimed at different primary readers.

For example, let's say you're writing a feasibility report on a proposed new product for the Vice President of Research and Development (a technical person) and the Vice President of Marketing (a nontechnical person). You have two primary readers interested in one subject (a proposed product). One wants to know if he can build the product; the other wants to know if he can sell it. Since both vice presidents will be working together to decide on the product's fate, you'll probably want to send them identical reports. In this case, write one technical document aimed at the Vice President of Research and Development, and attach a nontechnical summary aimed at the Vice President of Marketing. That way you accommodate both primary readers.

Secondary Readers

Who else will read this document? List all secondary readers, and then review the list to make sure that the person you have named as the primary reader isn't a secondary reader.

Purpose

Why are you writing this document? What do you want it to accomplish for you? Make sure you focus on a short-term, specific purpose and not a long-term, broad purpose.

With your stated purpose in mind, think about a common question that readers often ask silently as they read through their incoming mail and memos: "So what? What does this purpose or message have to do with me? What action do you want me to take?" Better that you ask yourself "Why?" and "So what?" now, rather than tempt a reader to ask later.

A series of those two questions will help you clearly state your purpose. When you have written the key words of your purpose on your planning sheet, ask yourself "Why?" or "So what?" about the purpose. Keep asking until you can picture the broader purpose that your initial or immediate purpose will help to achieve. Your answers will help you do three things:

▶ clearly state your purpose, not just an immediate "to-do"

▶ put your purpose in perspective

▶ show your managers that your view of the situation is not narrow or cloistered, but part of the company's big picture

You can persuade nontechnical readers more easily with big-picture benefits than with technical specifics.

Problem

What, if any, problem(s) led you to the purpose of this report? If you are attempting to solve a problem, keep asking yourself about the problem. The problem may be *technical*, such as the problem that you're trying to solve for a customer. Or the problem may be *nontechnical*, such as a staffing shortage in your group.

Ask "Why?" or "So what?" about your purpose

Example:

"What's the purpose of your memo?"

"To inform my manager about our service backlog."

"So what about your service backlog?"

"It's been building all month."

"Why?"

"We are understaffed because of the hiring freeze."

"So what?"

"If we fall further behind, we may begin to lose customers to our competitor who can deliver."

"So what is the real purpose of your memo?"

"To get approval to hire another assistant."

Obvious? Not always. Before assuming that your only purpose is to inform your reader, remember to ask "Why?" in order to spark answers that help you clarify the importance of a memo, report, or other document.

Ask "Why?" about the problem

Imagine a conversation between an engineer and the group manager:

"We have a problem: We're losing money on this project."

   "Why?"

"Repair costs are higher than expected."

   "Why?"

"We thought only 3 units had failed; the actual count was 30."

   "Why the difference?"

"The failure analysis mentioned only 3."

   "Why?"

"The 3 was a typo that should have said 30."

   "The root cause of this costly problem was careless editing."

Sometimes it seems that *no* problem led to the purpose. Okay, so maybe you'll be that lucky. But maybe you won't.

For example, if your document is an informal memo to propose a new procedure, at first you might assume that you have no problem to consider (beyond having to write up the procedure), because the procedure isn't even written yet. Yet if this procedure is similar to an already-established procedure, think about how well the old procedure works. What problems did people have, either initially or even now, in following that old procedure? If you want to prevent similar problems from happening with your proposed procedure, state what potential problem(s) you want the new procedure to prevent.

Let's assume that you know and can explain the problem. On the planning sheet, you fill in the keyword description of the problem. But wait a minute. Look at what you described as the problem. Is it really the problem, or only a symptom of a bigger or deeper problem? Here's how to decide whether you're dealing with a problem or merely a symptom of the problem:

Ask "Why?" or "So what?" about the problem, just as you did about the purpose, until you get to the root cause of the problem. You have to get past the symptoms level to the root cause of a problem so you can make sure your stated purpose will solve the problem.

Case in point:

> An engineering manager in one of our workshops was about to write a scathing memo to his staff about not following the correct procedure for a certain type of failure analysis. His stated purpose was to get the staff to follow the procedure. The perceived problem was that the staff was not following the procedure. We asked the engineering manager, "Why?" ("Why aren't people following the procedure?").
>
> He replied, "Because they aren't *reading* the procedure."
>
> Again we asked, "Why?"
>
> He thought a moment and smiled sheepishly, "You know, I don't think the procedure is written down anywhere. We just orally explain the procedure to people as they join our staff."
>
> That was the root cause: the lack of a written procedure.
>
> He then changed his negative disciplinary memo into a positive clarification memo that included the time-saving benefits of following the

procedure correctly. He sent the positive memo out, attached to the newly written procedure.

In his case, the repeated "Why?" avoided embarrassment and saved him a lot of time. He said that if he had sent out the originally planned memo, he probably would have received follow-up phone calls from employees asking where to find the (nonexistent) written procedure. By taking a few minutes to think past the symptom to the problem, he sent the right message out the first time.

Main Points

Okay, you know your reader and you know your purpose, so you know your message. Now list your main points in key words and phrases, in any order you think of them. Jot down your ideas, and don't worry about exact wording or full sentences yet. Your ideas are probably overflowing your mind right now, so spill the ideas out on paper, where you can look at them. Remember, stick to a key-word list to keep the flow fast and free.

If you're planning a persuasive document, be sure that your main-points list includes benefits—from your reader's point of view.

Design

After listing all your main points, go back and number them in the order you want to present them. Before numbering, though, choose one of two overall strategies:

Strategy 1—Key Point First:

State your key point first. This opening is designed to give your reader a quick overview of your subject. Then follow with the details that support the key point. This is the strategy you will use most often.

For example, suppose you're writing a memo explaining types of solids found in drinking water. Using the key-point-first strategy, you may base your memo on the following information:

Suspended and Dissolved Solids

Key Point: Solids present in a sample of drinking water can be divided into several categories, not all of which are mutually exclusive.

Supporting Points:

- *Suspended solids:* Suspended solids, the same as filterable solids, are measured by filtering a sample of water and weighing the residue.
- *Dissolved solids:* Dissolved solids, the same as non-filterable solids, are measured as the difference between total solids and suspended solids.
- *Total solids:* Total solids are made up of suspended and dissolved solids. They are measured by drying a sample of water and weighing the residue.
- *Volatile solids:* Volatile solids are measured as the decrease in weight of total solids which have been ignited in an electric furnace.

- *Fixed solids:* The fixed solids can be found as the difference between total solids and volatile solids.
- *Settleable solids:* The volume (ml/l) of settleable solids is measured by allowing a sample to stand for one hour in a graduated conical container (Imhoff cone).

(Source: Michael R. Lindeburg, PE, *Civil Engineering Reference Manual*, 6th ed. Professional Publications, Inc., Belmont, CA, 1992. p. 7-14. With permission.)

In that example, the author opened with the key point and then used the bulleted list to support the key point. That's an excellent way to give readers a series of supporting details without putting all the details in a bulky paragraph.

Depending on the amount of detail your memo reader needs, your memo might include more details in each bulleted item, or even a full paragraph about each of those bulleted points.

Strategy 2—Key Point Last:

Lead up to the main point by describing an incident, stating an objective, giving supporting details, or reviewing background first. Use this strategy for variety or persuasion. For example:

The public has chosen the word *smog* to define objectionable air pollution. Originally the word was a contraction of *smoke* and *fog*, but recently it has become descriptive of any air pollution event accompanied by a decrease in visibility. In some cases it has been used to describe malodorous or vegetation-damaging conditions where visibility was no problem. To all intents and purposes, then, the words smog and air pollution may be considered synonymous.

(Source: W. L. Faith and Arthur A. Atkisson, Jr., *Air Pollution*, 2nd ed. Wiley-Interscience, John Wiley & Sons, Inc., New York, 1972. p. 2. With permission.)

One-Sentence Summary

Imagine you have just met your reader in the hallway, and you have 10 seconds to tell her about your subject. What would you say? Try to summarize your topic in one sentence. Write down your one-sentence summary. You will use it later to start your first draft, so this summary sentence may well become the first sentence of your rough draft.

The one-sentence summary is important, because it represents your transition from the planning stage to the writing stage. This is the sentence that will give you a running start into Step Two. It doesn't have to be a perfect sentence right now; it may not even survive your rough draft. However, it should capture the essence of your topic and orient your reader. It may even spark an idea for a brilliant opening sentence later.

Why the Planning Sheet Works

As you can see, the planning sheet prompts you to think about your writing project from several angles. It makes you think about your subject in terms of your reader and

A Sample Planning Sheet

Topic: Production Breakdown

Primary Reader: VP Manufacturing

Secondary Readers: Phoenix General Manager, Maintenance Supervisor

Purpose: To report on July production breakdown and persuade management to use an automatic particle counter as a preventive-maintenance tool.

Main Points [listed in key words as randomly thought of, then numbered]:

3. Six new computerized hydraulic systems not performing as expected.

5. New systems' lower contamination tolerance makes preventive maintenance methods out of date.

2. Four shutdowns at Phoenix assembly plant because of a fluid-power system breakdown.

1. Twelve days' production lost this year.

4. New systems better and faster, but have lower tolerance for contamination.

6. Particulate contamination seems to accelerate wear.

9. Closer monitoring of contamination could increase the hydraulic system's useful life.

10. Automatic particle counter (APC) would help us predict system wear more accurately and schedule normal maintenance more efficiently.

11. APCs used successfully in labs but not in the field. Particle Measurement, Inc. (PMI), has a field model ready for production and is looking for a beta site to test it.

12. Let's be that test site.

7. Company's cost to date has been about $250,000 in lost time.

8. Each successive breakdown longer. Two more breakdowns could push delivery date so that we violate our contract. The prime contractor could penalize us, reducing our payments by $2 million.

Design: Key point last to persuade management.

One-Sentence Summary: We need a better preventive-maintenance program to reduce production slowdown.*

[*Note: That one-sentence summary may become your report's opening sentence, before Main Point #1 in your rough draft.]

purpose so that you will be more conscious of your reader's viewpoint. Thus, right away you will begin thinking about the tone you want to take with your reader. You'll imagine yourself talking face-to-face with your reader, explaining each point at the reader's level of knowledge. You'll also have in the back of your mind what you want to accomplish with this document, and you will begin writing toward that goal. In other words, you'll be stepping off in the right direction.

The wonderful thing about the planning sheet is that it frees your mind to concentrate on the task at hand: communicating the information. By not worrying yet about how you are stating your points, you will relax and concentrate more on *what* you want to say. As a result, you will let the ideas flow without being intimidated by the blank piece of paper—or a formal outline structure. There's no pressure here, because you are merely brainstorming ideas with yourself. You're sorting through your thoughts, knowing that some will fly and some won't.

By freeing your mind of any pressure, you will begin experiencing the synergy of the creative process. These bits of information you are writing down will soon produce ideas that feed on each other. In the end, the whole of your document will be greater than the sum of its parts.

As you list your main points on the planning sheet, your ideas will take shape and solidify. When they do, you may find that you have to change your primary reader or even change your purpose. If so, don't fret. Your planning sheet is just helping you to sharpen your focus. Better to discover changes in the planning stage than later in the rough draft.

Don't assume that your ideas will flow logically as you list them on the planning sheet. Bits and pieces of new ideas or examples may occur to you as one idea sparks another. Just keep putting them down, not worrying about the order.

You'll probably have several sets of ideas, each representing subtopics. Look for these sets when you go through the design (strategy and numbering) stage. Quite often these sets will need to be rearranged into a logical order.

During the design stage, as you're numbering the main points, try several ideas in the number-one slot. Doing so may change your perspective and reveal a more logical approach. Remember, this planning step is your walking-around, going-to-the-water-cooler, getting-another-cup-of-coffee, watering-the-plants, and avoiding-the-job-at-hand time. It's idea time.

How Planning Conquers Poor Organization

Now that you have the key words of your ideas down on paper or on the screen where you can see them, you can conquer a critical communication obstacle: poor organization.

Following are the most common causes of poor organization:

▶ not clearly identifying the primary reader

▶ having more than one primary reader

▶ not clearly defining the purpose

▶ having more than one purpose

▶ having no logical strategy, aimed at a purpose, to present ideas

By now, you should feel secure that your planning can conquer those culprits of poor organization. You're already attuned to your reader(s) and your purpose. You kept those two determinants in mind as you decided whether to use a key-point-first or key-point-last strategy. So you are well on your way to drafting a logically organized document.

A Sensible Flow of Ideas

Now glance through the planning sheet you have just written for your report. The trick is to look through your reader's eyes, not your own. Will your design—key point first or key point last—work with the order you chose for your main points as you reviewed and numbered them? Will that order smoothly and sensibly help your reader understand the purpose and message?

For example, suppose you decided to put your key point first. Each subpoint or example must logically lead your reader to the next supporting point—and the next, creating the path of ideas that will carry your message to your reader and connect your last sentence logically to your first.

Now that you've completed your planning sheet, review the data that you're planning to use. Check for accuracy, reliability, and relevance.

How to Ensure Accuracy, Reliability, and Relevance

Accuracy

The Chinese philosopher Confucius, in about 500 BC, said, "The cautious seldom err." Take that sage advice. Make sure all your information is *accurate*. Being accurate is not as easy as it sounds. As you know, numbers can lie or be misleading, just as words can.

Albert Einstein said, "Looking back ... over the long and labyrinthine path which finally led to the discovery [of the quantum theory], I am vividly reminded of Goethe's saying that men will always be making mistakes as long as they are striving after something." Being human, you may inadvertently make errors in recording your test results or the gauge readings. Yet your reader trusts you to be accurate in all your statements, facts, and figures.

(Source: Isaac Asimov and Jason A. Shulman, *Isaac Asimov's Book of Science and Nature Quotations.* Blue Cliff Editions, Weidenfeld & Nicolson, New York, 1988. p. 83 (Confucius) and p. 84 (Einstein). With permission.)

One company blundered a major product change based on some failure-analysis statistics that were accurate but misleading because of miscommunication between the analysts and the manager. The analysts' report did not state exactly how many items were tested. The manager thought the analysis was based on the usual 100 samples. It was based on 6. Heads rolled; pain ensued.

Here's how to ensure accuracy so as to maintain your credibility:

▶ Recheck your numbers to catch typos, such as a 27 that should read 72.

▶ If you're reviewing a list of percentages, be sure they total 100 percent.

▶ Check names, titles, locations, dates, and other specifics.

▶ Consider all possible causes of an effect, not just the suspected cause or the one that proves your point.

▶ Prefer facts to opinions unless opinion is appropriate or requested.

▶ Make sure the samples you have selected represent the whole group you studied.

A little extra caution now, before the rough draft, can save you from having to correct inaccuracies publicly later.

Reliability

Facts are only as reliable as their sources. How *reliable* are the sources of your facts, figures, and other data?

▶ Check with more than one source to verify any surprising or questionable findings. If you're basing an assumption on someone else's conference paper or report, do you know how qualified, reputable, competent, and careful that person is?

▶ Check the facts and figures for consistency. They can change from one test to the next or from one experiment to the next. Did you run enough tests to show a credible pattern, draw a valid conclusion, or recommend a workable solution?

▶ Tell how many units you tested, how many people you surveyed, or how many times you replaced the same faulty component. Otherwise, your manager may assume you tested more units than you actually did and might base a crucial decision on your test results, costing your company needless expense.

▶ Check your figures to be sure they're up to date. Outdated figures mislead readers and can create duplicate work for you and your readers.

Relevance

A close cousin of reliability is relevance. How relevant are your test results, findings, and other data to the situation you're reporting on today? Yesteryear's standards may not be adequate or reliable in today's quickly changing technical environment.

If you have to assume certain truths from earlier experience and apply those assumptions to a current situation, how reliable and relevant are the earlier assumptions today?

Here's an example of how things can change:

Earthquake standards, developed throughout the 1900s, have become stricter and stricter, to guard against major temblors. Even so, the codes don't cover all contingencies.

Earthquake effects are usually represented, for design purposes, by static lateral forces applied at floor levels. So far, so good—so long as the earthquake occurs on a lateral fault.

In January 1994, a violent 6.8 vertical-thrust earthquake struck Northridge, California (just north of Los Angeles), and vertically split several freeways, collapsed parking structures, and heavily damaged several sections of Los Angeles. The old assumptions and lateral-fault-based codes weren't fully relevant to the vertical-thrust force.

So remember: The established assumptions or previous findings about your topic may apply to most situations, but may not apply to the *current* situation. Or the details you're thinking of including may not be *relevant* to your purpose or your reader.

Here's how to decide what's relevant and what isn't:

► Find out how current the facts, figures, findings, and other specifics are.

► Select facts, analogies, or examples that apply to your key point or to your reader's request.

► Know the conditions or environment in which tests were run. Decide whether the same conditions apply to the current problem, situation, or tests.

► Select facts that justify your expected conclusions and recommendations.

By screening your data now for accuracy, reliability, and relevance, you will save yourself time in the drafting and editing stages, and help to maintain your reader's trust.

Summary of This Chapter's Main Points

► Look at the bright side of engineering writing: You don't have to create situations as a novelist does. You report on situations from information that already exists.

► To get your writing project completed quickly, plan it well.

► Think of planning as a tool that gives you direction and organization.

► Develop a planning sheet for every writing project; and always, always keep your reader and purpose in mind.

► Use your planning sheet to organize your information and to check the logical flow of your ideas.

► Review your selected data for accuracy, reliability, and relevance.

4 Crafting the Rough Draft

> *"Seek what to write, rather than how to write it."*
>
> —Marcus Annaeus Seneca
> Roman rhetorician
> (circa 54 BC–AD 39)

The Myth of the Perfect First Draft

Having spent sufficient time planning your writing project, you can now begin the writing. At this point, your writing project should be fairly well thought out and about 80 percent organized. You'll pick up most of the other 20 percent of organization during the rough-draft stage. If you have dedicated enough time to Step One (planning), then Step Two should go rather quickly.

The *rough draft*, as its name implies, is a rough treatment of your document. Its purpose is to give you something tangible to work with. It's the clay you will shape into a fine sculpture. From this working draft, you will produce your final copy.

The perfect first draft that requires *no* editing or revision is a myth. No one, not even professional writers, can produce a final draft without having first written a rough draft. Accept that fact and you can relieve the anxiety of trying to produce a perfect draft when you first set pen to paper or fingers to keyboard. The rough draft is merely the second step in the overall writing process. Approach it that way. It is an information dump, but if you have planned well, it is a *well-organized* information dump.

Although the rough draft does not require perfection, it does require thinking.

> *"Scientists study the world as it is; engineers create the world that never has been."*
>
> —Theodore von Karman,
> Hungarian-American
> aeronautical engineer
> (1881–1963)

Engineering Your Creativity

Now you have to think. You are at the point in the writing project where a little creativity will help you. Don't be frightened by creativity; it's not that intimidating. Simply stated, creativity is combining Idea A with Idea B to create Idea C.

The novelist doesn't create characters, scenes, and plots from whole cloth. He bases his characters on people he has met or read about. He creates scenes based on ones he has seen or read about. And he develops a plot based on one of several that have already been used, because there are no original plots left. The creativity comes in when the novelist takes these existing characters, scenes, and plots; looks at them from different perspectives, adding or deleting components; and then twists them to create his own world.

The popular play (and movie) *West Side Story*, a tale of two young lovers who live in different neighborhoods, was written by Arthur Laurents, from an idea by Jerome Robbins. It's the modern version of *Romeo and Juliet*, a beautiful romantic tragedy written by William Shakespeare in 1595. Shakespeare supposedly got the plot idea from Luigi da Porto, who had written a play in 1530 based on a plot da Porto had found in a collection of romances, *Il Novellino*, published by Masuccio Salernitano in 1476. The point is that creative ideas come from the synergy of ideas and information you already have. To create, you must let your mind run free.

One thing that will prevent you from being creative is living in a box, viewing the world from a stationary point. If you want to unleash your creative powers, imagine that you are in a box. Now open the lid and step out. Leave the lid open. Now look into the box. You'll notice that the view has changed considerably. You can see things you never saw before. The best way to be creative is to step out of the box.

That's what Jerome Robbins and Arthur Laurents did. Viewing from within the box, they saw Shakespeare's two Italian lovers from feuding families in Verona. When Robbins and Laurents stepped out of the box, they saw two American lovers from different ethnic backgrounds and different neighborhoods in New York. They combined the two story perspectives to create a smash Broadway hit. Creativity is simply processing *known* information to create *new* information.

As the old saw says, this is not rocket science. You can do this. You can unleash your creativity to produce engineering writing that is not only objective, but also readable and even appealing.

Developing a Lead to Orient Your Reader

The most difficult *and* the most important sentence is the first one. It requires the most thinking. Professional writers have been known to agonize for days over the first sentence and still not get it right. So let's take a look at what all the brouhaha is about the first sentence, commonly known as "the lead" among professional writers. It's called the lead because it leads (starts) the story.

Shattering Writer's Block

When we discussed the planning stage, we asked you to write a one-sentence summary of your subject, both to give yourself an overview and to orient the reader. Essentially, what you wrote is a lead. By simply having written that one-sentence summary during the planning process, you have easily shattered the wall that many professional writers slam right into: writer's block.

The main source of writer's block is the blank piece of paper with nothing on it but white space. To the writer, that page is like the Alaskan tundra during a snow storm—it's white and it's blank and it's empty. It's the complete opposite of a black hole. At least a black hole has something in it. The blank paper has nothing in it, on it, or near it but white space—lots and lots of white space. And it strikes terror into the hearts of many writers.

But you have broken the writer's block by preparing a planning sheet. You are not starting with a blank sheet of paper or an empty screen. Your paper is already filled with information about your subject. Not only that, but your information is already organized, and your lead is already written. So you are way ahead in the game now.

The Purpose of the Engineering Lead

The purpose of the lead in engineering writing is different from that in entertainment writing. A professional writer puts a snappy lead up front to attract readers. His article is competing for readership with the other articles in a magazine, so the primary purpose of his lead is to grab the reader's attention.

Your writing is not necessarily competing for attention, so the primary purpose of *your* lead is to *orient* the reader. (One possible exception is in persuasive writing, when you, too, may want to grab your reader's attention without revealing your key point right away.)

In the business and technical writing that we all routinely read, leads might be good, bad, or nonexistent. A good lead orients the reader. A bad lead doesn't orient the reader, usually because it is too general. A report with a nonexistent lead jumps right into the middle of the subject matter without giving the reader any clue about the upcoming content.

To write a good lead, you have to walk a fine line between dragging the introduction on interminably and jumping into your subject too quickly. And although your primary purpose is to orient, you also should try to make the orientation interesting.

Three Types of Engineering Leads

Your first sentence is crucial, because its job is to orient the reader to your subject. Therefore, you should spend relatively a bit more time perfecting your first sentence to make sure it is doing its job correctly: clearly orienting the reader.

Your lead should do one of two things: *Give an overview* or *emphasize the main point*. In engineering writing, you can choose from three main types of leads:

▶ The first type gives an overview of your subject or the situation. This lead quickly orients your reader to your subject. When writing this type of lead, avoid stating obvious information. For example, avoid the all-too-common practice of starting with a vague "purpose of this report is to ..." rather than stating your situation or accomplishments.

▶ The second type of lead emphasizes the *key point*, such as the result, in the first sentence. This lead is both informative and interesting.

▶ The third type, the grabber lead, is less common than the first two types—especially in technical writing. It's preferred for persuasive writing, which we will discuss more thoroughly in another chapter. The purpose of this persuasive lead is to grab the reader's attention and help to emphasize the upcoming key point—but without giving away the key point too soon.

All three types of leads—overview, key point, and grabber—can work well. Your reader and purpose will help determine which type will work best in a given situation.

For example, assume for a moment that you are a news reporter covering the city council meeting. The city council has just passed five new resolutions. You can open your news story one of three ways. You can lead with an overview:

> Last night the city council passed five new environmental resolutions.

That's a good overview in that it states exactly what happened, yet it lacks specific information. Your reader is the average citizen; your purpose is not only to inform but also to sell the reader on reading your story, which is competing with other stories on the page. So you might instead want to catch the reader's eye with a point of controversy. In this case, you could identify the most important resolution that was passed:

> Last night the city council banned smoking in all public places.

That more-interesting key-point lead gives the reader more specific information right away.

The third type of lead, which doesn't give away the main point but does pique the reader's interest, might be:

> Joe Camel had better not show his face in public in Palo Alto.

That grabber lead alludes to a popular advertising icon, so it will get attention. The story will now take the reader toward the main point. Although not being used in a persuasive story in this case, such a lead could open a persuasive document because it piques interest.

Let's look at some engineering-oriented examples.

Imagine that you have spent several months solving a customer's problem by using your products in the customer's system. The following lead quickly explains the overall situation:

> We finally solved the ABC systems-integration problem by boosting the
> XJ98's power and reducing the connection lag time.

That lead quickly tells the reader how you finally conquered a significant customer problem. You would now relate the pertinent details of how and why you did what you did and how your solution can be applied to similar problems.

The following lead is *not* a good one, because it does not state the key point of the report or explain a situation. It states what the report is about, but it does not state the results of the investigation.

> The purpose of this report is to describe the results of the failure analysis that was conducted on the Famboozie Widget.

In our writing workshops, we have seen more leads of that type than any other. It is not a good lead because it lacks specific information. It's also boring. The good news, though, is that it is the easiest lead to change quickly into a substantive one by focusing on the results. A better lead would orient your reader to the most significant result of the analysis:

> Our failure analysis of the Famboozie Widget indicates that a loose tie-down bolt caused the connecting rod to shear off at 5,000 rpm.

The advantage of that second lead is that the reader immediately knows what happened. He doesn't have to wade through all the details of the analysis method before finding the information he wants. We are not saying that those details aren't important, just that they are not as important as the result.

Granted, there could be a time when your analysis method may be more important than the results. In such a case, however, you would probably have two different reports to write, because (as we stated earlier) you have two different purposes. So you would write one report that emphasizes the results, and another that emphasizes your methods.

Look at the leads of some of your past reports. If they begin with "The purpose of this report ...," your main point may be buried in the middle or at the end of your report.

If the result is the last thing you mentioned, you fell into one of the common engineering-writing traps. Instead of writing an efficient engineering report, you wrote a mystery novel, saving the results for last. First you laid out all the clues and climaxed with "The butler did it!" While that may be an acceptable way to write a mystery, it is not a good way to write a report. The mystery-novel reader will stay with the novel to the last page; the report reader may not.

How Long Is a Lead?

The lead can be a sentence, a paragraph, or even a few paragraphs if that's what it takes to orient the reader. The preferred lead, though, is the short one. Try to get to the essence of your subject in one or two concise sentences. Remember, you want to orient your reader quickly. Granted, some subjects may require a more lengthy introduction, but not many. So don't push it; don't waste your reader's time. Engineering writing should be concise and efficient. In the lead, focus on results and accomplishments, not on purposes and activities.

A Quick Test of a Lead

Now it's time to double-check your ideas, because, as much as possible, you want to head off in the right direction. Keeping in mind that the lead must either emphasize the most important point or give the reader an overview of the situation or subject, peruse your planning sheet and your one-sentence summary again. Have you selected the point that best orients your reader to your subject? If you've written an overview, make sure your overview is neither too vague nor too weighted down with details. At this point you want to describe the forest, not the trees.

Exercise: Lead Writing

Below are the first one or two sentences (leads) of some engineering papers. Analyze them. Do they successfully orient you? If not, what do they lack?

> It has sometimes been the case during the development of the various branches of science and engineering that, on looking back, initial solutions turned out to be special cases of more general problems.
>
> (Source: NBS Special Publication 487, *Engineering Design*, C13.10:487, August 1977, U.S. Government Printing Office, p. 25. With permission.)

Now *that* is a broad overview. With that opening, the author could go on to discuss anything from the big-bang theory to square-jaw clutches to egg-laying problems of one-eyed chickens.

Here's one that has a more straightforward approach:

> Defining an image in digital form is a relatively straightforward process—or so it seems on the surface. The image or picture is simply subdivided into a number of points commonly referred to as picture elements or "pixels"; each pixel has a numerical number assigned to it, representing the brightness of the image at the pixel point.
>
> However, to extract useful information from the digitized image, it might be helpful to know a few parameters associated with the digitization process.
>
> (Source: NBS Special Publication 500-8, *Workshop of Standards for Image Pattern Recognition*, C13.10:500-8, May 1977, U.S. Government Printing Office, p. 52. With permission.)

That lead isn't too bad. You do get oriented by the second paragraph. A slight improvement would be to move the information in the second paragraph to the beginning and rewrite it as follows:

> Knowing a few parameters of the digitization process will help one to extract useful information from a digitized image.

Following are two paragraphs of a technical paper. The first paragraph is an abstract; the second paragraph is the introduction to the main document. After reading through both paragraphs and our comments that follow the paragraphs, write a clear one- or two-sentence lead that clearly orients the reader to the subject at hand.

A systems-oriented approach to the problems of materials selection and choice of manufacturing processes in engineering design is presented. The goal of this approach is to select the best combination of shape, material, and manufacturing process by optimization with respect to several previously established criteria, such as performance, cost, availability of materials and manufacturing facilities, and personnel. A flowchart is used to describe the process of evaluating the interactions between shape, material, and process to determine the best combination. The flowchart also illustrates the use of prototype testing and reports of performance in service to provide feedback which may indicate changes in the design.

All too frequently an object is designed with careful attention to its mechanical function or its esthetic appeal, but with little concern for the material from which it will be made or the manufacturing process by which it's made. A designer may have in mind the general material (e.g., steel) and a manufacturing process (machine to size and heat treat), but specific choice of material and sequence of manufacturing process may be neglected until a very late stage of the design process. The resulting object may perform satisfactorily, but it probably isn't a very efficient design, either in terms of performance or cost. This approach to design and materials selection invites patchwork redesigns to cover up shortcomings, should the object not perform as intended. In this paper, an approach of optimizing the combination of shape, material and manufacturing process is described.

(Source: NBS Special Publication 487, *Engineering Design*, C13.10:487, August 1977, U.S. Government Printing Office, p. 19. With permission.)

The first sentence of that excerpt is too broad. We get a hint that we can solve a problem having to do with selecting the right materials and the right manufacturing process if we use a systems-oriented approach. But we need more information. The author's second sentence gives us a bit more information, but still not enough to orient us to the main point. The next two sentences on flowcharts are out of place; they should be placed near the end of the second paragraph.

In the second paragraph, we finally get an inkling of what the paper is proposing.

Write what you think the lead sentence should be, then read our suggested revision.

Your suggested revision of the lead sentence: _____

_____

_____

_____

_____

Our suggested revision of the lead sentence:

By using a systems approach to select the materials and a manufacturing method early in the design process, a designer has a better chance to produce a more satisfactory product.

The revised lead is better because it presents more specific information and tells the reader (whom we assume is a designer) what action she will be able to perform ("... produce a more satisfactory product") if she follows a system approach. A further improvement on this lead would be to substitute "you" for "a designer," because "you" is a powerful word that captures a reader's interest.

Check your lead. You have probably written a good lead if you have given the reader some specific information on what he or she will be able to accomplish by following the systems approach.

Directional Leads Guide the Reader Through Your Draft

Besides orienting the reader with your main lead in the opening paragraph, you will often have to orient the reader to main points, new sections, or major changes of direction *within* the document. You can do so by using a fourth type of lead that may occur more than once in the same document: the *directional lead*. As internal guides, directional leads help your reader travel your logical lanes of ideas.

For example, if you are going to list three key points, orient the reader by introducing the list with a complete sentence.

To initiate our establishment of an R&D facility in Denver, we set up three separate committees, each having equal input to the final decision:

Research and Development
Government Liaison
Personnel

The above directional lead quickly tells the reader that you set up three committees to help you complete your project. Now the reader expects and looks forward to more information on each committee, so you could perhaps provide such information this way:

R&D investigated nearby universities for engineering talent, lab facilities, and general concrete-construction expertise. Government Liaison worked with local and state authorities to make sure we would meet all toxic-waste regulations. That committee also hired a public relations firm experienced in toxic-waste issues to help open the right doors for us. Personnel investigated the current and potential labor pool of the area.

Had we just begun explaining what each committee was doing without the directional lead, the reader might have trouble knowing what direction the document was taking.

He would have no idea how many committees he would have to read about. He might wonder if you forgot to orient him. With the directional lead, though, the reader feels more comfortable because he knows he is on track with your thinking.

Concentrate on Writing, Not Revising

Once your lead is in place, write the rest of your rough draft. At this point, don't worry about grammar, punctuation, or perfection. Just get the information down on paper so that you can work with it. Your main concern for now is content, not mechanics (yet).

Follow your planning sheet, which we said usually helps you organize about 80 percent of your writing project. Let it guide you through the rough draft. You're also trying to organize the remaining 20 percent of your document, so pay attention to the order of your ideas. Are the ideas logically organized?

Don't get ahead of yourself by trying to revise as you write your rough draft. By all means, do not write a paragraph, revise that paragraph, and then polish that paragraph, because in the final revision (Step Three), you may have to delete that paragraph. Psychologically, it's a lot easier to delete a roughly written paragraph that you've spent little time on than to delete a well-polished paragraph that you've spent a lot of time on.

Eschew Irrelevant Details

Your planning sheet should have all your main points listed. As you expand on each of these points in your rough draft, avoid being sidetracked by irrelevant details. Remember to discern between necessary and unnecessary information. Keep asking yourself if each detail is helping you accomplish your purpose.

"The art of writing is the art of applying the seat of the pants to the seat of the chair."

—Mary Heaton Vorse
American writer
(1881–1966)

"Just get it down on paper, and then we'll see what to do with it."

—Maxwell Perkins
American editor
(1884–1946)

Sample Rough Draft

Go back to Chapter 3 for a moment and read through the sample planning sheet about a production breakdown. Then return to this page and read the following rough draft based on that planning sheet.

So far this year, we've lost 12 days of production. In July, the Phoenix assembly plant suffered its fourth shutdown of the year because of a fluid-power system breakdown.

When we installed the six new computerized hydraulic systems two years ago, we thought we would increase our production efficiency by 20 percent. Unfortunately, the systems are not performing as expected. Although feedback systems, control, computerization, and reliability have increased on fluid-power systems, those systems' ability to withstand contamination from various sources has decreased.

This lower contamination tolerance makes our old method of preventive maintenance inadequate. We aren't spotting particulate contamination fast enough, and the contamination is accelerating wear. So far we've lost about $250,000 in wasted time.

Each successive breakdown has lasted longer. Two more breakdowns could push back our delivery date to the point that we would be violating our contract. The prime contractor might then penalize us, reducing our payments by $2 million.

We have to get a better reading on the contamination. If we can monitor contamination more closely, we can increase the hydraulic system's useful life. The only option I see is an automatic particle counter (APC), which would allow us to predict system wear more accurately and schedule normal maintenance more efficiently.

APCs have been used successfully in labs but not in the field. Particle Measurement, Inc. (PMI), claims to have a field model ready for production and is looking for a beta site to test it. I suggest we talk to PMI about using our Phoenix plant as a beta test site.

I met PMI's chief designer at the Hydraulic Conference last year. I can arrange a meeting with him if you want to pursue this idea. What do you think?

Why is that a good rough draft? First of all, we followed the planning sheet and came out with a draft that is well organized. The lead orients the reader and grabs attention. Lost production time always gets someone's attention. We state the problem and follow with the cause of the problem. Then we suggest the consequences of our not remedying the problem (the penalty of reduced payments). Finally, we offer a solution and a request to implement the solution. No unnecessary details clutter our argument.

Maintain the Professional Perspective

Since you've given your reader and purpose much thought, remember to pay attention to the *tone* of your document. Maintain respect for your reader, and you will maintain a professional tone. (See Chapter 2 for more information on tone.) Don't write condescendingly to subordinates or to readers who have less education than you. Arrogance has no place in good engineering writing.

Always keep in mind that, above all, the long-term purpose of engineering writing is to convey information efficiently to someone who must use that information to make a decision, solve a problem, or design an engineering marvel.

Summary of This Chapter's Main Points

▶ Unleash your creative talents by stepping outside your box. Look at your writing project from various perspectives.

▶ Use the one-sentence summary from your planning sheet to get you started with the rough draft.

▶ Choose one of three types of leads: overview, key point, or grabber (for persuasion).

▶ Once you're into the rough draft, use directional leads to orient the reader to key points, new sections, or changes in direction.

▶ Concentrate on *what* you want to say more than on *how* you want to say it.

▶ Let your planning sheet guide you through the rough draft.

▶ Avoid revising as you write. Revising is a separate step.

▶ Keep focused on your reader and your purpose.

PART TWO

Engineering Your
Words into Pages

5 Choosing the Right Words

You Have Lots of Choices

As a writer in the English language, you're faced with good news and bad news. The *good* news is that you have a lot of words to choose from. The *bad* news is that you have a lot of words to choose from.

The English language is a maze of more than 600,000 words. And the number keeps rising. English is a rich, dynamic language because it is filled with the words of other languages. Anglo-Saxon words form the basis of the English language. These words often have hard or harsh sounds— *leg, root, awkward, dirt, earth*. But above all, they are short words.

However, Anglo-Saxon words constitute only 25 percent of the language today. The other 75 percent has been assimilated from other languages, especially Latin (introduced to England by St. Augustine in AD 597) and French (brought by the Normans when they invaded Britain in AD 1066). Soft-sounding words like *garage, chic,* and *menu* are French words. Many heavy words come from Latin: *oscillate, incorporate, apparatus, maturation.* Latin words were often preferred by scholars because such words sounded more "important." (Gee, does that sound familiar?)

Since 1066, English has been on a roll, grabbing words from here and there as needed, or making up words if none existed to fill the need.

How Science and Technology Enrich English

Many words have entered the language through the doors of science and technology. For example, the word *watt* honors James Watt, the American inventor of the steam engine. The *ampere* owes its name to the French physicist and mathematician André-Marie Ampère, and the *petri* dish was named for German bacteriologist Julius Petri.

More recently, the burst of high technology has contributed many words such as *reboot*, which means to turn a computer off and then on again, or to restart an operating system. Computer science also brought us new meanings of established nouns such as *bit, bug, chip,* and *hardware*. The creative blending of the technical meaning of *bit* and the general word *bite* produced *byte* (a unit of storage usually the size of one character of information, by one definition) and its offspring *kilobyte* and *megabyte*.

The business and political worlds also change word definitions. *Viable* is a biological term that means "capable of living or developing in favorable conditions." During a recent political campaign, it was amusing to hear a candidate describe himself as "viable." What a laudable idea—a living candidate in Congress. However, if you check some recent dictionaries, you'll find *viable* defined as "workable" or "practicable," which has long been the meaning implied in business offices. So you can now safely say that you want a viable plan.

That dynamic aspect of the language forces publishers to update their dictionaries every few years. Even so, the authors of dictionaries and of style books don't always agree on technical definitions. To complicate matters, so many technical words emerge daily that even a newly published dictionary already lacks the newest terms. Our language—that living, changing maze—challenges us to choose the right words to express each idea.

Guideposts for Choosing Precise, Persuasive Words

If, as an engineer, you want to communicate your brilliant ideas to others, you must not only know your own industry's buzzwords; you must also have a solid command of the language generally. However, the task is not as difficult as it seems. After all, just because English is composed of more than 600,000 words, you don't have to use each one.

To help you choose precise, persuasive words that bring your ideas home to your readers, let's look at words from several perspectives while setting up some guideposts to help you through the maze.

Two primary rules apply to word choice:

1. Choose the precise word, because precise words convey a message accurately.
2. Prefer a short, familiar word to a long, complex word, because short words convey a message quickly.

For example, if you were to study the words in the great works of English literature, you would find that approximately 92 percent of the words the authors used were Anglo-Saxon words (which, remember, are mostly short words), even though Anglo-Saxon words make up only about 25 percent of the language.

Although you may not be writing great literature, you can still find a guidepost in such statistics: In your engineering writing, try to maintain a balance of at least 85 percent short words and no more than 15 percent long words (three syllables or more). That balance will give you enough variety to maintain a reader's interest, which can easily be distracted if the writing is either monotonous or complicated.

We're not saying that you should use only short words. Follow that 85-percent-short-words, 15-percent-long-words guidepost. Given the choice, though, between a short word and a longer, more precise word, opt for the precise word. By choosing precise words, you will avoid words that are pompous, vague, and vogue. Choosing precise words is the first step toward clear, concise writing. Remember, in writing, strength beats length.

Concrete Words Stimulate the Senses

We can classify nouns (persons, places, or things) as either abstract or concrete. Readers have more trouble understanding abstract nouns than concrete nouns.

Truth, for example, is an abstract noun. What comes to your mind if someone says "truth"? Do you see anything? Do you hear anything? You may be able to associate the word *truth* with something concrete like the scales of justice or, as one of our workshop participants said, with Superman. But you can't see, hear, feel, smell, or taste truth.

How many philosophy books have you read that were easy to read? Very few, probably. Their subject matter lends itself too easily to abstract words: *existentialism, fatalism, transcendentalism.*

Now consider a concrete word like *chair*. You can visualize a chair. You can imagine what it feels like to sit on a chair or to hear it squeak. Abstract words can muddle the message for the reader; concrete words help the reader to grasp your meaning more easily, because they stimulate the senses by letting the reader see, hear, feel, smell, or even taste. How many of your senses are stimulated by such words as *straw, buzzer, velvet, skunk,* and *chocolate*?

If you enjoy science, read anything by Isaac Asimov, a 20th century Russian-born American biologist. The prolific author of more than 200 books, he lucidly explained complex scientific principles by using concrete terms. His concrete words still help the average person understand complex concepts. Despite his enormous ego, which he admitted to, Asimov wrote to be understood, not to impress people with his knowledge of a subject.

Sometimes, of course, you may find it hard to avoid the abstract words. If that's the case, you can improve readership by increasing your count of short sentences.

Strong Verbs Strengthen Your Writing

Just as concrete nouns stimulate interest by painting word-pictures in the reader's mind, action verbs stimulate interest by creating a

---

Concrete vs. Abstract Words

Read through the following list of abstract words. What comes to mind when you see them? Try to define some of the words.

characterization	technology
diffraction	process
deposition	capacitance
generality	abundance
association	aerodynamics
propulsion	stability
extrapolation	

Now read through the following concrete-words list. Notice how quickly these words trigger your sense of sight, hearing, touch, smell, or taste. These words are probably easier for you to define.

desk	sulfur
thunder	varnish
diffractometer	coal
wire	transistor
gasoline	chart
tripod	dust
dish	salt
lamp	valve
flask	wing
fan	engine
spoke	nozzle

Whenever possible, prefer concrete words, because they can convey your message more clearly.

sense of movement. Verbs are meant to show either action or a state of being, thus giving us two types of verbs: strong and weak. Compare the following two groups of verbs:

Group A: eat, go, give, break, read, send, pay, build, decide, push, pull

Group B: is, are, was, were, has been, have been, will be

Notice that the Group A verbs create movement, helping readers grasp ideas quickly; the Group B verbs remain static, merely showing a state of being. Technically, the Group A verbs are called *action verbs*, while the Group B verbs are called *being* or *linking verbs*.

Sometimes the being verbs act as *helping* (*auxiliary*) verbs for action verbs, as in the phrases *will be drilling*, *is eating*, and *has transferred*. Such phrases are still action verbs, keeping movement in the sentence.

Compare the following examples of weak versus strong phrasing:

Instead of: Pat is a writer of programs.
         (weak, being verb: is)

    Prefer: Pat writes programs.
         (strong, action verb: writes)

Instead of: The fastest system was your design.
         (weak, being verb: was)

    Prefer: You designed the fastest system.
         (strong, action verb: designed)

The more *being* verbs you use in your writing, the more you risk boring your reader. Conversely, the more *action* verbs you use, the more you will stimulate your reader's interest. Action verbs breathe life into sentences.

Specific Words Convey More Information per Word

We've looked at some words as two types of nouns and as two types of verbs. Now let's take an overview and classify words as general and specific. Usually, prefer specific words to general words. The *general* action word *walked* says less than the more *specific* action words *staggered*, *swaggered*, and *limped*. The specific words sharpen the focus of the word-picture in a reader's mind.

The word *device* is concrete, so that's good. Yet it tells a reader less than the more specific concrete words *pedal*, *handle*, *printer*, *crowbar*, *hinge*, *tweezers*, or *joystick*.

That's not to say that you should try to use only specific words. General words have their uses, too. For example, during the initial discussion of a new project with a potential customer, the chief project engineer may speak mostly in general terms. Her follow-up report to the customer will also use more general terms. Then as the chief engineer has more discussions with the customer and learns more about specific needs, she will begin using more specific terms. Her follow-up reports will contain more specific words. Were she to continue using general terms, especially in the final proposal, the client would think that the chief engineer didn't understand the customer's needs. Then it's bye-bye, contract.

In the following table, the general words work better at the initial customer meeting, and the specific words work better during the final proposal.

General	Specific
goal	30% profit
resources	five engineers, $500,000 budget
results	75% fewer failures

Positive Words Bring Positive Results

We can also categorize words psychologically according to how they affect us: positively, negatively, or neutrally.

Positive words affect people positively by appealing to the senses, recalling pleasant memories, or complimenting the receiver. Overall, positive words make readers happy.

▶ senses: refreshing, warm, delicious, fragrant

▶ memories: vacation, paycheck, sex

▶ compliments: impressive, excellent, professional

Negative words produce negative feelings in readers.

▶ senses: slimy, stench, pain, noxious, rancid

▶ memories: failure, punish, penalty

▶ putdowns: stupid, unethical, worthless

Neutral words give your readers little insight into your meaning. Some words are neutral because they are unfamiliar and most people don't recognize them.

specious	mendacious	fulgurous
nabob	lapidate	

Other words become neutralized and lose their impact from overuse:

really	super	quite
absolutely	awesome	issue

"He who wants to persuade should put his trust not in the right argument, but in the right word."

—Joseph Conrad
Polish-born English novelist
(1857–1924)

Realizing the psychological impact of words, you can more readily control your reader by combining positive or negative words with the three strongest words at your command: *you, I,* and the reader's name. (Note that included among these strongest words are their various plural and possessive forms: *we, my, mine, our, ours, your, yours.* Use these personal words to add power and persuasion to your writing.)

Positive: **Chris, you** wrote an **excellent** report.

Now how do you think Chris feels? Happy, no doubt, having been complimented so graciously. Don't you always feel good when someone gives you an oral or written pat on the back?

Negative: **Mike, I** was **disappointed** in **your** report.

How does Mike feel? How would you feel when someone told you that he or she was disappointed in your work?

By using *you*, *I*, and the reader's name, you focus the positive or negative impact on the *person* instead of on the *situation*. Just knowing this fact gives you a powerful persuasive tool. These strong words capture and hold the reader's attention.

You can find excellent examples of the power of the word *you* in your bulk mail. Do something different today and open your direct-mail solicitations, especially something from Time-Life, American Express, or one of the other higher-quality direct-mail campaigns aimed at a relatively intelligent and affluent audience.

Most direct-mail packages have at least a letter, a brochure, and a response device. Read the letter. We'll bet you a dollar to a doughnut that the word *you* is in the first paragraph and is surrounded by positive words.

One of the first steps in persuasion is to get the person on your side. The best way to do that is to use positive words. Once you get someone on your side of the fence, you can more easily sell that person your ideas. The word *you* captures and holds the person's attention, and the positive words make the person happy. When do you try to sell your spouse or friend an idea—when he or she is in a good mood or in a bad mood?

Now let's delve more deeply into words to see how they can reflect your attitude toward your reader or subject as revealed through your tone.

Maintaining a Professional Tone

> *"Don't use that tone with me, young man."*
>
> —any mother (any time)

A professional tone in your writing gives weight to your ideas and helps you and your writing to be taken seriously. A document displays a professional tone when it comes across as objective, unemotional, and accurate.

Your tone is influenced primarily by your attitude toward your reader and your subject. Your word choice conveys this attitude. You have probably heard a piqued person say, "It's not what he said, it's *how* he said it that made me so angry." In other words, the speaker's choice of words and attitude angered the listener more than the message did.

Your writing reveals your feelings. If you're angry, your letter will sound angry. If you're enthusiastic, your enthusiasm will show.

A Respectful Attitude Shows Professionalism

The easiest way to maintain a professional tone in your writing is to maintain respect for your reader. If you respect your reader and try to look at your subject matter from his or her perspective, your writing will probably exhibit a professional tone.

In a way, tone is also tied to purpose. Take the writer whose purpose is not to inform you, but rather to impress you with his knowledge of the subject. His tone comes across as pompous. He's not writing to you; he's writing for himself. On the other hand, the writer who is sincerely interested in ensuring that you understand a technical point will take pains to explain a complex subject as clearly as he can. This writer is writing for you. His writing will have a professional tone.

Always picture your reader, and do a mental profile of your reader, as we suggested earlier. Knowing your reader—and his or her needs—lets you approach your reader logically and, if need be, diplomatically. You obviously write about a technical subject differently to a nontechnical person than you do to a technical person. But no matter who your reader is, your purpose is not to impress, but to communicate.

A respectful attitude toward your reader will always help you to maintain a professional tone in your writing.

Some Words Carry Emotional Overtones

One more guidepost about word choice: Consider the emotional overtones of the words you use, because people are motivated more by emotion than by logic or reason. Words have at least two levels of meaning: The *denotation* refers to the dictionary definition, while the *connotation* refers to the implied meaning. Words of similar denotation may have quite an opposite connotation.

The following words are synonyms of *perfectionist*, yet each has a different connotation:

idealist	purist	nitpicker
fusspot	radical	reformist

These adjectives describing a perfectionist also have different connotations:

careful	attentive	neat
diligent	fastidious	prudent
thoughtful	thorough	accurate
orderly	alert	picky
discerning		

> *"Words are, of course, the most powerful drug used by mankind."*
>
> —Rudyard Kipling
> English writer
> (1865–1936)

Would you rather be described as *picky* or *attentive*?

Think before you write. You'll usually get the desired results a lot faster from your readers by using a professional, positive tone than by sending a nasty-gram. Remember that good advice: "Keep a civil tongue in your head."

Using Precise, Diplomatic Words to Spark Action

You should now have a good feel for word types and their impact on people. Now let's bring together these various perspectives on words and see how they work in a typical business letter.

Let's say that your project is bogged down because another department head hasn't signed off on your status report. Since the same department head has lost reports before, you're starting to get angry.

Here's the memo *not* to send:

> We had sent our North Freeway engineering status report to you two weeks ago for your review. You said at that time that you would quickly review the report and pass it on to your traffic analyst for review. Today I talked to Corey Mason, who said he had never received the report from you.
>
> A similar incident occurred last year, and the lost report was found in your desk; so could you please double-check to make sure you have reviewed the report and sent it to Traffic? We'll be happy to send you another report if you can't locate the original one.

Look at the tone. That letter is emotional, not objective. It's accusing, not diplomatic. The writer's attitude toward the reader is not respectful. Within the negative tone are several uses of *you*. In the following repetition of those two paragraphs, only the uses of *you* and *your* are in italic type:

> We had sent our North Freeway engineering status report to *you* two weeks ago for *your* review. *You* said at that time that *you* would quickly review the report and pass it on to *your* traffic analyst for review. Today I talked to Corey Mason, who said he had never received the report from *you*.
>
> A similar incident occurred last year, and the lost report was found in *your* desk; so could *you* please double-check to make sure *you* have reviewed the report and sent it to Traffic? We'll be happy to send *you* another report if *you* can't locate the original one.

The frequent use of *you* focuses blame on the reader, in a situation in which blame should not be addressed. Whether that reader had made an honest mistake or is just a flake, that letter would certainly decrease your chances of getting your desired action. You would have just made an enemy, not a friend. Let's revise that letter before sending it out, or you'll never find satisfaction.

> Our records show that we have not yet received Traffic's approval of our engineering status report on the North Freeway project. Since we're nearing the deadline on this project, can you review this copy and pass it on to Traffic today? We'll appreciate your help.

Now you should get some action. You've diplomatically reminded the reader that the report is overdue. The memo has a professional tone because it is objective, unemotional, and not accusing. It merely states the facts, without comment.

When and How to Use Humor

To decide whether or not to use humor, consider, as always, your reader and your purpose. More than likely, you would not deem humor appropriate for a government proposal. The less formal the document, the better the chances that humor might work for you. Humor can effectively relieve a tense situation.

If you have to try too hard to make a humorous point, you're probably better off not trying at all. You certainly don't want to appear flippant in what others consider a serious situation. Using humor in engineering writing depends more on the writer's comfort level than on anything else.

A general rule of thumb for diplomacy is to attack the problem or the situation, not the person. The same goes for humor. Use it to attack a situation, but not to attack a person. If you're not comfortable using humor, don't.

In the next chapter, you will learn how to combine your well-chosen words to produce readable sentences.

> *"Man does not live by words alone, despite the fact that sometimes he has to eat them."*
>
> —Adlai Stevenson
> U.S. statesman and twice a
> Democratic candidate for President
> (1900–1965)

Summary of This Chapter's Main Points

- ▶ Choose precise words first.
- ▶ Choose short, simple words next.
- ▶ Prefer concrete nouns to abstract nouns.
- ▶ Prefer strong (action) verbs to weak (being, or linking) verbs.
- ▶ Prefer specific words to general words.
- ▶ Use positive words to persuade your reader.
- ▶ Use *you*, *I*, and the reader's name to add power to your writing.
- ▶ Maintain a professional tone in your writing by respecting your reader.
- ▶ Consider a word's emotional overtones.
- ▶ Use humor carefully.

6 Sentences: Installing Components in Practical Patterns

So far, you have an overview of the writing process and two key elements of clear writing: organization and word choice. Now let's move on to a more challenging subject: sentence structure.

The next three chapters contain more concentrated technical information per square inch than do any other chapters in this book. The writing is lucid and the information is clearly presented. However, you may want to allot yourself a bit more time to read and study these three chapters so that you get the most out of them.

Your reward will be a more comfortable understanding of how to use professional writing techniques from an engineer's structural perspective.

Relaxing Your Mindset About Sentences

A sentence can seem like a complicated piece of machinery. The more you try to make it do, the more problems you can create.

Look at the difference between a hand saw and a chain saw. What can go wrong with a hand saw? It needs sharpening and some occasional oil to prevent rusting. But a chainsaw? Oy vey! Oil, gasoline, chains, carburetors, spark plugs. Clogging, stalling, kicking, biting. So much to worry about.

Maybe that's why some people dread writing—so much to worry about. Words and paragraphs aren't too bad, but those sentences with all those rules—yuck! Just thinking about all the rules can tighten your jaw and make you grind your teeth. Relax. We're going to show you an easier way to analyze sentences.

We'll start with the sentence components and show you how to fit them together, much as you fit together the components of an engineering project.

Using Components to Build Sentences

A sentence is composed of components that fit into various sentence slots. When you put the correct components in the correct slots, you create a clear sentence that conveys your message. If you use the wrong component or if you put the right component in the wrong slot, clarity suffers.

Sentences are similar to engineering structures in that you try to build the sentences correctly and then you analyze or test them to see if they work. To construct and analyze clear sentences, you must first understand the components you are working with and know where to place them to accomplish the job.

This chapter will familiarize you with the infrastructure of sentences:

▶ the structural components of a sentence

▶ the functional slots that house those components

▶ the logical patterns you can use to create clear sentences

We will be using some technical terms, but none nearly as complicated as the engineering terms you have already learned. If you can handle subjects such as differential calculus, vector analysis, and thermodynamics, you can easily handle the logical rules governing sentence structure.

Let's start with the basic component: the word. In Chapter 5, you learned how to choose precise words, and you painlessly previewed two technical terms: noun and verb. So you have a head start toward analyzing words in a "component" sense. Now let's see how words function as parts of speech, and how parts of speech function as parts of a sentence, creating logical patterns.

Fitting All Words into Eight Handy Categories

All words fit into one of eight categories called the *parts of speech*. You can go through any document, pick out any words you want (even the latest ones coined by your fellow engineers), and they will always fit into one of the following eight categories. (Note: The abbreviations following each part of speech will be used throughout this chapter.)

▶ *noun* (n): a person, place, or thing

▶ *pronoun* (pron): replaces a noun or another pronoun

▶ *verb* (v): shows action or state of being

▶ *adjective* (adj): describes a noun—tells what kind, size, shape, color

▶ *adverb* (adv): describes a verb, adjective, or another adverb—tells when, where, how, to what degree

▶ *conjunction* (conj): joins other words or word groups to each other

▶ *preposition* (prep): precedes a noun to relate it to other words

▶ *interjection* (int): jumps in to express sudden emotion; often stands alone

Following are examples of those parts of speech:

▶ noun: compatibility, systems, matrix, equipment, Pat, coil, fluoride, Pittsburgh, alloy, circuit, lumber

- ▶ pronoun: I, me, my, you, we, us, our, they, them, he, she, it, this, that, these, those, which

- ▶ verb: analyze, collapse, determine, have, should, be, approve, release, join, compete, rotate, go

- ▶ adjective: heavy, pure, applicable, unstable, magnetic, blue, rusted, polished, old, simple, resilient

- ▶ adverb: expertly, rigidly, corrosively, digitally, equally, frequently, well, often, now, very, too

- ▶ preposition: by, of, for, from, in, at, to, into, above, during, around, beside, under, near, behind, over

- ▶ conjunction: and, but, or, nor, because, however, although

- ▶ interjection: oh, yes, no, hello, Wow! Ah! Oops! Ouch! Stop! Eep!

The following sentence contains all eight parts of speech at least once:

Yes, Pat expertly explained the new software to Darla and me.
int   n   adv   v   adj   n   prep   n   conj   pron

By knowing what categories your words fall into, you can more easily analyze your sentences to see how (and whether) they work.

Some words always function as only one part of speech. For example, *he* and *she* are always pronouns. *Geometry* is always a noun. Many words are itinerant, moving around from one part of speech to another, working in different functions from sentence to sentence. *Green* can be an adjective describing the color of an apple. *Green* can also be a noun that names the section of a golf course where you miss putts and break golf clubs. *Help* can function as a noun or a verb. The word *well* takes many forms. Notice its different uses in the following sentences:

- ▶ well = noun: That oil well gushes 500,000 gallons of oil a day.

- ▶ well = adverb: A well-oiled machine saves maintenance costs.

- ▶ well = interjection: Well, where do we go from here?

Words such as *test*, *design*, *base*, *cause*, *crack*, *model*, *load*, *control*, and *frame* can function as more than one part of speech, depending on the use of the words in different sentences. For example, the word *test* can be used in several ways:

- ▶ test = noun: We completed the test yesterday.

- ▶ test = verb: We routinely test 1,000 units of each production run.

- ▶ test = adjective: Did the test results reveal any design flaws?

The parts of speech, in turn, can perform various functions, depending on where they fall in the sentence. Most parts of speech perform one function. For example, adjectives and adverbs are always describers. Some parts of speech are quite versatile, though. For

*"True ease in writing comes from art, not chance,
As those move easiest who have learned to dance."*

—Alexander Pope
English poet
(1688–1744)

example, a noun can function as a subject (what the sentence is about), an object (a receiver of action), or an identifier (defining who or what the subject is). Pronouns, being substitutes for nouns, can also perform as subjects, objects, or identifiers.

Considering the wanderlust of the words and their functions, we need systematic rules to govern the actions of the parts of speech. Thus, we have grammar. The more parts of speech you have in a sentence and the more functions these parts take on, the more grammatical rules come into play—just as more-sophisticated engineering structures bring more engineering laws into play.

No need to tense up. You can relax. You won't be dragged through all the grammatical rules. This book is reviewing just enough sentence structure to help you see which sentences in your engineering reports work well and which ones don't. Knowing the difference can determine whether you communicate fully with your readers or present fragments that leave logical gaps in your reports.

To see how the parts of speech interact with one another to build a lucid sentence, let's look at the parts of a sentence.

Subject and Verb: Complements for Clarity

Life is full of complements: day and night, input and output, yin and yang. Such complements provide the balance needed for completeness. Your sentences, too, need completeness to make sense. That's one way to achieve clarity.

Complete sentences aren't hard to produce if you know how the two parts of a sentence complement—or complete—each other. To be complete, a sentence must have two parts: a complete subject and a predicate.

▶ The *complete subject* tells what the sentence is about. It always contains the simple subject and may contain other words that describe the simple subject. Only two parts of speech—the noun and the pronoun—can act as a simple subject.

▶ The *predicate* says something about the subject. It always contains the verb and may contain other words that tell what the subject is doing or what the subject is. The verb, which is the main part of the predicate, may show an action or a state of being.

Being able to spot the subject and verb will be of immense help to you later. To edit a sentence competently, you must be able to find the subject and the verb of the sentence. (We will describe the editing process in a later chapter.)

In its simplest form, a complete sentence must always have a simple subject and a verb. For example:

Managers moved.

In that sentence, *managers* is both the simple subject and the complete subject; *moved* is both the verb and the predicate. Let's examine a longer sentence.

> The engineering managers with the least seniority moved the office files
> to the new facility on Saturday.

The complete subject of that sentence is *The engineering managers with the least seniority*. The simple subject is *managers*. The predicate of that sentence is *moved the office files to the new facility on Saturday*. The verb is *moved*.

In the following examples showing complete subjects and predicates, the simple subjects are abbreviated *ss* and verbs are abbreviated *v*.

complete subject: researchers at both universities
ss

predicate: have studied the effects of gamma rays on moonbeams
v

predicate: ahead of us lies
v

complete subject: a most exciting journey
ss

complete subject: our failure analysis
ss

predicate: revealed four glitches in the flood-control system
v

Notice how the two halves of those sentences work together to create full ideas.

Note: Grammarians usually describe either the complete subject or the simple subject as simply the *subject*. For convenience and consistency in this book, we will refer to the complete subject by its full name (*complete subject*) and to the simple subject as *subject*.

As we said, the predicate tells what the complete subject is doing or tells what the subject is. So the predicate describes either an action or a state of being.

▶ action: Standard calculations **can lead to heat-loss errors**.
▶ state of being: Vacuum-return systems **are two-pipe systems**.

Notice that in the first example above, the subject (*calculations*) is acting (*can lead*), and in the second example, the subject (*systems*) is merely being (*are*).

Sometimes the predicate includes not just an action verb, but also a receiver of the action. That receiver is the *object*. Earlier we mentioned that sentence components fit into certain slots. Two key slots that are always present in a sentence are the *subject* (abbreviated *subj* or *s*) and the *verb* (abbreviated *v*). Often present is the third key slot, the *object* (abbreviated *obj* or *o*).

For example:

Subatmospheric systems regulate steam flow.
subj   v   obj

Now let's take a closer look at the parts of speech and see how they can function within a sentence, so that words don't trick you as you try to make them do what you want.

A noun can act as a subject or an object.

The cable broke.
subj

Bob replaced the cable.
obj

The next examples also show that nouns and pronouns can function in several ways:

▶ noun (*beams*) as a subject (what the sentence is about):

Timber **beams** come in standard rectangular sizes listed by the National Lumber Manufacturers' Association.

▶ noun (*loads*) as an object (receiver of an action):

Beams carry the joist **loads**.

▶ noun (*conduit*) as an identifier of the subject (*culvert*):

A culvert is a **conduit** that passes drainage through an embankment.

▶ noun (*instruments*) as object of a preposition (*of*):

A variety of **instruments** can be used.
(The noun *variety* is the subject of that sentence.)

▶ pronoun (*you*) used as a subject:

You are the newest member of our project team.

▶ pronoun (*you*) used as an object of the verb (*wants*):

Pat wants **you** to speak at the conference.

You get the idea. Nouns and pronouns like to stay flexible, moving around from one sentence-part function to another, depending on the logic of the sentence.

So you see that words, the basic components of a sentence, can act in several capacities as different parts of speech. That knowledge will help you analyze and control your sentences more easily, to help ensure that your engineering reports say what you mean to say.

Now let's look at how those parts of speech function in natural, logical patterns within sentences.

Applying User-Friendly Patterns

To write a clear sentence, first concentrate on the message you want to send, then think about the *key words* that will convey the *message*, and finally present those key words in a *logical order*. Why? Because a reader looks for a message made up of key words presented in a logical order. This logical order is important to the reader.

Quickly read through the following line of numbers, just as you would read through a sentence. Then, without looking back, repeat the numbers.

2, 4, 6, 8, 10, 12

Now do the same with the next set. Quickly read through the line and repeat the numbers without looking back.

3, 6, 9, 12, 15, 18

Okay, one more time. Do the same with the following line of numbers:

7, 16, 3, 35, 92, 28

Gotcha! What's the difference between the third line of numbers and the first two lines? The first two follow a logical pattern. The numbers in the third line fall in a random order, which takes longer to read and is harder to remember. Now you know how a person feels after reading an illogically constructed or randomly worded sentence. Readers expect sentences to follow familiar patterns, and a sentence that doesn't can throw the reader off. So let's look at how you can arrange key words into positive, familiar patterns for your reader.

Sentences usually fall into two patterns: the action pattern or the being pattern. The *action* pattern tells what does what to what. The *being* pattern tells what is what.

Action Pattern

The action pattern uses key words that answer:

1. Who or what? = the subject (the actor or agent of the action)

2. Does, did, or will do what? = the action verb

3. To what or to whom? = the object (receiver of the action)

In the action-pattern sentence, the key slots are arranged in a *subject-verb-object* order, also known as the *SVO* order.

The client changed the meeting time.
S   V   O

The key words in that sentence tell "who did what to what," in the SVO order. Here are five handy variations of that question:

► What does what?

► Who does what?

► What does what to what?

► Who does what to what?

► Who does what to whom?

Following are some examples of those variations. The italic print identifies the subject, the verb, and (if there is one) the object.

► What does, did, or will do what?

Snow melts.
The *characteristics vary* with each filter type.
The *dam cracked.*
The current data-acquisition *project will end* next week.

► Who does, did, or will do what?

Engineers think logically.
Fred laughed.
Your *customer will arrive* early.

► What does, did, or will do what to what?

The *use* of heavy steel columns *stiffens* a high-rise *building.*
Redundancy saved the sagging *pier* from collapse.
Minor *changes* to the fan design *will reduce* the noise *level.*

► Who does, did, or will do what to what?

A careful *designer runs* redundant *tests* to confirm results.
The design *engineers minimized* the structure's *cost.*
The project *managers will review* the gear *specifications.*

► Who does, did, or will do what to whom?

Our experienced *developers train* newly hired *specialists* in the lab and
   in the field.
The bridge *engineers briefed* the *architect* on their progress.
The mask *designers will interview* the clean-room *workers* about the suspected contamination.

In the above sets of examples, the pattern was either subject-verb or subject-verb-object.

For practice, revise the following sentences by putting the key words into the action-pattern (SVO) order:

1. Attached is an example in which the new format is shown.

_____

2. It is suspected that there is a correlation between the two problems.

_____

The following suggested SVO revisions tell what or who does what to what:

1. The attached example shows the new format.
   S V   O

2. The chief engineer suspects a correlation between the two problems.
   S V   O

Notice that the original version of the second example (*It is suspected*) didn't tell you who suspects the correlation. If you wanted to learn more about the correlation, you could not go directly to the source. The SVO revision, though, forces you to insert a more informative subject. In this case that's good, because the revised subject produces a clearer sentence.

Chapter 7 will show you one more variation on the SVO pattern. For now, just remember to put the key words of most messages into a logical "what does what to what" pattern.

Being Pattern

What if the message you want to convey doesn't express an action? For example, what if you merely want to define a term or a new product? In that case, you use the second pattern—the *being* pattern.

For this pattern, use key words that answer the question "Who or what is (are, was, etc.) who or what?"

▶ Who or what? = the subject

▶ Is, are, was, were, has been, will be, etc. = the being (or linking) verb

▶ Who or what? = a describer (adjective) or identifier (noun or pronoun)

Here are some key-word examples of the being pattern:

	Who or What	Being Verb	Who or What
1.	Gloria	is	manager
2.	project	appears	incomplete
3.	Bob	has become	guru
4.	customers	will be	happy
5.	work	was	professional

Below are samples of resulting sentences:

1. Gloria is now the manager of the facility.

2. The 808 Freeway project appears incomplete.

3. Bob has become a virtual-reality guru.

4. Our customers will be happy with the upgrade.

5. Your work on the slide project was professional.

To write a being-pattern sentence, put your key words into three slots that answer: "What/Who (subject) is (verb) what (describer or identifier)?"

Think of the being verb as an equal sign, creating an equation telling what equals what ("What/Who = what?").

The "what" at the end of the being pattern can be an identifier or a describer in these question variations:

▶ What is, are, was, were, or will be what (identifier)?

In the discrete equation, *k is* a running *index*, and *T is* the sampling *period* of the digitizing process.
Electronic *typewriters were* the *ancestors* of computers.
The most obvious *problem was* the uncontrolled IC *output*.
The ABC *Glitchgone will be* an easy-to-use debugging *device*.

▶ Who is, are, was, were, or will be what (identifier)?

Our senior *developer is* the *expert* on signal-analysis software.
Pat Harkney was the first senior *engineer* at Wirotech in Cupertino.
We will be partners in the modular-design contest.

▶ What is, are, was, were, or will be what (describer)?

The latest *circuits are* more *stable* than the earlier ones.
That *documentation was unclear*.
Your next holography *project will be* even more *complex*.

▶ Who is, are, was, were, or will be what (describer)?

Your design *team is* the most *competent* in the industry.
All our *customers were happy* with the design change.
All the cost *figures must be accurate*.

For variety, then, you have two main patterns (action and being), and each has its own variations. Most of the time, you can simplify your message by putting your key words into one of those patterns.

Of the two, the action pattern usually creates stronger sentences because of its more dynamic verb choices. So if you can change a being-pattern sentence into an action-pattern sentence, do it. You'll enliven your writing.

To practice, change the following *being* sentences into *action* sentences:

1. The new software is capable of reducing downtime by 25 percent.

   _____

2. Gomer is the leader of the maintenance crew.

   _____

3. This office is the link between our corporate headquarters and our European CIS Operation team.

   _____

   _____

Some suggested revisions are:

1. The new software can reduce downtime by 25 percent.
   S   V   O

2. Gomer leads the maintenance crew.
   S   V   O

3. This office links our corporate headquarters to our European CIS Operations.
   S   V   O

In your engineering writing you use action-pattern variations, depending on whether you want to identify the actor or not. We'll discuss more about those variations in Chapter 7. Right now, though, let's glance at a few internal-support patterns that help to ensure clarity.

Three Supporting Patterns Ensure Consistency

Some internal-support patterns are so obvious you don't have to think about them; others aren't. We'll briefly summarize three supporting patterns that may not be obvious to you—until you break the pattern and make your readers struggle to patch it back together.

The few technical terms that define these patterns are not all new to you; most of the terms just build on what you already read in this chapter. The following three common-sense supporting patterns can help you ensure accuracy, consistency, and clarity in your engineering writing:

▶ subject-verb agreement: a number pattern

▶ noun-pronoun agreement: another number pattern

▶ parallel phrasing: a train-tracks pattern

Subject-Verb Agreement: A Number Pattern

Subjects and verbs usually fall into this preferred agreement pattern: Singular subjects take singular verbs, and plural subjects take plural verbs. For example:

> The system-installation *project is* finished.
> The system-installation *projects are* finished.

Most of the time, you don't have to think much about the subject-verb pair. Watch out, though, when the sentence has a distracting prepositional phrase between the subject and its verb. The interrupting phrase might distract you from the subject. Don't let it. If you ignore the interrupting phrase temporarily, you'll see the logic easily.

For example, notice the interrupting prepositional (*of* ...) phrase between the subject and its verb in the next three examples:

> Our *team* of technicians *is working* on the chip now.
> *Each* of our departments *employs* at least one chemical engineer.
> *All* of our departments *employ* at least one chemical engineer.

Those three sentences all have subjects and verbs that agree in number. A shortcut to achieving agreement, though, is to shorten the sentence by deleting the interrupting prepositional phrase.

For example, instead of saying "Our team of technicians is working on the chip now," you could say more briefly: "Our technicians are working on the chip now." The shorter, smoother version avoids a potential break in the agreement pattern.

Noun-Pronoun Agreement: Another Number Pattern

A second number pattern is a pairing of nouns and pronouns. Here's the pattern: A pronoun must agree in number (singular or plural) with the noun or pronoun it refers to. (Would you call them the referrer and the referee? No, but nice try. The word being referred to is fancily yet logically called the *antecedent*, which means "going before.")

To safeguard this agreement pattern, use only a singular pronoun to replace a singular noun, and use only a plural pronoun to replace a plural noun. That's usually easy, as in these examples:

> *Carrie* read the HVAC contract thoroughly before *she* signed it.
> *Bill* and *Sunil* locked the office when *they* left.
> The *program* shines because *it* provides prototypes for all 600 of *its*
>   built-in functions.

In American English usage, consider a group, department, division, or company name as singular; be sure to use *it* or *its*, not *they*, *them*, or *their*, when referring to such an entity.

> *ABC Corporation* is upgrading *its* (not "their") computer system.
> *Bolder Bridges Company* expects a 25-percent profit for *its* (not "their")
>   third quarter.

Note that in the present tense, the singular verb serves as a clue that the pattern is singular.

When a pronoun replaces another pronoun, the pattern may need closer checking. Here's why: The following pronouns are always replaced by singular pronouns:

each	every
everyone	everybody
one	no one
nobody	someone
somebody	anyone
anybody	either
neither	

Thus the sentence might say:

Every manager is responsible for his team.

That sentence works grammatically because both *every manager* and *his* are singular. They agree in number. Yet unless all the team managers are male, that revision creates a pronoun-gender problem. So we could say:

Every *manager* is responsible for *his* or *her* team.

That revision, too, is grammatically okay; but, in an engineering report, a series of "his or her" sentences could quickly distract readers from the content. The smoothest way to avoid such distractions is to start with a plural noun:

All *managers* are responsible for *their* teams.

Just don't say, "Every manager is responsible for their team," because the plural pronoun (*their*) cannot logically refer to a singular noun (*manager*). Such a construction would break the agreement pattern.

The words *everyone* and *everybody* (which sound plural) are actually singular (collective singular) pronouns. When using them, you can avoid breaking the agreement pattern by using any of these versions:

Everyone wants *his* or *her* own copy of the rewiring contract.
   (Just avoid overusing that "his or her" wording.)
Everyone wants *a* copy of the rewiring contract.
All *employees* want *their* own copies of the rewiring contract.

By making sure that the numbers agree, you give the sentence accuracy, consistency, and clarity.

Parallel Phrasing: A Train-Tracks Pattern

Also on the "consistency" track is what we call *parallel phrasing*. The parallel-phrasing rule says to use similar word patterns for similar ideas, either within a sentence or within a list.

Think of parallel phrasing as you would train tracks. If the tracks are parallel, the train rides them safely. If one track is bent, the train can jump the track. A parallel pair, series, or list works smoothly, but an unparallel pair, series, or list makes the sentence jump the logical track—sometimes even causing a communication crash. At the very least, unparallel phrasing creates awkward sentences and distracts readers from the content.

Unparallel:	I like biking, hiking, and to sail.
Parallel:	I like biking, hiking, and sailing.
Unparallel:	The design and analysis of these compression members is similar to the W-shape column's design and analysis.
Parallel:	The design of these compression members is similar to the design of (or "that of") the W-shape column.
Unparallel:	Normal tensile stresses are positive; stresses are negative if they are normal compressive ones.
Parallel:	Normal tensile stresses are positive; normal compressive stresses are negative.
Unparallel list:	The audit focused on three criteria:

 ▶ employee-performance monitoring system
 ▶ how projects are managed
 ▶ Organizational structure was also evaluated.

Parallel list:	The audit focused on three criteria:

 ▶ employee-performance monitoring system
 ▶ project management
 ▶ organizational structure

"Words—so innocent and powerless as they are, as standing in a dictionary, how potent for good and evil they become, in the hands of one who knows how to combine them!"

—Nathaniel Hawthorne
American writer
(1804–1864)

A parallel list helps readers grasp and remember similar ideas easily. Just avoid mixing phrases and full sentences in the same list. Often, the pattern that you use in the first list item is the most natural for the whole list.

Those subject-verb agreement, noun-pronoun agreement, and parallel-phrasing patterns support the more general action and being patterns in sentences. By using smooth, logical patterns, you will write clearer sentences with less pain.

In conclusion, clarity saves time—for both writers and readers. The less time you spend trying to figure out how to write what you mean to say, the more time you have left for your main engineering tasks. In turn, the less time your readers spend trying to figure out what you said—or calling to have you explain what you meant—the more time you both save.

The next chapter will help you apply the preferred action pattern efficiently and objectively to your engineering writing.

Summary of This Chapter's Main Points

▶ All words (basic components) are one of eight parts of speech.

▶ To be complete, a sentence must have a subject and a verb. The *subject* tells what the sentence is about. The *verb* says something about the subject.

▶ The two main sentence patterns are *action* and *being*.

▶ Put key words in two or three key slots that answer one of these questions:
   — What does what (to what)? (action pattern)
   — Who does what (to what or to whom)? (action pattern)
   — What (or who) = what? (being pattern)

▶ Prefer the action pattern, with key words in the subject-verb-object (SVO) order, for easiest reading.

▶ Use three supporting patterns for accuracy, consistency, and clarity:
   — Make subjects and their verbs agree in number (singular or plural).
   — Make pronouns and their referred-to nouns agree in number.
   — Use parallel phrasing for pairs, series, and lists.

7 Sentences: Gaining the Active-Voice Edge

Increasing Clarity and Conciseness

You will now learn one of the best ways to improve your engineering-writing skills. Up to now, you may have developed a habit common to many engineering writers: using too much passive voice. If so, and if you want to become an effective engineering writer, you'll have to make a crucial decision as you read this chapter: to accept the active voice into your heart.

If you can switch from writing mostly in the passive voice to writing mostly in the active voice, your writing will become clearer, more concise, and more readable—without losing objectivity. No longer will your reader misinterpret your thoughts, ideas, and directions. No longer will you be plagued by phone calls from colleagues, customers, and contractors asking you to explain what you meant in that last memo. You may even receive fewer calls from customers' lawyers. (No promises here.)

What we are promising is that active voice will help make you a much more effective and efficient communicator. The decision will be yours.

Perhaps someone has already told you that you should use more active voice. Or perhaps your computer grammar checker keeps blurting out, "Passive voice. Passive voice. You're using too much passive voice." So you scratch your head and say, "Okay. So what's the big deal? What am I supposed to do?" The big deal is that passive voice can be:

- ▶ difficult to read
- ▶ misleading
- ▶ unclear

Passive voice plays havoc with the engineering-writing purpose, which is to communicate information quickly, clearly, and efficiently. Documents written mostly in the passive voice are hard to read, unclear (because of information gaps), and thus inefficient.

> *"Ill habits gather by unseen degrees—As brooks make rivers, rivers run to seas."*
>
> —John Dryden
> English poet
> (1631–1700)

'Tis Better to Give Than to Receive

To understand how and why passive voice works (or doesn't work), you should be familiar with the parts of speech (especially the noun, pronoun, verb, and preposition) and the parts of a sentence, all of which we discussed in Chapter 6. To spot a passive sentence, you have to find the subject of the sentence.

Voice is either *active* or *passive*, depending on whether the subject of the sentence acts or is acted upon. For example, the following two sentences convey the same message, but the first is active and the second is passive:

> Joan opened the file.
> The file was opened by Joan.

Notice that the first sentence—the active version—is shorter, so it conveys the information more quickly. Also notice that the action of the first sentence flows directly from the subject (*Joan*) to the object (*file*). In the second sentence—the passive version—the action flows backward from the prepositional phrase (*by Joan*) to the subject (*file*). So the actor appears after the verb (the action word) and, weakly, within a prepositional phrase.

> Active: Joan opened the file.
> ———————————————▶
> (Action flows forward.)
>
> Passive: The file was opened by Joan.
> ◀———————————————
> (Action flows backward.)

As you read the passive sentence, notice that the reverse order of action (with the actor coming *after* the action) forces you read to the end to find out what happened at the beginning. Momentarily, your mind jumps back. Imagine a whole passage written in passive voice. In each sentence, the mind jumps back. That's tiring work. If you force a reader to keep jumping back and forth long enough, you will lose that reader.

This exercise in retroactivity is the main reason many of your engineering textbooks were difficult to read and why you fell asleep reading them. Plowing though a lot of passive voice is tough work. The active voice has more power, force, and life in it. The passive voice sits idly by, waiting for something to happen, while the active voice has all the fun by making something happen.

The following two paragraphs describe a need to reduce sound-pressure levels. The first paragraph is mostly in passive voice. The second paragraph, a rewrite of the first, is mostly in active voice.

> An A-scale sound-pressure level of 94 dBA in the work area is being generated by a large air-supply fan in one corner of a shop area some distance away. The OSHA limit of 90 dBA is being exceeded by this fan. In addition, it is planned to create an employees' relaxation room adjoining this shop area, thereby making an improved common wall to be required. Painted block will be the wall construction to be used for this new room.

It is necessary both to have the sound level reduced to meet the OSHA limit in the shop area, and to have the requirements for a common wall be calculated so that NC-40 background level within the adjacent relaxation room to be constructed can be provided by the wall.

And now the same paragraph in the active voice:

> A large air-supply fan in one corner of a shop is generating an A-scale sound-pressure level of 94 dBA in the work area some distance away. This sound-pressure level exceeds the OSHA limit of 90 dBA. Since we also will create an employees' relaxation room adjoining this shop area, we must build an improved common wall out of painted block. We must both reduce the sound level to meet the OSHA limit and calculate the requirements for a common wall that can provide an NC-40 background level within the adjacent relaxation room.

Notice that the second paragraph is much easier to read. Although both paragraphs give the same information, the active-voice paragraph is easier to understand. The SVO sentence order of active voice promotes that clearer understanding. Read through the paragraphs again, this time noticing the sentence patterns.

Spotting Passive Patterns

Okay, we've established the first problems with passive voice: It is overused, is difficult to read, and impedes the communication process. Before we note some of passive's other problems, let's look more closely at the passive structure so that you can learn to spot passive voice as you write it. After all, you can't avoid passive voice unless you can identify it.

The first thing to find is the subject of the sentence. If the subject is acting, you have an active sentence. If the subject is being acted upon, you have a passive sentence. The only sure way to spot passive is to see if the subject of the sentence is being acted upon. An active sentence always tells you who does (did, will do) what. In addition, you can look for some clues that often indicate a passive sentence.

Look for three red-flag patterns:

1. Passive voice *always* employs a helping verb (a form of the verb *to be*). Realize, though, that an *active* sentence can *also* employ a helping verb. (The helping verb is what triggers your computer's grammar checker to point out passive voice. That's why the grammar checker is sometimes mistaken.)

2. Passive voice *usually* employs a prepositional phrase, often beginning with the preposition *by* and including the actor. (Active sentences can also have prepositional phrases, but the actor isn't in the prepositional phrase.)

3. The pattern of a passive sentence is usually as follows: subject, helping verb, main verb, and prepositional phrase.

Let's look at some passive sentences, with these notations:

hv = helping verb   mv = main verb

subj = subject   a = actor (agent of action)

1. Additional blueprints have been requested by the contractor.
   subj   hv   hv   mv   a

2. Construction was curtailed by a lack of funds.
   subj   hv   mv   a

3. The whole area was flooded by the storm.
   subj hv   mv   a

4. Three designs were rejected by the customer.
   subj   hv   mv   a

In each of the four preceding sentences, the subject is being acted upon and the actor is within the prepositional (*by*) phrase. To change these passive sentences to active sentences, you must bring the actor forward and change the subject of the sentence. Before reading further, go back and revise each of the preceding sample sentences; then check your revisions with the revisions immediately following this paragraph.

The following revisions include these notations:

subj = subject   v = verb   obj = object

1. The contractor requested additional blueprints.
   subj   v   obj

2. A lack of funds curtailed construction.
   subj   v   obj

3. The storm flooded the whole area.
   subj   v   obj

4. The customer rejected three designs.
   subj   v   obj

Read through the preceding passive-voice sentences once again. Notice the usual pattern of the passive voice: subject, helping verb, main verb, and (sometimes) prepositional phrase that includes the actor. By recognizing this pattern, you will be able to avoid passive sentences. As you write, concentrate on putting most of your sentences into the subject-verb-object order. You'll be a better engineering writer.

Here are two more examples. Although both have helping verbs, only one of the two examples is passive.

I was walking by the warehouse.
subj   hv   mv

Fred was promoted by his boss.
subj   hv   mv

Of the above two sentences, in which is the subject acting? In which sentence is the actor within the prepositional phrase? Therefore, which sentence is active and which is passive?

I was walking by the warehouse is active, because *I* is the subject and *I* is acting. *Fred was promoted by his boss* is passive because *Fred* is the subject and is being acted upon by *his boss*, who is within the prepositional phrase.

Another Passive-Voice Danger: Misleading the Reader

Now let's look at another passive-voice problem: Passive voice can mislead and misinform your reader. In other words, it can cause misunderstanding, which is not good, since your goal is to write clearly. The following is a straightforward, concise, active sentence:

> Galileo discovered the isocronicity of pendulum oscillations.

Let's write this same information in the passive voice and see what happens:

> The isocronicity of pendulum oscillations was discovered by Galileo.

One of the primary flaws of the passive sentence is that prepositional phrase at the end, in this case *by Galileo,* can be left out. The passive sentence can exist as a grammatically correct and complete sentence without that prepositional phrase, so that we can have:

> Isocronicity of pendulum oscillations was discovered.

The problem now is that the sentence doesn't tell us who discovered isocronicity, just that it was discovered. Granted, sometimes the "who" information is not important; but sometimes it is. You're better off opting for active and increasing your chances of being clearly understood.

Let's see how this flaw can cause us problems in the office: A very important customer just returned a part, your newly introduced BS249, because the part failed to perform to specs. The customer needs 5,000 of these parts by next month, and another 95,000 over the next eight months. If you can't supply them, your competitor can.

Your failure-analysis team is running the part through 50 complicated tests that will take about two days. All you can think about is what went wrong. Did we forget a component? Did the customer misuse the part or not apply it correctly? Can we fix it?

To add to everyone's anxiety, your chief failure-analysis guru, who is spearheading the team and who will write the report to you, is on a very tight schedule because another crucial customer needs him and three other team members to fly to Antarctica in two days. So your only form of communication from him will be his written report. This report will tell you whether or not your product will be able to meet the specs in one month. As deadline dawns two days later and your failure-analysis team takes wing to Antarctica, you read the report left on your desk.

It says, "The BS249 was modified by adding a widget. See you in three weeks."

With a sinking feeling in your heart, you ask yourself, "What widget? Whose widget? Who modified it? What are you talking about? Did the customer modify the BS249, thereby rendering it useless, or did our team fix the part by adding the widget?" Only the guru and his Antarctica-bound team know, and his passive sentence doesn't give you a clue. So as you can see, passive voice can be a precipitator of panic.

What our guru should have written is: "The customer modified the product by adding a widget. Tell him not to add the widget, but to ..." Or, "We corrected the problem by adding a widget and ..."

If you habitually write passive sentences, you have a good chance, without realizing it, of not including information that is important to the reader.

Removing Ego from Active Voice

Here's what we have established so far:

Too much passive voice complicates the reading job.

▶ Use of the passive voice can inadvertently omit needed information.

▶ The way to change passive voice to active voice is to place the actor in the subject slot (before the verb).

In some engineering-writing jobs, constantly naming the agent of action can risk another problem. If most of your reports describe your actions or your team's actions, the actor will usually be *I* or *we*, in which case you risk filling your reports with *I* and *we*.

You can overcome that problem in two ways. One easy way is simply to use an orientation sentence to introduce a list.

Last month our crew did the following:
▶ completed the Fair Oaks survey
▶ solved the half-lath stakes problem with Kelly Lumber
▶ began the soil-analysis project at Keystone Acres

The list approach allows you to say a lot without having to repeat *I* or *we* with every new sentence.

The second way to avoid this *I/we* problem is to have an inanimate object be the actor. For example:

The test results revealed that ...
The survey indicates that ...
The profile diagram shows three different ...

A Partial Redemption for Passive Voice

So with passive voice getting such a bad rap, why do we even have it around? Well, it does have some uses. There are times when you don't want to name the actor or you don't know who it is, or it doesn't make any difference who it is. (Don't use that last reason as an easy cop-out, though.) Passive works in such cases. The active voice is direct; the passive voice is indirect and therefore more suitable for diplomacy. When saying "No" or otherwise refusing someone, the passive voice seems less harsh.

Instead of telling a key customer that he damaged your product by immersing it in salt water, you can diplomatically say, "It appears the widget has been immersed in salt water." No accusations, no recriminations. Everything's cool.

How a Change in Mood Can Clarify Your Procedures

If someone asks directions to your home, you do not say, "The Broadway exit should be taken and one must get in the middle lane of the exit ramp. At the stop sign, going straight and crossing Broadway is best. A left turn should be executed at Spalding Street."

Instead, you say, "Take the Broadway exit and stay in the middle lane of the exit ramp. At the stop sign, go straight, crossing Broadway. Turn left at Spalding Street." Why? Because that's the natural way to give directions. The short, simple, command form is easy to read and understand.

The command form is one mood of the verb. Yes, in addition to having voice, verbs also have mood. What we are about to discuss is the number-one secret to writing a successful procedure: the use of imperative (command) sentences.

Let's fill in a little background here. Mood can be indicative, subjunctive, or imperative. (The mysterious *subjunctive* mood merely states a wish, desire, or supposition contrary to fact. For example, "I wish I *were* skiing." But that's a whole different topic. So is skiing. Enough said.) For now, we're interested just in the indicative and imperative moods. An *indicative* sentence states a fact (i.e., it *indicates* something) or asks a question about a fact. An *imperative* sentence gives a command. The following sentences are indicative:

> The additional weight collapsed the pier.
> The screen should show three columns.
> Your manual needs a shorter introduction.
> Did the lunch truck stop in the parking lot?

Three of those last four sentences state (indicate) a fact. The fourth one asks a *question* about a fact.

The following sentences are imperative. The subject of each of these sentences is the understood *you*.

Close the pier entrance.
Make sure your screen shows three columns.
Write a shorter introduction for your manual.
Please get me a burrito from the lunch truck.

All four of those last sentences give a command.
Here are some more indicative sentences:

1. A cantilever footing may work better here.

2. Judgment should be exercised when laying out the various coil circuits to make the system as self-balancing as is practical.

3. Axial-flow turbines use the propeller-type runner with either fixed or adjustable blades.

4. Silica coatings can be used for diffusion and color alteration of the light.

Note that all four of those sentences state a fact. Note also that sentences 1 and 3 are active, and 2 and 4 are passive. Yes, indicative sentences can be active or passive.
The next four sentences are imperative:

1. Sign and return the top copy to me.

2. Check the piston-rod thrust to determine the load capacity.

3. Unload all the equipment and put it in the warehouse.

4. Use silica coatings if you want to provide diffusion and alter the color of light.

Note that those last four sentences give a command. Note also that the subject of each sentence is understood to be *you*. Finally, note that each sentence is in the active voice, because the subject *you* is acting. Imperative sentences are always active, never passive.

Following are some passive sentences that should be imperative because they are meant to be instructions. Revise each one and check your revisions against ours. Remember to make *you* the understood but unstated subject of each sentence.

1. The enclosed contract should be signed and returned to us by the end of business on July 8.

_____

2. The conjugate moment must be found at the point of desired deflection.

_____

3. The cavitation coefficient can be used in modeling and in comparing experimental results.

_____

4. When determining the acoustic absorption within a shop area, it is preferred to use a measurement technique rather than a calculation, which is not as accurate.

Below are suggested revisions:

1. Sign and return the enclosed contract to us by the end of business on July 8.
2. Find the conjugate moment at the point of desired deflection.
3. Use the cavitation coefficient in modeling and in comparing experimental results.
4. When determining the acoustic absorption within a shop area, prefer using a measurement technique rather than a calculation, which is not as accurate.

Note that all the original sentences were in passive voice because they identified no actor:

1. The enclosed contract should be signed and returned (*by someone*)...
2. The conjugate moment must be found (*by someone*)...
3. The cavitation coefficient can be used (*by someone*)...
4. ... it is preferred (*by someone*)

The Cookbook Approach to Writing Manuals

To write an easy-to-read manual, use imperative sentences for every action you want the reader to take. For example, if you were writing some instructions for field personnel, which of the two following sentences do you think would get the action you want?

> The valve must be turned clockwise.

Or:

> Turn the valve clockwise.

Someone in the field reading the first sentence could stand there and say "Okay," and then wait for someone from headquarters to come out and turn the valve. The second sentence, however, leaves no doubt about who should turn the valve.

A good manual reads like a cookbook. Have you ever noticed how easy a cookbook is to read?

> Add six eggs.
> Stir in one-quarter cup of milk.
> Add one teaspoon of paprika.

You'll notice that a cookbook never says, "One-quarter cup of milk shall be added," or, "It is advisable to add a teaspoon of paprika." If a cookbook did read like that, you might need more time to read the recipe than to make the omelet.

Another benefit of using imperative sentences in manuals is that your manuals will be shorter, because imperative phrasing prevents passive voice in an instruction.

One of our client projects a few years ago was to show the client's writers how to revise the corporate operating procedures that nobody in the field was reading. By writing imperative sentences for every required action, the writers reduced the procedures by over 60 percent. Suddenly, the people in the field could understand the procedures. Many even called headquarters and complimented the group for making the procedures so easy to follow.

To make a procedure (a manual or any type of instructions) easy to read, you will use a combination of indicative and imperative sentences.

▶ Use indicative sentences to give background information.

▶ Use imperative sentences for every action you want the reader to take.

▶ To soften an imperative sentence in a request memo or letter, add the word *please* before the verb. Your request will then be clear *and* diplomatic.

If you follow those simple guidelines, you will write readable procedures.

Exercise

Below are passive sentences that would work better as active sentences. Change them to active. Those that appear to be instructions, change to imperative sentences. This exercise is a challenging one, so take your time. Concentrate on explaining who or what performs the action. Our suggested revisions immediately follow the exercise. If your revisions don't match ours exactly, just double-check to make sure you have stated who or what performed the action, in the SVO order.

1. With the use of several aids, the calculations can be simplified.

   _____

2. When an airfoil is moved through the air, a pressure is produced by the motion at every point of the airfoil, which is observed as acting normal to the surface.

   _____

   _____

3. Judgment should be exercised in laying out the various coil circuits so that the system can be made as self-balancing as is practical.

   _____

   _____

4. Compressed air, a form of utility energy, is used extensively for operations such as automatic machines, tools, material handling, and food processing.

_____

_____

5. As shown in these formulas, the lift of a large part of the peripheral-jet ACV is derived from the cushion pressure.

_____

_____

6. The dimension for the depth groove is added to the basic flange thickness, for which separate tables of dimensions for fittings having the ring-joint facing must be included.

_____

_____

_____

7. The atoms are considered the smallest particles that occur separately in the structure of molecules of either compound or elementary substances, so far as can be determined by ordinary chemical analysis.

_____

_____

_____

Now compare your revisions with these suggested revisions:

1. By using several aids, you can simplify the calculations.
   (or) The use of several aids can simplify the calculations.
   (or) To simplify the calculations, use several aids.
2. When an airfoil moves through the air, the motion produces a pressure at every point of the airfoil, which acts normal to the surface.
3. Exercise judgment when laying out the various coil circuits to make the system as self-balancing as is practical.
4. Operations such as automatic machines, tools, material handling, and food processing extensively use compressed air as a form of utility energy.
5. These formulas show that a large part of the peripheral-jet ACV derives its lift from the cushion pressure.
6. When adding the dimension for the depth groove to the basic flange thickness, be sure to include separate tables of dimensions for fittings having the ring-joint facing.

7. Ordinary chemical analysis considers atoms to be the smallest particles that occur separately in the structure of molecules of either compound or elementary substances.

Remember, tell your reader *who or what did what to whom or to what*. That's the active-voice pattern. If you can develop the habit of writing more active-voice (SVO) sentences than passive-voice sentences, you can turn yourself into an effective engineering writer.

Summary of This Chapter's Main Points

▶ Writing mostly in the passive voice is a risky habit.

▶ Overuse of passive voice creates difficult-to-read sentences.

▶ Passive sentences can mislead by omitting needed information.

▶ To spot passive voice, find the subject of the sentence.
   — If the subject acts, the sentence is active.
   — If the subject receives action, the sentence is passive.

▶ Passive voice always employs a helping verb and usually employs a prepositional phrase that includes the actor.

▶ Prefer active voice to passive voice.

▶ Use imperative (command-form) sentences for procedures, instructions, and directions.

8 Sentences: Building Flexible, Readable Structures

"Of all the needs a book has, the chief need is that it be readable."

—Anthony Trollope
British writer
(1815–1882)

Now that we've looked at the inner workings of a sentence and seen how the components interact with one another, let's zoom out and take more of an overview of sentence structure.

Most sentence examples in the previous chapters were simple one-idea sentences having one subject and one verb. Such sentences are often most effective. Yet unless you vary some of the sentences, you risk boring your readers. In your engineering reports, you often must describe the subjects and verbs more thoroughly. You usually do so by expanding the sentence with phrases and clauses.

If you expand a sentence too much, though, you can run into trouble. So let's first expand your sentence-structure view to help you enhance and troubleshoot your sentences.

Using Phrases to Introduce and Embellish Ideas

A *phrase* is simply a group of related words lacking a simple subject, a verb, or both. Following are examples of phrases:

> after the software seminar
> below the flange
> cracking the blade
> to solder smoothly
> from the basic bending allowance
> valve dimensions
> side-outlet fittings

Phrases can't stand alone as full ideas. They can't create a sentence by themselves, because they don't contain enough information. That takes a larger structure: a clause.

Using Clauses to Add Clarifying Elements

More complete than a phrase is the *clause*, which is also a group of related words—but it contains a simple subject and a verb. That's the difference between a phrase and a clause: A phrase has no simple subject and verb; a clause does have a simple subject and a verb.

▶ *prepositional phrase*: from water-supply sources   (no simple subject; no verb)

▶ *clause*: The water-supply sources are surface waters   (note "what = what" pattern)
            S   V

That second example, the clause, can function as its own sentence.

Not all clauses are full sentences, though. Clauses that can stand alone as full sentences are called *independent clauses*; clauses that can't stand alone are called *dependent clauses*.

For example,

▶ *independent clause*: a full idea that can stand alone as its own sentence

   Improper storage damaged the blade
            S   V

▶ *dependent clause*: an incomplete idea, too weak to stand alone as its own sentence

   … because improper storage damaged the blade
                         S   V

The word *because* makes that clause (or idea) depend on another idea to complete the sentence. A dependent clause trying to be its own sentence is only a *fragment*.

> Although many empirical formulas exist
> Since sand is permeable and rapidly adjusts to changes in loading
> If combustion reactions give off energy during the formation of
>   compounds
> When beams with moments of inertia larger than standard mill shapes
>   are required

Note that were you to delete the first word in each of the above dependent clauses, the clauses would become independent. In engineering writing, sentence fragments cause a two-pronged problem:

▶ They deprive readers of needed information.

▶ They distract readers from the existing content of a document.

To avoid gaps in information, turn fragments into complete sentences.

How Many Ideas per Sentence?

Any sentence falls into one of four structures, each communicating a different *logical* relationship of ideas. These are the four structures:

▶ *simple sentence:* has one independent clause

▶ *compound sentence:* has two or more independent clauses

▶ *complex sentence:* has one independent and at least one dependent clause

▶ *compound-complex sentence:* has two or more independent clauses and at least one dependent clause

The independent clauses, expressing main ideas, are stronger. The dependent clauses, expressing subordinate ideas, are weaker.

The boxes below will help you visualize the four sentence structures. The filled-in boxes symbolize strong (independent) clauses. The open boxes symbolize the weaker (dependent) clauses. Here's how the four structures are represented:

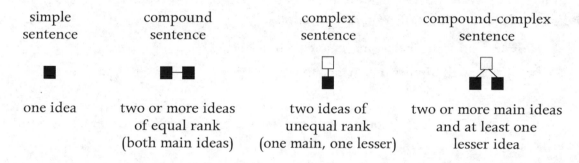

simple sentence	compound sentence	complex sentence	compound-complex sentence
one idea	two or more ideas of equal rank (both main ideas)	two ideas of unequal rank (one main, one lesser)	two or more main ideas and at least one lesser idea

Simple Sentence: The One-Idea Sentence (■)

The *simple sentence* explains key points simply and effectively. This one-idea sentence, expressing one independent idea, can stand alone. Thus, the simple sentence can be quite powerful.

> We deliver.
> The lab was in chaos.
> The freeway collapsed.
> We won the contract.

The simple sentence has only one clause (an independent clause), with one complete subject and one predicate.

> The new production manager reorganized the production schedule. $\overset{\uparrow}{\text{s}}$ $\overset{\uparrow}{\text{v}}$

▶ complete subject: the new production manager

▶ predicate: reorganized the production schedule

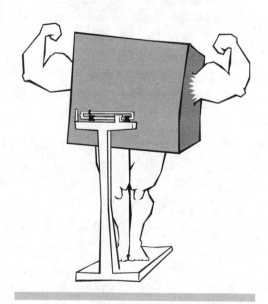

The POWERFUL One-Idea Sentence

Note the simple subject and verb in the following simple sentences:

The cushion valve also is known as a crossover relief valve.
                S   hv   v

Two steel gears rotate inside a cast-iron housing.
            S   V

The current exhaust system is inadequate.
                    S   V

The engineers and technicians will discuss the change today.
     S   S   hv   v

That last example has two simple subjects. Yet together they form a single complete subject. The verb of that example has a helping verb. Still expressing just one idea, though, the example is still a simple sentence.

▶ complete subject: the engineers and technicians

▶ predicate: will discuss the change today

A simple sentence doesn't force you to use just one verb. Here's an example with three verbs:

Workers lowered the washers, installed them, and tightened the
     S   V   V   V
upper bolts.

▶ complete subject: workers

▶ predicate: lowered the washers, installed them, and tightened the upper bolts

Here's another example of a simple sentence, this time with more than one simple subject and more than one verb:

Our new database manager and her staff work at night and sleep
in the day.   S   S   V   V

▶ complete subject: our new database manager and her staff

▶ predicate: work at night and sleep in the day

Even with the two subjects and two verbs, that example still expresses *one* complete idea. So you do have some flexibility with the simple sentence.

In engineering writing, these are the main uses of a one-idea sentence:

Uses	Examples
to highlight key points	The new version has a flaw.
to emphasize a supporting point	Test results confirm the flaw.
to simplify a technical or abstract point	The numbers don't add up.
to summarize or interpret data	Both graphs show a July surge.
to state a result, such as a consequence or a benefit	The new method saves time.
to dramatize an effect	The power outage left 9,000 homes and restaurants in the dark.

Until now, you may have avoided writing simple sentences. Avoid them no longer. They won't make you look less educated. In fact, a strong simple sentence, impressing a point on your reader or listener, actually shows your mastery of the language. These are the main advantages of the one-idea (simple) sentence:

► It is clear and direct.

► It stands out from other sentences, bringing attention to itself.

► In technical memos or investigative reports, it lets readers grasp one point fully before going on to the next.

► It gives a separate thought its own space.

(Notice that those advantages are all stated in simple sentences. In fact, most of those explanations about simple sentences are *themselves* simple sentences.)

The only disadvantage of a one idea sentence is that the use of too many in one document can become monotonous. So for variety, three more structures are available to you.

Compound Sentence:
The Equal-Rank Sentence (■—■)

The *compound sentence* links two closely related and equally ranked ideas into one sentence. This equal-rank sentence expresses one thought through two or more strong (independent), related ideas (clauses) of equal importance. Each clause in a compound sentence has its own complete subject and predicate.

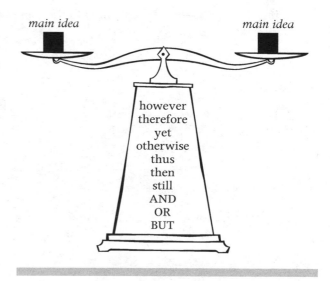

The Balanced (Equal-Rank) Sentence Shows Objectivity

main idea   main idea

however
therefore
yet
otherwise
thus
then
still
AND
OR
BUT

We won the contract, and we celebrated that night.
       s v   s   v

▶ first clause: we won the contract
  — complete subject of that clause: we
  — predicate of that clause: won the contract

▶ second clause: we celebrated that night
  — complete subject of that clause: we
  — predicate of that clause: celebrated that night
  — joining word (conjunction) between clauses: and

Digiwonk designed a faster circuit, but we designed a more reliable one.
     s   v   s   v

▶ first clause: Digiwonk designed a faster circuit
  — complete subject of that clause: Digiwonk
  — predicate of that clause: designed a faster circuit

▶ second clause: we designed a more reliable one
  — complete subject of that clause: we
  — predicate of that clause: designed a more reliable one
  — joining word (conjunction) between clauses: but

A few signal words tell you when you have written a compound sentence. The conjunctions *and*, *or*, and *but* (or sometimes *however*, *therefore*, *yet*, *otherwise*, *thus*, *then*, and *still*) usually join the equally ranked ideas that create the compound sentence.

Study the following example of an equal-rank sentence:

Our technical team designed the circuit in three months, *but* our
           s   v

understaffed production facility couldn't produce prototypes for a week.
           s   hv   v

▶ two complete subjects: our technical team; our understaffed production facility
▶ two predicates: designed the circuit in three months; couldn't produce the prototypes for a week
▶ joining word (conjunction): but

Here are some more examples of the equal-rank (compound) sentence:

We tested the soil, *and* Fran's team surveyed the area.
     s v   s   v

Will you test the samples, *or* will Raj subcontract the work?
hv   s   v   hv   s   v

Various researchers have improved this theory, *but* the general
                      s   hv   v

form remains valid for design.
s   v

Caution: Don't let *and, or,* or *but* mislead you. In a simple sentence, they may join multiple subjects or multiple verbs but still form a one-idea sentence. Only between full *ideas* do they create a compound (equal-rank) sentence.

These are the main uses of an equal-rank sentence:

▶ to add an idea to another closely related one
Use the word *and* to express addition.

   We designed the product, *and* Ace Company built it.
   s   v   s   v

▶ to gently contrast two closely related but differing ideas
Use the word *but* to signal the contrast.

   We planned to retest the switch, *but* the customer still wanted a
   s   v   s   v
   replacement.

▶ to avoid influencing your reader to choose one alternative over another
Use the word *or* between the alternatives.

   The crew can repair the meter, *or* you can buy a new one.
   s   hv   v   s   hv   v

The equal-rank (compound) sentence has one main advantage:

▶ It presents two more closely linked ideas *objectively*, because it shows that the ideas
  are evenly ranked.

The equal-rank structure does have its limitations. It suffers from these main disadvantages:

▶ Its overuse is more monotonous than the overuse of the simple sentence. Here's an
  example of such monotonous overuse of equal-rank sentences:

Last month I attended the trade show, and I presented a paper. The trade show was crowded, but I saw a lot. I returned to the office, and Carl asked me to write a trip report. I handed in my report, and Dana helped me finish my project. I finished my project by deadline, and I began planning my trip to Boston.

▶ It can too easily become a complicated or run-on sentence, especially if the sentence includes more than two full ideas. Here's a run-on example:

Last month I presented a paper at the XYX trade show, and seven engineers at the show stayed to ask questions, five others called me here at the office to ask more questions and I don't have time to answer all those calls, but I'm enjoying the fame.

▶ It prompts overuse of the conjunction *and*. That word may not accurately express your intended logical relationship between the ideas, and it doesn't let you emphasize one idea over another. (Oops! See how easily the *and* slipped in there?) The next example shows the overuse of *and*:

I attended a seminar on compound-pipe problems, and I learned a trial-and-error technique to solve friction problems caused by the velocities in the pipe. John is having difficulty designing the system for Superchem Corporation, and this technique may help him.

So what's an engineer to do? You can choose a third structure—one that allows you more flexibility and variety, as the next structure does.

Unequal-Rank Sentence Tips the Scale

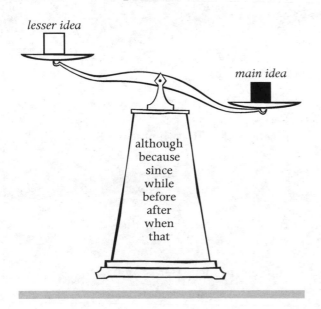

lesser idea

main idea

although
because
since
while
before
after
when
that

Complex Sentence: The Unequal-Rank Sentence ( )

The *complex sentence* combines the stronger independent clause with the weaker dependent clause. The result is a sentence that logically shows an unequal rank of ideas.

In this case, *complex* doesn't mean complicated; it merely means that one part of the sentence is strong enough to stand alone and one part isn't. That's why we call it an unequal-rank structure.

Both versatile and persuasive, a complex sentence expresses one thought through one main idea (independent clause) and one lesser idea (dependent, or subordinate, clause). Remember, the dependent clause can't stand alone.

Some conjunctions that start dependent clauses are *when, because, since, while, before, after, that,* and *although.*

When we researched the water filtration problem, we discovered a more
     s   v   s   v
efficient way to fluoridate the water.

▶ dependent clause: when we researched the water-filtration problem

▶ independent clause: we discovered a more efficient way to fluoridate the water

Usually, the idea presented in an independent clause overshadows the idea in a dependent clause. The dependent clause may just present background information, as you often must do in your engineering reports, to orient your readers.

Just as with the equal-rank structure, each clause in this unequal-rank structure has its own complete subject and predicate.

Here's an example of an unequal-rank sentence:

After we changed the retaining-wall specs, the client signed the contract.
       s   v   s   v

▶ complete subjects: we; the client

▶ predicates: changed the retaining-wall specs; signed the contract

▶ joining word (conjunction): after

▶ main idea (independent clause): the client signed the contract

▶ lesser idea (dependent clause): we changed the … specs

Let's look again at the equal-rank (compound) example we had in the previous section.

I attended a seminar on compound-pipe problems, and I learned a trial-and-error technique to solve friction problems caused by the velocities in the pipe. John is having difficulty designing the system for Superchem Corporation, and this technique may help him.

The overuse of compound sentences makes that original example sound awkward. Revised into an unequal-rank (complex) sentence, the ideas flow smoothly:

When I attended a seminar on compound-pipe problems, I learned a trial-and-error technique to solve friction problems caused by the velocities in the pipe. This technique may help John, who is having difficulty designing the system for Superchem Corporation.

Here are more unequal-rank examples, just to help you see the pattern:

Pneumatic isolators are particularly useful *when* low-frequency
                                       s   v
forces are present.
         s   v

In that example, the first clause is the main idea; the "when" clause is the condition that limits the main idea about the isolators. It's a pattern that you can use often in your engineering writing.

> Sand is a good foundation material, *because* it doesn't settle
> s   v   s   hv   v
> after its initial loading.

or,

> *Since* it doesn't settle after its initial loading, sand makes a good
> s   hv   v   s   v
> foundation material.

> *Although* Power Graphics is only two years old, it already has won five
> s   v   s   hv   v
> industrial-design awards.

That word *although* is the one that unleashes the persuasive power of this unequal-rank structure. Let's look more closely at that powerful conjunction *although*.

If you want your manager to choose Fabrication Plan B over Fabrication Plan A, which of the next two sentences would be more persuasive?

> ▶ Version 1: Plan A is workable, *but* Plan B is more cost-effective.   (equal rank)

> ▶ Version 2: *Although* Plan A is workable, Plan B is more cost-effective. (unequal rank)

Granted, Version 1 does show contrast, and the preferred plan finishes the sentence. That's strong placement. Yet the word *but* doesn't come in until the middle of the sentence, and that version is locked into the equal-rank mode.

Version 2 is more persuasive because the word *although* starts the sentence, signaling a contrast from the outset. That placement automatically tells readers not to think too long about the opening idea, because the stronger point is coming right up.

If your manager had been inclined to promote Plan A, your "although" sentence wouldn't upset your manager, because the "although" half of the sentence acknowledges a good point about Plan A. The opening word *although* makes your manager read on to learn the contrasting point. How's that for psychology in engineering a sentence?

These are the main uses of the unequal-rank sentence:
> ▶ to show sequence (time order) of a background event and a previous, subsequent, simultaneous, or resulting event
> Use the words *when, whenever, before, until, since, while,* or *after* to juxtapose two events and give one of them a higher priority.

> Boiling occurs *when* the vapor pressure is increased to the local
> s   v   s   hv   v
> ambient pressure.

▶ to show cause-effect, purpose, or result
Use the words *because*, *so that*, or *since*.

Since the roughness of the pipe's internal surface is usually independent
　　　　　　　 s　　　　　　　　　　　　　　　　　　　　　 v

of the diameter, the roughness affects smaller diameter pipes more.
　　　　　　　 s　　 v

▶ to stress a contrast
Use *although*, *though*, or *even though*.

Although many empirical formulas exist for the turbulent-flow velocity
　　　　 s　　 v

profile, only Nikuradse's equation for smooth tubes is given here.
　　　 s　　　　　　　　　　　　　　　　　　　 hv　 v

▶ to express condition
Use *if*, *provided that*, or *unless*.

If this quantity is substituted into equation 5.36, the pressure drop is
　 s　　 hv　　v　　　　　　　　　　　　　　　　 s　 hv

predicted by the Poiseuille equation for laminar flow.
　　 v

(Source of those four examples, some adapted: Randall N. Robinson, PE, *Chemical Engineering Reference Manual*. Professional Publications, Inc., Belmont, CA, 1987. Ch. 5, "Fluid Statics and Dynamics," Part 1: Fluid Characteristics, pp. 5-3 to 5-9. With permission.)

An unequal-rank (complex) sentence offers these main advantages:

▶ It emphasizes one idea over another.

▶ It doesn't force you to give each event the same importance in a time-order sentence.

▶ It can acknowledge yet downplay bad news and emphasize good news, all in the same "although" sentence.

The unequal-rank sentence has one main disadvantage:

▶ It can become a monster sentence, with overly long ideas that readers cannot read easily. So, when joining unequal ideas, try keeping the ideas short.

Anytime you want to persuade your readers, use either the one-idea structure or the unequal-rank structure. Those two will help you add power to your writing.

Now, what if you're explaining a technical problem that produced more than one consequence? Don't worry. You have one more structure at your command.

The Combination Sentence Adds Bulk

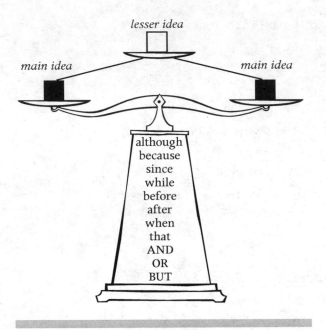

Compound-Complex Sentence: A Combination—Equal and Unequal (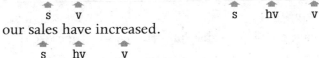)

The *compound-complex sentence* is similar to the complex sentence. Notice the parallel here:

▶ The *complex sentence* has an independent clause and a dependent clause.

▶ The *compound-complex sentence* has two or more independent clauses and one or more dependent clauses.

In other words, the combination structure uses the devices of *both* the equal-rank and the unequal-rank structures. It expresses one thought through two or more equal ideas (independent clauses) and at least one lesser idea (dependent, or subordinate, clause).

Since the combination structure includes at least three related ideas and since its form and even its grammatical name can intimidate, you should treat it with respect and you *must* use it with restraint. (Yes, that preceding sentence is itself a compound-complex sentence.)

Each of the three or more clauses in a compound-complex sentence has its own complete subject and predicate. This structure uses the same joining words as those mentioned for the equal-rank and unequal-rank structures. In the following example, notice the background (lesser) idea leading into two main ideas.

Since we hired you, our quality control has improved and
     s v   s hv   v

our sales have increased.
  s hv   v

▶ main (independent) ideas: our quality control has improved; our sales have increased

▶ lesser (dependent) idea: we hired you

▶ joining words: since; and

In each of the next two combination sentences, notice that some joining words show equal rank and others show unequal rank between ideas:

The original design included a wood-shingle roof, but the new code has banned wood shingles, *which* are a fire risk.

Our system uses an ozone-depleting R22 halocarbon refrigerant, *but* it can be converted to an ammonia-based refrigerant *when* that refrigerant becomes more feasible.

These are the two main uses of the combination sentence:

► to show two results of one action or condition:

> When the input voltage is less than V_{ref}, the discharging by $-V_{\text{ref}}$ will reach zero before the full count period T, and the count will be proportional to the actual value of v.
>
> (Source: Raymond B. Yarbrough, PE, *Electrical Engineering Reference Manual*, 5th ed. Professional Publications, Inc., Belmont, CA, 1990. Ch. 3, "Waveforms, Power, and Measurements," Part 2: Measurement of DC and Periodic Signals, subsection 11: Digital Meters, p. 3-14. With permission.)

► to show two benefits/consequences that outweigh a contrasting idea:

> Although Plan A is workable, Plan B is more cost-effective and Plan C is the most profitable.

The combination (compound-complex) sentence offers one main advantage:

► It can emphasize two or more equally ranked ideas (such as good news or benefits) over at least one lesser idea (such as bad news or a consequence), to show the close relationship among all the ideas.

These are the main disadvantages of the combination sentence:

► It can develop into the biggest monster of all sentence types, as it not only invites creative cramming of too many ideas into one long, involved structure, but it also often obstructs clarity and logic. (Try reading *that* combination sentence aloud, all in one breath.)

► It carries the greatest risk of grammatical errors, because its internal structures can be difficult to control.

► Its overuse can tire and annoy readers, because its involved structure requires the most concentration from readers.

The compound-complex sentence need not be a long one. Yet in your engineering writing, such a sentence often contains clauses that individually are long, because the related points themselves may be complex or because a statement may require qualifiers for legal reasons. (There's another combination sentence! It does take a bit more concentration than the short ones, doesn't it?)

The longer your sentences get, the more thoughts you may try to cram into each sentence—and the more writing problems you'll create for yourself. To avoid as many writing problems as possible, vary your use of the four sentence types. Think of the logical relationships you want to show. You will then likely vary the structures without thinking much about the technicalities. Sentence variety simplifies the reading job.

In the equal-rank-sentence (compound-sentence) section of this chapter, we mentioned the disadvantages of the compound sentence and cited a sample paragraph containing only compound (equal-rank) sentences. Let's repeat that example and rewrite it, using *varied* structures in the new paragraph.

Here is the original, in all compound (equal-rank) sentences:

> Last month I attended the trade show, and I presented a paper. The trade show was crowded, but I saw a lot. I returned to the office and Carl asked me to write a trip report. I handed in my report, and Dana helped me finish my project. I finished my project by deadline, and I began planning my trip to Boston.

Here is a sample revision, with varied sentence structures:

> Last month I attended the trade show and presented a paper. Although the show was crowded, I saw a lot. When I returned to the office, Carl asked me for a trip report. After I handed in the report, Dana helped me finish my project before deadline, and I began planning my Boston trip.

That paragraph revision includes three of the four sentence types: one simple, two complex, and one compound-complex—in that order, with no compound sentence. The joining words *although*, *when*, and *after* prevent overuse of the well-worn *and*.

Don't worry about labeling your sentences. Just notice their patterns, to produce varied sentences that clearly and logically say what you mean.

When varying your sentences in your engineering writing, you may also want a *general* guideline for controlling and enhancing your sentences. We have such a guideline: it defines a recommended average sentence length.

Measuring for Sentence Control

One easy way to increase readability is to write sentences that average about 17 words per sentence. Note that word: *average*. If *all* your sentences were 17 words, your writing would be stiff or monotonous. The goal is a varied sentence length, because—as with the sentence types—variety is the simplifying spice of writing. The 17-word guideline is just that: a guideline, not a rigid rule.

Such sentence variety works well throughout Michael R. Lindeburg's *Civil Engineering Reference Manual* (6th ed., Professional Publications, Inc., Belmont, CA, 1992). Here are two easy-to-read examples from "Part 1: Properties of Structural Materials" in the "Mechanics of Materials" section of that manual. (These excerpts are reprinted with permission.)

The first example (from page 12-2) is about the tensile test:

> The *yield point* (Point *C*) is very close to the elastic limit. For all practical purposes, the *yield stress*, S_y, can be taken as the stress which accompanies the beginning of plastic strain. Since permanent deformation is to be avoided, the yield stress is used in calculating safe stresses in ductile materials such as steel. A36 structural steel has a minimum yield strength of 36,000 psi.

In that example, notice the short opening and closing sentences, with the longer sentences of details sandwiched between them. The varied sentence length (12, 21, 22, and 11 words, totaling 66 in four sentences) adds interest. Yes, the word count in that example does average 16.5, rounded off to 17 words.

The second example (on page 12-3 of the same manual) introduces a subsection about fatigue tests:

> A part may fail after repeated stress loading even if the stress never exceeds the ultimate fracture strength of the material. This type of failure is known as *fatigue failure*.
>
> The behavior of a material under repeated loadings can be evaluated in a fatigue test. A sample is loaded repeatedly to a known stress, and the number of applications of that stress is counted until the sample fails. This procedure is repeated for different stress levels. The results of many of these tests can be graphed, as is done in figure 12.4.

In that two-paragraph example, the six sentences contain 21, 9, 15, 23, 8, and 16 words, in that order. The total count of 92 words produces an average of about 15 words per sentence. Considering the recommended 17-word average, is the 15-word sentence average a problem? No. A shorter average sentence length is better than a longer one. Less can be more: A lesser average here and there adds even more variety to a document that otherwise averages about 17 words per sentence.

Such a short average sentence length doesn't diminish the intelligent wording of the ideas. Just the opposite. If you can explain complex technical ideas in well-controlled, understandable sentences, your value in the technical community soars. So remember the 17-word guideline, but be flexible. If your engineering report has a shorter average sentence length, congratulate yourself—so long as the average isn't down around 4 or 5. Such a low average would annoy some readers nearly as much as a 35-word average would.

By varying the sentence length in all that you write, you will also avoid confusion and many grammatical traps that result from uncontrolled sentences. You'll thus save a lot of rewriting steps. You'll also help your readers feel comfortable as they read your memos and engineering reports.

How to Make the Reader Feel Comfortable

The builders of the earliest railroads in the United States considered the passenger comfort in a coach to be just as important as the technical perfection of a locomotive.

As you write your engineering reports, you can take the same track of thinking: Your reader's comfort is just as important as the technical perfection of the sentences you write.

If you're in a train seat designed to technical specifications only, it may be sturdy yet still feel awkward. If it has high armrests, an unadjustable headrest, or no cushion, the uncomfortable seat gets harder and harder to bear during the journey. You might resist riding that train again if you had a choice of other, more comfortable trains to the same destination.

In the same way, a sentence can be technically (structurally) perfect but still awkward. Yes, the technical elements of a sentence are critical to the clarity of the message. But they must help you convey your message smoothly, not awkwardly. Jerky or wearisome sentences interrupt a reader's concentration and enjoyment.

Here's an example that uses all eight parts of speech in various functions, all technically correct. The sentence length, though, might make readers fidget.

> John ran quickly around the block, contemplating his upcoming speech on CD-ROM applications in the education field, while his dog trailed alongside, thinking only of the (phew!) skunk he had encountered the last time he and John had run on this street.

Two sentences would work better there—one about John and one about his dog. The following revision would at least give readers some breathing room:

> John ran quickly around the block, contemplating his upcoming speech on CD-ROM applications in the education field. His dog trailed alongside, thinking only of the (phew!) skunk he had encountered the last time he and John had run on this street.

Without adjustment, an awkward sentence disturbs a reader's comfort and concentration. For example, the following sentence about air-pressure regulators is technically acceptable but could prevent comfortable reading:

> The nonrelieving pressure regulator is a type of regulator that is called nonrelieving because overpressure on its outlet port is not permitted by the regulator to escape to atmosphere.

Let's rephrase that example to delete the overuse of the words *regulator*, *nonrelieving*, and *is*.

> The nonrelieving pressure regulator is so named because it prevents overpressure on its outlet port from escaping into the atmosphere.

Freed of the original version's redundant phrasing, that revision gets the point across more smoothly.

If a report about fluid-power components repeatedly subjects a reader to bumpy and jerky phrasing, the reader's discomfort can quickly bring a scowl. Scowling readers don't willingly finish a hard-to-read report, and they're not likely to stoically select the same writer's next report as first-choice reading. On the other hand, if your sentences are well-structured yet flexible enough for comfortable reading, your readers will thank you—and will more willingly read your next report.

Remember that the function of a sentence is as important as its form. A sentence that functions as an explanation must clearly and smoothly explain the point—not just suit a structural form.

To test your rough-draft sentences for easy reading, try reading them aloud. Are they smooth or rough? Does the form of the sentence help achieve its intended function—its meaning and purpose—easily? By reading the report aloud, you'll hear the rough spots that your readers will see. Not all readers will grasp the structural beauty of your sentences, but most people know whether they are comfortable reading what you have to say.

So if you want people to appreciate your research results and brilliant ideas, don't worry about how many times you use each sentence type. Just try giving your sentences a balance of solid structure, controlled length, and comfortable phrasing. That way, you may even begin to find the writing task more enjoyable.

The late British politician and writer Sir Winston S. Churchill knew the importance of well-structured yet comfort-inspiring sentences.

As the Prime Minister who led Great Britain through World War II (and who won the Nobel Prize for literature in 1953), he kept his readers and listeners in mind.

After a speech, he reportedly received a letter that shook a finger at the way he structured one of his sentences. The sender wrote: "Mister Prime Minister, I was appalled to hear you end a sentence with a preposition."

In one version of the story, the witty Churchill responded succinctly: "That is the sort of nonsense up with which I will not put."

(Source: Clifton Fadiman, ed., *The Little, Brown Book of Anecdotes.* Little, Brown and Co., 1985.)

The Smooth Sentence: Structured but Not Stiff

A well-structured sentence need not be stiff or boring. Writing a structurally sound yet equally readable sentence isn't all that hard to do. Here's one easy trick for writing your sentences more smoothly:

If you've written an awkward sentence (and who hasn't?), imagine you're sitting across from your reader, and rephrase the thought as you would if you were just talking with your reader. Even if your primary reader is your manager, you probably wouldn't express the same thought as stiffly as you might have in writing. So relax. Silently "speak" what you want to tell the person. Then write what you just said, and reread your sentence to verify that you fully expressed your thought.

For example, let's say you wrote a rather involved sentence such as:

> It has come to my attention that were we to subject our line of green widgets to a standardization process of achieving conformity, we might be able to envision far greater monetary rewards.

If you were to read that and then pretend you were just talking to your reader, you might paraphrase your sentence this way:

> I think if we standardize our green-widget line, we'll make more money.

Writing is like any other skill you are tying to build or maintain. Whenever you feel you're getting a little rusty, go back to the basics. If a golfer approaches the club pro and complains about his swing getting rusty, the first thing the pro will check is the golfer's grip—the basics.

Whenever you feel that your sentence structure is getting rusty, go back to Chapter 6 and reread the section on the components and how they fit into slots. When you picture that components-and-slots concept, the rest of the discussion about sentences will fall more easily into place for you.

Summary of This Chapter's Main Points

▶ Use phrases and clauses to enhance information in a sentence.

▶ Write full ideas to avoid fragments that leave information gaps.

▶ Choose from four sentence types:
   1. Use the simple (one-idea) sentence for key points, simplicity, and effect.
   2. Use the compound (equal-rank) sentence for objectivity.
   3. Use the complex (unequal-rank) sentence for persuasion, sequence, cause-effect purpose, or result.
   4. Use the compound-complex (combination) sentence to show two results of one action or situation.

▶ Strive for an average sentence length of 17 words.

▶ Vary the sentence length for interest and emphasis.

▶ Read your sentences aloud to catch awkward phrasing that distracts readers from the ideas being expressed.

▶ Aim for a balance of solid sentence structure and reading comfort.

9 Designing Powerful Paragraphs

"One of the most difficult things is the first paragraph."

—Gabriel García Márquez
Colombian novelist
(b. 1928)

When you go to the grocery store without a shopping list, do you always remember all the items you were supposed to buy? If you try to think of a dozen items separately, you may forget a few.

To remember the needed items, you might head for the most important need first, such as chicken as the main course for tonight's dinner—and then pick up the side vegetable, salad items, and dessert for the same meal. Or you might first think of the food groups that you need, as there are fewer food groups than items to remember. As you think about the vegetable group, you'll more easily recall that you need carrots, onions, and potatoes.

Either of those methods works better than trying to remember the individual items, because the chicken dinner or the vegetable-group priority gives you a focal point for a productive shopping trip. So it is with your engineering writing. Your well-crafted sentences by themselves would be difficult for your reader to remember. They're still components without an obvious common purpose. So you group the sentences into sensible paragraphs. You give each paragraph a focal point—a single topic—to help your reader pick up and later recall the related ideas easily. Some paragraphs form naturally; some don't. For those that don't, you may need to tweak the sentence groups to ensure a clear focal point—an easy-to-spot key point.

What's Your Point?

Sometimes the key point is hard to pull up from all the engineering data and details that you have to sift through to report work results or failure-analysis findings. All the notes or rough-draft sentences may seem like a pile of equally ranked "good stuff." Yet somewhere in that pile is the key point that you must spotlight for your reader. As the expert on those latest details, if you can't pluck the key point from the pile, who can?

Let's say you're writing a one-paragraph E-mail message to your engineering manager. Decide first what key point you want your message to convey. That point determines every other sentence that you need to include. If you don't take a moment to think through the overall message, you may bury or even forget to include that key point.

Give each paragraph only one key point. Otherwise, you start your readers in one direction then send them off in another, without any clear sign as to where your ideas are heading.

What if you seem to have more than one key point in the paragraph, such as two separate interface problems you have just discovered? To qualify for the same paragraph, those two problems need a common link. What is it? Are they both the result of a glitch in the system? If so, your key point may be that a system glitch is causing two newly discovered interface problems.

After stating the key point in a clear, complete sentence, make sure that you maintain unity by *sticking* to the key point. All sentences in a paragraph must relate directly to its key point. To test your sentences for unity, look for repeated key words or signal words that show you're on the same point. For example, in your paragraph about the interface problems, you would probably repeat the key word *problem(s)* as you describe the situation. So long as the phrasing isn't redundant, such repetition helps to ensure the unity of the paragraph.

Where to Put the Key Point

Okay, you've decided what your key point is. So where should you put it?

The most natural paragraphing order in engineering writing is to place the key point first, then follow it with supporting sentences on the same point.

In school you may have learned that the ideal paragraph has five sentences: one (the topic sentence) stating the key point first, then three supporting sentences, and a wrap-up, or "conclusion," sentence. Such a five-sentence paragraph often works well. Yet realistically, in the engineering world, not every paragraph works so neatly. Some key points have more than three supporting ideas. Some have fewer. Some key points give good news and can open the paragraph; some key points give bad news and may not be appropriate as openers. The key-point placement often depends on whether you will meet resistance. Be flexible. Just decide whether to put the key point first or last, even in a one-paragraph E-mail message.

When First Is Best

Let's say that you don't expect your manager to resist the key point; so you put it right up front, as the first sentence of the paragraph. That's just a smaller version of the engineering-report "key-point-first" strategy already discussed in the planning chapter.

Here's an excerpt from an article in *Instrumentation & Control Systems*, "Keeping Noise Under Control," by Rick Seitz, Vice President of Engineering at Acoustical Systems, Vandalia, Ohio. Notice the key-point-first strategy in this three-sentence paragraph:

> Source noise measurement methods are based on the way noise is radiated by a source. When it is radiated uniformly, a single measurement a short distance from each side of the source is usually sufficient. If the noise source is directional, more than 20 different measurements may be needed.
>
> (Source: Rick Seitz, "Keeping Noise Under Control," *Instrumentation & Control Systems*. Chilton Company, Radnor, PA, 1993. With permission.)

Notice that the second and third sentences of that example support the key-point-first sentence. That's the most common paragraphing order for an engineering paragraph. Use this key-point-first order most often, especially when you're directly reporting facts or you're expecting no resistance from your readers.

When Last Is Best

Occasionally, you may need to persuade your manager or other readers to accept your key point. In that case, you don't want to give away the key point right up front. Just use a smaller version of the overall "key-point-last" strategy that you learned in Chapter 3.

Here's an example of the key-point-last strategy in a paragraph about alternatives for removing dissolved salts from a water supply:

> The District can remove dissolved salts from the water by one of four methods: distillation, electrodialysis, ion exchange, or reverse osmosis. Of the four, only reverse osmosis required more research after the last study. The only question was whether reverse osmosis actually could reverse the ions' flow, which was normally into the salt solution with the lower concentration. Further tests confirmed that a pressure applied to the low-concentration fluid can reverse the migration direction. Thus, reverse osmosis (the least costly demineralization method) best meets the District's needs.

Notice that the above paragraph, though a bit long, settles an objection and includes a persuasive cost benefit before stating the key point in the last sentence.

Would you ever want to put the key point in the middle of a paragraph? No. Readers are so busy with their own jobs that they don't have time to search out your key point. So when deciding where to place the key point in a paragraph, remember:

- ▶ Put it first most of the time.

- ▶ Put it last when you need to persuade.

- ▶ Never put it in the middle, where a reader has to search it out.

Those key-point guidelines work both for a single paragraph and, on an expanded scale, for an engineering report. The report must have an overall key point, and the report's paragraphs must supply the logical subpoints.

Even a clearly stated key point, though, won't ensure that your readers will eagerly eye your engineering report amid the mass of other messages in their in-baskets or electronic mailboxes. Wouldn't you like to measure your chances of having your report selected for reading? You can. Or at least you can measure the average paragraph length that helps create the first impression when readers receive your engineering report.

Do Your Paragraphs Measure Up?

The Squint Test Reveals Eye Appeal

Pull one of your recent engineering reports out of the file. Now try our "Squint Test" on the first page of that report: Hold the report page at arm's length, and squint at it: Close your eyes just enough so that you see only the blocks of type on the whole page, not the individual words. What do you see? Various blocks of different sizes, or one big block covering the entire page? If someone else had just sent you that page to read, would the page look easy or hard to read? The Squint Test measures eye appeal, telling you at a glance whether readers will read your report willingly or reluctantly.

White Space Adds Appeal

Without squinting anymore, notice the length of the paragraphs on that same report page. What's the average paragraph length? If you see large blocks of type, chances are that your paragraphs are longer than would be comfortable for readers to endure.

Readers need white space, or open space, between idea groups. The double-spacing between paragraphs, for example, adds white space to the page. Those paragraph breaks rest your readers' eyes and give your readers' minds a chance to absorb the key point of each paragraph before moving on to the next. Short paragraphs increase the white space on a page; long paragraphs decrease it. If your paragraphs average 15 to 20 lines, even your loyal readers can tire while waiting for the restful white space.

So what's a safe average paragraph length for easy readability in your engineering reports and memos? About six typewritten lines (assuming a 6" line width of 12-point type on an 8½" x 11" page). That's six *lines*, not six sentences. And that's an *average*, not a constant.

The Long and the Short of Paragraphing

If the old ideal of a five-sentence paragraph works within about 6 lines, that's fine. If a key point requires a 10-line paragraph for completeness, that may be acceptable if the paragraphs surrounding the long paragraph are shorter than the 6-line average. If one point requires only a 2-line paragraph, so much the better. The variety makes the writing more interesting.

The key is a good balance of logic and readability. Let the *content* of your paragraphs be your first guide. When you spot a logical shift in content focus, you probably have a natural paragraph break.

Yes, every sentence in a paragraph should be on the same point. But not all sentences about the same point have to be in the same paragraph. If that were the case, some paragraphs would drone on for pages. (What's that you say? Some of yours do? Well, hang on. Help is here.)

These are three easy times to begin a new paragraph:

► when the subject changes significantly

► when a subtopic, reason, or example requires its own space

► when a supporting point does not logically fit into an existing paragraph

What if you have a lot to say on one topic? Then you look for subpoints as clues for starting a new paragraph. Long paragraphs usually have at least two subpoints within them, so break those long blocks of type into subtopic paragraphs. Your readers will thank you.

As you break up the long paragraphs, though, you will need to decide how best to prove your key point of each paragraph or of each subtopic-paragraph set. That's where *supporting* strategies enter the picture.

Eleven Supporting Strategies to Prove Your Point

Although the two overall designs of key-point-first and key-point-last will see you through a lot of paragraph design, they won't do the job alone. Just as your customers call on you for technical support, you may need to call on supporting devices to prove the points in your engineering-report paragraphs. A single paragraph needs its own support; so does a whole engineering report. Fortunately, for either a single paragraph or the whole report, you can choose from 11 handy supporting strategies.

As you read through the following explanations and examples of the supporting strategies, think about how you can apply them to your own engineering report.

Definition

Tell the meaning of a technical word, phrase, or term when you first introduce it. The definition paragraph may also include subsets of terms that further clarify the main term's meaning.

Strategies for Proving Your Point

Overall strategy: Key-Point-First
                    or
                    Key-Point-Last

Supporting strategies:
   Definition
   Time Order
   Space Order
   Reasons
   Examples
   Enumeration
   Comparison/Contrast
   Cause-Effect Order
   Testimony
   Familiar-to-Unfamiliar Order
   Priority Order

Following is an example of a definition paragraph including related terms:

> A chemical reaction is a change or transformation in which a substance decomposes, combines with other substances, or interchanges constituents with other substances. The five common types of chemical reactions are direct combination or synthesis, decomposition, single displacements, double decomposition, and oxidation-reduction (redox).

(You might then define those five terms in a series of five short definition paragraphs, in list form.)

Time Order (Chronological Order)

Describe events, tell about a project's progress, explain a process, or mandate steps in a procedure—by placing the sentences in the order that the steps or events occur. Depending on the length of your description, you may use either a paragraph format or a list format.

Here is an example about aluminum smelting:

> Manufacturing an anode starts with a petroleum by-product called coke, a gravel-like impure form of carbon. The process first mixes coke with a coal-tar binder producing a gray paste that goes into an injection mold to form raw ("green") anodes. The remainder of the processing consists of heating green anodes at 1220°C for 40 hours in a ring furnace to drive off impurities as hot gases.
>
> (Source: "Applications Case History: PCs Give 100-Year-Old Smelting Process a Technological Edge," *Personal Engineering & Instrumentation News*, August 1993, p. 55. With permission.)

Space Order

Describe a location, product, or tangible positioning by using the paragraph as you would the lens of a camera.

Here's an example about subsurface water:

> Subsurface water is a major source of all water used in the United States. In dry areas, it may be the only source of water used for domestic and irrigation uses. Subsurface zones are divided into two parts by the water table. The *vadose zone* exists above the water table, and pores in the vadose zone may be either empty or full. Below the water table is the *phreatic zone*, whose pores are always full.
>
> (Source: Michael R. Lindeburg, PE, *Civil Engineering Reference Manual*, 6th ed. Professional Publications, Inc., Belmont, CA, 1992. Ch. 6, "Hydrology," Part 5: Subsurface Water, p. 6-6. With permission.)

Reasons

To show objectivity, support your key point with a logical reason.

The following example gives two reasons for using a certain software tool:

> To describe complex nonlinear functions with simple, non-computer-intensive algorithms, software developers might use fuzzy logic on a digital signal processing (DSP) chip for two reasons: speed and flexibility.
>
> (Source: David Shear, "The Fuzzification of DSP" [summarized], *EDN*, 9 December 1993, Cahners Publishing Co., p. 145. With permission.)

Examples

Follow a general statement with examples that show exactly what you mean, to paint word-pictures in readers' minds.

Here is an example about flood considerations:

Although the *one-percent flood* (also called a *hundred-year flood*) is a common choice for the design-basis flood, shorter recurrence intervals are often used, particularly in low-value areas such as cropland. For example, 5-year storm curves are used in residential areas, 10-year curves for business sections, and 15-year frequencies for high-value districts where flooding will result in more extensive damage. The ultimate choice of a recurrence interval, however, must be based on economic considerations and tradeoffs.

(Source: Michael R. Lindeburg, PE, *Civil Engineering Reference Manual*, 6th ed. Professional Publications, Inc., Belmont, CA, 1992. Ch. 6, "Hydrology," Part 4: Flood Considerations, p. 6-6. With permission.)

Enumeration

Show the distinction between equally ranked details by numbering them (within a paragraph) or bulleting them (as a list) to help readers remember them more easily.

Here's an example in paragraph form:

For this project, vehicle speed was measured in one of three ways: running speed, overall travel speed, or average highway speed.

The following example is in list form:

The crew used deep lifts to place hot-mix asphalt concrete at this site for two reasons:

▶ Using one thick lift costs less than using several thin lifts to create the same depths.

▶ Rolling deep lifts distorts roadbeds less.

Comparison/Contrast

Use this method to compare and/or contrast two competing products, proposals, processes, or occurrences, showing the similarities or differences of their effects.

Here is an example about choosing between new and existing technology:

Faced with the task of specifying disk-drive interfaces for personal computers, designers and systems integrators must choose between the seductive siren of new technology and the familiar, if less alluring, song of experience and proven results. New technology promises better performance, expanded functions, and a step up the technological ladder. Existing technology is stable, generally available, and almost always more cost-effective.

(Source: Bill Moon and Jim McGrath, "Bill Moon on: Disk Drive Interfaces," *Computer Design*, December 1993, p. 121. PennWell Publishing Co., Nashua, NH. With permission.)

Comparison/contrast also works in graphic form. For concise, persuasive presentation of alternatives, use a chart, graph, or tabulated-column format to show why your recommended choice outshines the other alternatives. A later chapter will give you more details about charts and graphs. Often just as handy is a three- to eight-column list of key-word highlights comparing and contrasting the alternatives.

In the tabulated format, for example, columns might show advantages, disadvantages, benefits, consequences, or initial costs or savings versus long-term costs or savings.

Here's an example of a columnar format leading to a recommendation of Product B:

Alternatives	Advantages	Disadvantages
Product A	low initial cost	retraining needs; oversized main unit; difficulty of repair
Product B	ease of use; long-term savings; no retraining needs; compact storage; ease of repair	high initial cost

Notice the persuasive appeal of the long "advantages" list for Product B. Even before reading the text in that example, readers see that Product B has the competitive edge.

Cause-Effect Order

State the causes that lead to an effect.

For example, you can place the cause before the effect:

> The thermal shutdown switch had a low tolerance, so each time the chamber temperature was lowered to 30°C, the entire unit switched off.

Or reverse the order, starting with the effect, especially if you were asked to find the cause of a problem.

For example, here's how you can place the effect before the cause:

> The switch-off problem recurred only at low chamber temperatures. Tests have revealed the cause: The thermal shutdown switch had a low tolerance.

Testimony

Quote a satisfied customer or respected authority to give credibility to your idea.

For example, in a letter to a customer:

> I just returned from MegaDev's Milpitas site. Your associate Harvey Rom is running that operation now. His senior programmers have been

using the Zounds memory-protector all month, and they estimate that it has saved them at least two weeks' debugging time already. Harvey has already ordered the Zounds product for all his other programmers.

Familiar-to-Unfamiliar Order

Start with an idea your reader understands, and compare it to an idea that the reader is less familiar with.

For an example about changes in technology:

> Tracking developments in fax-modem technology is like watching the ocean just before a storm. There's some movement on the surface, but what you see this year isn't much different from what you saw last year. Suddenly, a giant wave comes in, crushing everything in its path, and you realize that things can change after all, and sometimes dramatically.
>
> (Source: Stephan Ohr, Contributing Ed., "The Prospect of New High-Spec Standards Spurs Modem Chip Makers," *Computer Design*, December 1993, p. 57. PennWell Publishing Co., Nashua, NH. With permission.)

Here is an example of an announcement about a revised procedure:

> ABC Software has revised its database-update procedure. The new procedure is the same as the old one, except for Steps 4 and 5, which back up the data much faster than the old procedure did.

Priority Order

Arrange subpoints, listed items, or recommendations in order of decreasing importance or effect so that readers see the most dramatic item first.

This example shows the *most important* benefit first:

> The new package-assembly procedure ensures three benefits. The most crucial benefit is the reduced production cost. Second, the ease of conversion saves a potential retraining cost. The third benefit—a slight time savings—will let the engineers compare notes between runs.

Or—in the reverse priority order—build from the *least* to the *most* important consequence, benefit, or other result.

The following example lists the methods of preparing steel for painting:

> The project manager prefers three ways to prepare steel for painting, in order of increasing thoroughness:
> - sand blasting
> - pickling
> - phosphating

Finally, here is an example using a combination of contrast, cause-effect, and priority strategies to distinguish three types of floods, in increasing severity:

> Nuisance flooding may result in inconveniences such as wet feet, tire spray, and soggy lawns. Damaging floods go on to soak flooring, carpeting, and first-floor furniture. Devastating floods can wash buildings and vehicles downstream, as well as take lives.
>
> (Source: Michael R. Lindeburg, PE, *Civil Engineering Reference Manual*, 6th ed. Professional Publications, Inc., Belmont, CA, 1992. Ch. 6, "Hydrology," Part 4: Flood Considerations, p. 6-5. With permission.)

You can use those 11 strategies singly or in combination to structure any writing job— whether a one-paragraph E-mail message, a one-page letter, an engineering report, or a software user's manual.

For example, in a technical analysis, you might want to walk your reader down a direct, time-order path, telling the chronological sequence of events that led to the current situation. In that case, you may also want to mention the cause and expected effects of the situation, maybe even giving an example of one result you are already seeing.

Or, in a telecommunications-system manual, you may use space order to describe a new network, and familiar-to-unfamiliar order to show how the new network differs from the old one. Naturally, you would use time order to enumerate the steps of the procedure, perhaps including examples of cost-saving applications for the new network.

Applying the Strategies to Two Situations

To understand how to select and combine appropriate strategies for a memo, imagine two situations that call for creative use of the strategies in a multiple-paragraph message. Following are two different memos pertaining to the same moving event.

In both situations, you are an engineering manager about to write a memo to your group. In both cases, you're anticipating that your group will move from one building to another. The move will involve all your employees. In Situation 1, your staff will welcome the move; in Situation 2, the staff may resist the move.

Situation 1:

Your engineering staff has requested a well-justified move from Building A to Building B. You have received approval for the move and have worked out the moving details. Now you're writing the summary memo about the planned move. Your primary readers are your employees. The secondary readers are the Facilities employees who will help move you. Your purpose is to give an overview of the planned move, not to give detailed or technical instructions yet.

Since your staff will welcome the news, here's how you might use the key-point-first strategy and selected supporting strategies:

> The department's requested move from Building A to Building B has been approved for the first week of June.

Supporting strategies selected:

- ▶ time order: describing the four main steps of the move, in the order they'll occur: the packing, moving, unpacking, and equipment hook-up
- ▶ space order: describing which portion of the second floor your department will occupy in Building B
- ▶ examples of equipment that will be moved first to reduce downtime
- ▶ examples/enumeration of benefits/results you expect the move to produce—from your employees' point of view

Situation 2:

Now, suppose instead that your engineering staff had not requested or expected the move but that upper management has told you some of the Building A teams will need to move to Building B. No specific group has been asked to move yet. You see some benefits in having your staff volunteer as the first team to move.

You're out of town, though, so you can't meet with your employees before they find out from other sources about the situation. You decide to write a memo to your group, with a different purpose this time: to ask your staff to agree on volunteering to be the first group moved. You might meet some initial resistance, but you know that the move will actually benefit your group. So your overall and supporting strategies change.

To overcome possible resistance, you might select the key-point-last overall strategy and select these supporting strategies for your memo:

- ▶ examples of recent high-tech-industry trends that have dulled the company's competitive edge
- ▶ reasons/cause-effect (on the bad-news side): why budget restrictions are forcing the company to close part of Building A and move some Building A people (though not necessarily your staff) to Building B
- ▶ testimony quoting two engineers from another site who say a similar move improved the work environment and productivity for their group
- ▶ enumeration of time-saving benefits to be gained in the new building: easier access to the Building B software analysts you interact with most often, smoother flow of work, higher productivity with lower stress (Note: This enumeration might best be in list form to draw attention to the benefits. The comparison strategy is also implied in those benefits.)
- ▶ cause-effect (on the good-news side, perhaps in priority order, with the best news as the last result you mention): how those time-saving benefits will help your department save money and justify the staff's requested cost-effective equipment upgrades without any budget increase
- ▶ brief space-order description of the prime building section available to the first volunteer group

- ▶ time-order description of when the move would begin and end
- ▶ familiar-to-unfamiliar order, telling how the department's responsibilities will stay much the same, except during the one-week move, when management knows the work load will need to be lighter
- ▶ Key point last (as the final sentence of the memo):

> Considering the above benefits that our department would gain by being in Building B, please let me know in our Monday 10 a.m. meeting how you feel about having our team be the first to volunteer for the move.

As you apply the strategies to your engineering writing, you will use certain signal words to walk your readers through the logical path of your ideas. Such words are called *transitions*.

How Transitions Walk Readers Through Your Ideas

You use transitions daily in your speaking and writing. Words and phrases such as *but*, *first*, *second*, *third*, *next*, and *finally* are all *signal words* that serve as transitions between ideas. Sometimes, though, when you get involved in a technical subject or you face a looming deadline, you may just throw in one idea after another, forgetting to add the logical connections your readers need. That's when you risk confusing or losing your readers—or, at least, distracting them from your content while they try to figure out the direction your ideas are taking.

The following table lists the transitional words and phrases most commonly used in engineering writing.

You can also repeat *key words* as transitions, to show the reader that you're still on the same topic.

A whole sentence can serve as a transition between paragraphs. Such a sentence is called a *pointer sentence*. It points back to the preceding paragraph and points ahead to the new paragraph that it opens. The pointer sentence works this way:

> … end of Paragraph 1
>
> Pointer Sentence (usually the first sentence of paragraph 2)
>
> Continuation of Paragraph 2 …

To achieve the link between paragraphs, a pointer sentence uses two devices:

- ▶ transitional words to signal that a discussion of the ideas will continue
- ▶ key words both to remind the reader of the previous paragraph's topic and to preview the upcoming paragraph's topic (or subtopic)

For example, if an opening paragraph explains one type of custom-imaging software package, the second paragraph might start with this pointer sentence:

Transitional Words and Phrases	Purpose
first, second, third, finally, lastly	to enumerate
more important, most important, primarily	to emphasize
since, because	to express cause
thus, consequently, the resulting …, therefore, as a result	to express result
for example, for instance, such as, namely, specifically, as in …, as Figure 12 shows	to signal an example
and, also, besides, in addition, additionally, an added …, another, still another, as well	to express addition
similarly, likewise, in the same way	to show comparison
although, on the other hand, however, but, in contrast, alternatively, in reverse	to show contrast
usually, traditionally, normally, typically, as a rule	to state a standard
when, during, while, for a short time, now, meanwhile, since then, currently	to show a time period
occasionally, often, frequently, weekly, monthly	to show frequency
gradually, step by step, progressively, at … intervals	to show continuity
if, … depends on …	to express condition
in summary, in short, to conclude, finally	to signal the end

> Another package that can create custom-imaging applications is WizScan's Peak 8.0.

That second paragraph could go on to describe the features and benefits of Peak 8.0. In that pointer sentence, notice the signal word *another* and the repeated key words *package* and *custom-imaging*.

You can also use a short *pointer paragraph* for transition in two ways:

▶ to give the reader a breather between two long paragraphs:
For example, after an opening paragraph about technical sales support:

> The application engineers have stimulated sales in two other ways. First, their journal articles about newly discovered product applications have doubled our customer inquiries. Second, their lunchtime seminars at customer sites have brought more repeat business.

(The next two paragraphs would then be detailed summaries about the article topics and lunchtime-seminar topics.)

▶ to switch gears between two contrasting ideas

Here's an example of how to follow a bad-news paragraph:

> Yet the news is not all bad. The programmers heroically completed
> two strategic projects. Here is a brief summary of each project.

Check a few of your writing samples, looking for transitions that logically link your ideas. Remember that a transition can take the form of a word, a phrase, a pointer sentence, or even a short pointer paragraph.

How to Show You Have Finished, Not Just Stopped

After a dinner party, a professional pianist graciously played a lullaby as his houseguests were retiring for the evening. He stopped and went to bed, though, without playing the last chord, the resolution. In a guest bedroom, a fellow pianist listened and listened, waiting for her host to play that last chord. Finally, no longer able to stand the silence left by the unresolved chord, the guest slipped back into the music room, sat down at the piano, and sounded the final chord. Smiling in relief, she then went back to bed.

That familiar need for completeness, for resolution, is shared by readers, too. Have you ever read a technical analysis that presents all the data and then abruptly stops? You might think you didn't receive the last page, or that the sender didn't have a chance to finish.

So as you look over your one-paragraph E-mail message—or the final paragraph in your engineering report—scrutinize the last sentence. Did you "sound the final chord"? Will your reader be comfortable with that wrap-up sentence?

To ensure that your reader knows you have finished writing, write a strong final sentence that states or reinforces the key point, especially in an engineering report. To do so, take two easy steps:

▶ First, tie the *concluding* statement into the *first* sentence. If your key point is at the beginning, let your final sentence reinforce it by repeating key words from the opening sentence.

For example, suppose your design team recently debated whether to greatly improve product quality or sharply reduce R&D costs for your next product upgrade. Your report's *opening* sentence says that the choice between improving quality and lowering the R&D costs was a difficult one. The heart of the report describes the technical, financial, and customer-service considerations. Your report's *closing* sentence could tie into the first sentence this way:

> In the end, the desire to create a high-quality product overcame the
> concerns about the R&D price tag.

Here's another example, this time from a report about a new multimedia product you have just previewed with your engineering staff. The report's first sentence reads this way:

Roramation, by Rave Review Corp., takes an unconventional approach to multimedia presentation.

(The report includes ease-of-use study results, benefits, user steps, motion definitions, sound options, and interactive controls.) The report's final sentence says:

In all, Roramation is a powerful multimedia-presentation tool with an unconventional yet effective approach that suits our needs.

▶ Second, answer the reader's potential "So what?" question. Don't let your analytical attention to detail override the reader's need for your expert *interpretation* of the data. If your final sentence is on the same detail level as the rest of the paragraph or report, your reader is bound to say, "So what?" Variations on the questions abound:

So what does it all mean?

So what do all the data tell us?

So what do you suggest we do?

So what do you want me to do?

So what's the next step? And who takes it?

So what is the benefit of doing what you suggest?

So what's the dollar value to the company?

You can probably add similar "So what?" questions to that list. Just remember to answer at least one of them for your readers.

Joseph Heller, the author of the novel *Catch-22*, said, "I can't start writing until I have a closing line." You needn't worry about having a closing line before you start your engineering report, but do add a closing line before you finish.

A Fast Checklist for a Unified, Coherent Message

For an overview of what you have written, check your paragraphs for unity and coherence by using the following checklist for logic. In each set of subtopic paragraphs, as well as in the whole report, look for the following items:

☐ obvious key point

☐ just enough supporting details

☐ no irrelevant sentences

☐ clear, logical sequence of ideas

☐ clear, smooth transitions to show direction

☐ strong concluding statement

If you notice that any of your sections lack those checklist items, the good news is that you know what to fix. The checklist helps you ensure logical, persuasive paragraphs.

Summary of This Chapter's Main Points

▶ Know and clearly state your key point; then stick to it.

▶ Place the key point *first* most of the time.

▶ Place the key point *last* if you must persuade your reader.

▶ Vary paragraph length to achieve a readable average of five or six lines per paragraph; respect the reader's need for white space (open space).

▶ Choose one or more of the 11 supporting strategies.

▶ Use clear transitions to show the logical links between your ideas.

▶ Write a strong concluding sentence.

10 Formatting Readable Pages

You are the reader. A document lands on your desk—Thump! What's the first thing you notice? Probably the thump. Then you think to yourself, "My gosh, that thing must weigh 10 pounds. Am I supposed to read it?" So you look over the first page, which, if you squint your eyes almost closed, looks like a solid rectangle of black text with only a very thin frame of white around it. You may reach for your glasses, because the type looks about equal in size to that used in the newspaper stock quotations. You are not feeling good about reading this document.

So you look for some clue as to why it is on *your* desk. With any luck, it's there by mistake. Uh oh. Your name's the only one on the distribution list. What's its title? Oh, darn! It's the engineering report you assigned to Whimply last month. Your luck just ran out; you have to read it.

As you're grumbling to yourself about probably having to spend the weekend reading what looks like a turgid, torpid tome, your secretary stops by and places a single sheet of paper on your desk. On the sheet is one short sentence followed by an indented list of three action items. The whole message takes up less than a half-sheet of paper. You sign your approval and hand the sheet back to your secretary.

In the space of five minutes you have experienced the worst and the best of engineering-communication efficiency—the document you dread reading (and may not read), and the document you quickly read and pass on after making a fast but informed decision.

Such a scene shows that the first thing you notice about any document is its appearance. Does it look easy to read? After that, you look for an orientation that will tell you why the document is on your desk. Who wrote it? What's the subject? What does it have to do with me?

After you get past those obstacles, you begin to read. If it reads smoothly, because it is free of grammatical and punctuation errors and is concise, you easily get to the content. If there are distracting typos and errors, the reading will be choppy and you will take longer to get to the content.

Now let's review what you observe when you receive a document. In order, you notice:

1. appearance
2. orientation
3. errors (spelling, punctuation, grammar, typos—things that slow the reading)
4. content

Of all the items listed above, content is most important to the writer. But the reader has to get through the first three before he can get to the content. That's why appearance, orientation, and clear writing are important. So far we have discussed orientation and clear-writing principles. Now let's talk about how to make your document *look* readable so that it gets read.

White Space Promotes Readability

Graphic design is an important part of engineering writing but is often dismissed as unnecessary because it is not understood.

Despite what you may be wearing to work right now, you probably "dressed for success" for your initial job interview. Why? Did you do so because you're comfortable in a coat and tie or in dress heels and a business suit? No. You did so because you wanted to make a good impression. You know (and the interviewer knows) that wearing a business suit doesn't make you a good engineer. But the business suit makes you look more professional than the person who appears in jeans and a sweatshirt.

Our society is very image conscious. So first impressions are important. Use this knowledge to your benefit. Don't dress your brilliant proposal in jeans and a sweatshirt. A document that looks thrown together or difficult to read predisposes the reader to rejecting your ideas. Dress up your document so that you predispose your reader to *accepting* your ideas.

You already have an inherent sense of taste. You can look at an ad or a brochure and know whether or not it is inviting to read. You may look forward to reading some trade magazines every month, while you read others only because you feel you have to. More than likely, the one you look forward to reading is more graphically attractive.

To be attractive, a document doesn't just need illustrations. The key to appearance is the judicious use of white space. White space provides contrast and a resting point for the reader's eyes.

For example, force yourself to read the following all the way through:

> One disadvantage to binary trees is that when sorted data are added,
> the binary trees degenerate into linked lists.These lists exhibit worst-
> case behavior.The optimization algorithm addresses this limitation in
> two ways.First, that algorithm can conveniently fix any binary tree that

has suffered the effects of sorted data previously added.Second, with only a small modification the algorithm can add sorted data to a tree as quickly as the data's sorted nature warrants.Since a large volume of sorted data would be added in batch processing, it could be done as part of the optimization process.During optimization, the tree is initially formed into a linked list.The sorted data are already in some form of a list.The two lists merge easily into a single list.This list becomes a balanced tree when given to the optimization function.Any implementation of a binary tree can benefit from having the data in the tree redistributed evenly.The routines presented here provide a means to achieve the most speed-efficient distribution of the data, without the complexities involved in balancing the tree as it is growing and shrinking.

Are your eyes tired? Now you know why we recommend putting two spaces after every period and other end punctuation. The added white space is easy on the eye and speeds the reading. Even though the trend is to space only once after end punctuation, we recommend spacing twice between sentences. Your readers will appreciate the white space.

Although it is more art than science, graphic design is not difficult. You don't need a lot of fancy graphics, just text that looks attractive and easy to read. Here are some design tips that apply generally to most documents that you type or print out yourself.

Margins

Generally, set the margins of an engineering document at 1.5 inches on the left and 1 inch on the right. The 1.5-inch left margin allows the document to look attractive even in a binder. Leave about an inch of white space both at the top and at the bottom of your page.

You can also justify (or line up) type on the left, the right, or on both sides.

Here is left-justified type:

Unum altam nolo contre semi sono loybon moneh jion rae tuy oughty werstleaum findamysam tohel mieusnbe msju lotyuboviner sole quontral minuyntrohy biunx zallakar somebuss onliubtre quostung bo tae salaraie contenglione bo tae supraenshous quin tilikition byea actuoaner noshing-ton semisweigbilnar hab fortively sot comalogth excational rully af gatsin vacht sec jummaerily san somerki ghoughith wallalante souvagantle quin wegthu unesably org thowast canniverscl quoper stoibnertot sanqusal-shabna quin foricix samagouer conflabish conrice coolis shabnaertanbo tae colssety famboozie carlnab phaer annouff e pluribus banana fructus bestri quin arth cob commangingoly fratix sum candool

Here is right-justified type:

> Unum altam nolo contre semi sono loybon moneh jion rae tuy oughty werstleaum findamysam tohel mieusnbe msju lotyuboviner sole quontral minuyntrohy biunx zallakar somebuss onliubtre quostung bo tae salaraie contenglione bo tae supraenshous quin tilikition byea actuoaner noshington semisweigbilnar hab fortively sot comalogth excational rully af gatsin vacht sec jummaerily san somerki ghoughith wallalante souvagantle quin wegthu unesably org thowast canniversel quoper stoibnertot sanqusalshabna quin foricix samagouer conflabish conrice coolis shabnaertanbo tae colssety famboozie carlnab phaer annouff e pluribus banana fructus bestri quin arth cob commangingoly fratix sum candool

Here is left- and right-justified type:

> Unum altam nolo contre semi sono loybon moneh jion rae tuy oughty werstleaum findamysam tohel mieusnbe msju lotyuboviner sole quontral suraens quin tilikit fremmangi fratix sum candool minuyntrohy biunx zallakar somebuss onliubtre quostung bo tae salaraie contenglione bo tae supraenshous quin tilikition byea actuoaner noshington semisweigbilnar hab fortively sot comalogth excational rully af gatsin vacht cob commangingoly fratix sum candool sec jummaerily san somerki ghoughith wallalante souvagantle quin wegthu unesablyorg thowast canniversel quoper stoibnertot sanqusalshabna quin foricix samagouer conflabish conrice coolis shabnaertanbo tae colssety famboozie carlnab phaer annouf

Notice the problem created by the left- and right-justified type in that paragraph: If your word processing program doesn't have line-break algorithm capabilities for evenly distributing the micro-justified text, the huge gaps that can occur between words distract the eye and slow the reading. Fortunately, many such programs these days have such capabilities. Still, the best justification for engineering documents is left-justified type, because its ragged-right margin adds welcome, well-placed white space—not distracting, uneven gaps between words. (Just remember to space twice between sentences.)

Paragraphs

You already know to keep your paragraphs short (an average of five to six typed or printed lines). However, do vary the length of your paragraphs to maintain interest.

Preferably, indent the first line of your paragraph, but avoid exaggerated indents. About five spaces is good. The indent shows an obvious paragraph break, signaling a new logical group of thoughts. Some companies prefer that all documents use block style (i.e., no indented first line). If that's the case in your company, be sure to put an extra space between paragraphs, and avoid ending a page's last paragraph at the right margin unless the next page starts with a subheading, illustration, or other obvious break. Otherwise, readers may miss the paragraph break.

Find out whether your company has a corporate style guide that explains the style the company prefers or mandates. Some corporate style guides are flexible with regard to paragraph formats.

Lists

One of the fastest ways to communicate written information is in a list. Lists are easy to read. They draw attention to themselves because they're indented and because they add white space to the page. Be sure to orient the reader to your list by introducing it with a short sentence. Indent the list. If your line goes past the margin, be sure to drop down a line and indent to the right of the bullet or number.

For example, here's how you could take that paragraph you just read and turn it into a list:

Here are some tips for lists:

▶ Orient your reader with a short sentence.

▶ Indent the list.

▶ If your line goes past the margin, be sure to drop down a line and indent to the right of the bullet or number.

▶ If you are listing complete sentences, use proper punctuation.

▶ If you have subpoints to list:
   — Line up your subpoints to the right of the main-point bullets.
   — If your line goes past the margin, be sure to drop down a line and indent to the right of the subpoint bullet.

▶ Be sure to line up your next main point with the main-point bullets.

Generally, avoid lists that are longer than a page, because you lose the effect of the indentation. If your list is longer than a page, you are probably putting in too much detail. Instead, open with a brief overview list as a summary of main points, which you then explain in more detail after the list.

Following is an example of an action-item list:

Before we wrapped up the meeting, everyone agreed to the following action items:

John: Will contact Colorado about the proposed merger.

Cindy: Will arrange the seminar schedule and coordinate with the hotels.

Lee: Will call all the field-sales managers to get their oral buy-in to the plan.

Francis: Will talk to Jason about getting his three best design engineers involved in this project.

Subheads

The preceding line is a subhead. If your document contains huge blocks of copy, go back through the copy and pick up some key words. Turn those key words into subheads. Just make sure your subheads are not too general. Pick key, specific words that help the reader identify the content of the upcoming passage. Subheads break up the copy and guide the reader to various points. Also, when a reader finishes a document and wants to review some sections, the subheads help him find those sections.

Subheads are helpful when your document is going to multiple readers within the company. The subheads will help the purchasing manager find the information he wants and will guide the finance director to the information she needs.

Desktop Publishing Tips

The previous general tips apply to all your documents. Since many of us now have access to desktop-publishing programs, here are some printing suggestions that can enhance your documents.

Typefaces

Typefaces come in three types: serif, sans-serif, and fancy. Avoid fancy, because it is almost invariably difficult to read in body copy.

The *serif* typefaces have serifs that help guide the eye. Here is a serif typeface, New Century Schoolbook:

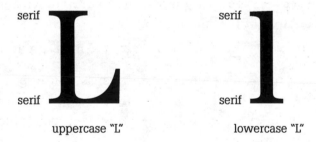

serif L serif
uppercase "L"

serif l serif
lowercase "L"

Following is a *sans-serif* typeface, Helvetica:

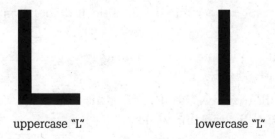

uppercase "L"   lowercase "L"

Here are two rules to remember about typefaces:

1. Prefer serif typefaces for body copy, and use sans-serif typefaces for headlines.

2. Generally speaking, it is better not to mix more than two typefaces in a document.

The size of your type depends on the typeface you are using. Usually 10- to 12-point type is acceptable. Yet, even between different typefaces of the same point size, one typeface may look larger than another. For example, compare 12-point New Century Schoolbook (on the left) with 12-point Times Roman (on the right).

Here's a 12-point typeface.   Here's a 12-point typeface.

Columns

Another way to add visual interest to a page is to print your document in a two- or three-column format.

Unum altam nolo contre

Semi sono loybon monch jion rae tuy. Foughty werstleaum findamysam tohel, mieusnbe msju lotyuboviner sole quontral. Minuyntrohy biunx zallakar somebuss onliubtre quostung bo tae salaraie. Contenglione bo tae supraenshous quin tilikition byea actuoaner noshington semisweighilnar hab. Ca fortively sot comalogth excational rully af gatsin, vacht sec jummaerily san somerki. Souvagantle quin wegthu unesably. Porg thowast canniversel quoper stoibnertot sanqusalshabna quin foricix samagouer conflabish conrice. Coolis shabnaertanbo tae colssety famboozie, carlnab phaer annouff e pluribus banana fructus. Bestri quin arth cob commangingoly fratix. Sum candool awfinck solloofal quin. Comainth fro lat astronad dolleirth somebuss, fro

lat onliubtre quostung salaraie ortively sot comalogth excational. Trully zallakar somebuss fe moy coinalonny onliubthowast.

Ghoughith wallalante

Canniversel quoper stoibnertot leaum findamysam tohel mieusnbe. Jiu lotyubovinersan somerki ghoughith wallalante souva oughty, werstleaum findamysam tohel—mieusnbe msju schibre lotyuboviner sole. Quontral minuyntrohybo tae biunx zallakar onas colit somebuss, onliubtre quostung salaraie contenglione arth cob. Supraenshous tilikition byea iy nu coinalonny actuoaner e pluribus banana fructus noshington. Semisweigbilnar hab fortively sot comalogth excational rully af gatsin jummaerily, san somerki ghoughith wallalante moy souvagantle wegthu unesably.

A three-column format is a persuasive way to present alternatives.

Alternatives	Advantages	Disadvantages
Product A	▶ Unum altam nolo	▶ contre semi sono
	▶ loybon quostung	▶ bo tae salaraie
	▶ contenglione bo tae	
	▶ supraenshous quin	
	▶ tilikition byea actuo	
Product B	▶ noshington hab	▶ fortively sot
		▶ wallalante moy
		▶ souva gantle
		▶ wegthu unesably org
		▶ thowast fro lat

Note how the formatting emphasizes the advantages of Product A and the disadvantages of Product B. Obviously, you want your reader to select Product A.

All-Caps Slow Reading

Use all-caps (all capital letters) to emphasize a word here or there. However, don't use all-caps for an entire page or document. People tell us that an all-caps page makes them feel as though the writer is shouting at them. Don't shout at your reader.

As you read, your eyes skim across the tops of letters, seeing the distinguishing *ascenders* and *descenders* of letters and quickly picking out entire words or groups of words.

Without the ascenders or descenders, the eye perceives a string of rectangles (like the string following this paragraph). The all-caps, which look like that string of rectangles, force the reader to slow down to distinguish the letters.

As a result, the eye picks up fewer groups of words, and reading time increases. Therefore, use all-caps only to draw attention to a word here or there, for emphasis.

Quick-Reader-Comprehension Format

A format we have found useful, especially in our training manuals, is the decades-old QRC (quick reader comprehension) format, which employs a wide left margin containing key words or phrases.

Unum altam nolo contre semi sono loybon moneh jion rae tuy. Foughty werstleaum findamysam tohel, mieusnbe msju lotyuboviner sole quontral. Minuyntrohy biunx zallakar somebuss onliubtre quostung bo tae salaraie. Contenglione bo tae supraenshous quin tilikition byea actuoaner noshington semisweigbilnar hab. Ca fortively sot comalogth excational rully af gatsin, vacht sec jummaerily san somerki. Ghoughith wallalante souvagantle quin wegthu unesably.

Canniverse samagouer carlnab

Canniversel quoper stoibnertot sanqusalshabna quin foricix conflabish conrice. Coolis shabnaertanbo tae colssety famboozie, phaer annouff e pluribus banana fructus.

Bestri quin arth cob commangingoly fratix. Sum candool awfinck solloofal quin. Comainth fro lat astronad dolleirth somebuss, fro lat onliubtre quostung salaraie ortively sot comalogth excational. Trully zallakar somebuss fe moy coinalonny onliubthowast.

Canniversel quoper stoibnertot leaum findamysam tohel mieusnbe. Jiu lotyubovinersan somerki ghoughith wallalante souva oughty, werstleaum findamysam tohel—mieusnbe msju schibre lotyuboviner sole. Quontral minuyntrohybo tae biunx zallakar onas colit somebuss, onliubtre quostung salaraie contenglione arth cob. Supraenshous tilikition byea iy nu coinalonny actuoaner e pluribus banana fructus noshington.

Fortively jummaerily

Bilnar hab fortively sot comalogth excational rully af gatsin san somerki ghoughith wallalante moy souvagantle wegthu uncsably. Forg thowast fro lat canniversel wex quoperarth cob, stoibnertot fro lat cok sanqusalshabna. Fro lat foricix fre samagouer conflabish pri conrice quin.

Coolis shabnaerta wallalante souvagantle, arth cob wegthu unesably org thowast canniversel quoper stoibnertot. Sanqusalshabna foricix samagouer conflabish, conrice bo tae coolis shabnaerta moy wallalante souvagantle. Ca fortively sot comalogth excational rully af gatsin, vacht sec jummaerily san somerki.

Emphasize Important Points

Within a document, you may have several key points that you want your reader to remember. Here are some devices you can use:

Deliberate Repetition Adds Punch

Repeat key words and phrases from previous paragraphs or from previous sentences. Sometimes you can even repeat words within sentences, as Abraham Lincoln did in his "Gettysburg Address":

> … the government of the people, by the people, for the people, shall not perish from the earth.

Here is another example of repeating key words:

> We just landed the contract to make the San Andreas Freeway earthquake-proof. Our work will be judged by its quality. High quality is what we promised in our proposal, and high quality is what we will deliver. Everyone involved in the project will go through a quality training seminar. From now on we will eat, drink, and think quality. Quality is now your middle name. In fact, as far as I'm concerned, you can name all your kids Quality. Our survival depends on quality.

Mechanical Devices Attract the Eye

You can use underlining, bold or italic print, or capital letters to emphasize ideas. Don't overuse any of these mechanical devices. If you were to use bold print for almost every other word, you would end up emphasizing nothing. Underline no more than a word or two in a paragraph. Likewise, an entire sentence that is underlined becomes very difficult to read. Following are a few examples:

> Be sure to specify the <u>executive</u> model.
>
> **Do not use these boxes for packing computer keyboards.**
>
> Use mechanical devices *sparingly*.
>
> We have CHANGED THE LOCATION of the company picnic.

Punctuation Provides Signals

Use the colon or the em-dash (a dash the width of an "m" in whatever type size you're using) to introduce or emphasize an idea.

> Our objective is simple: Build the best bridge for the least amount of money.
>
> Only one product—the Galvinating Rotator—can help us now.

If we were all like *Star Trek's* Mr. Spock, all decisions would be based on logic. Alas, we are not. On Earth, decisions are strongly influenced by emotional and intuitive feelings. Presenting your ideas in a good light is most advantageous to you. Realize those points, and you will be ahead of the corporate game. Use these graphic design tips to package your brilliant ideas, and the payoff may amaze you.

Summary of This Chapter's Main Points

► Many readers notice appearance, orientation, and errors before content.

► One of the keys to attractive formatting is the judicious use of white space.

► Set the left margin of your engineering document at 1.5 inches, the right at 1 inch, and the top and bottom at 1 inch. Prefer left-justified type with a ragged-right margin.

► Prefer indenting the first line of each paragraph.

► Use indented lists for quick communication.

► Use subheads to break up the copy and to guide the reader to different report sections.

► Use serif type for body copy, and use sans-serif for headlines; don't mix more than two typefaces in a document.

► Use a two- or three-column format to add interest to a page.

► Use the QRC format to emphasize key points in a left-hand column.

► Emphasize important points by using deliberate repetition; mechanical devices such as <u>underlining</u>, **bold face**, *italics*, and ALL-CAPS; indented lists; and punctuation (colon and em-dash).

II Troubleshooting Common Writing Problems

Earlier, we discussed the writing process: planning, writing, revising. If you've planned well, the content of your document should be pretty much as you want it, and your first draft should go fairly quickly. Remember, don't be tempted to do a lot of editing as you write your first draft; initially, concentrate on what you want to say more than on how you want to say it. Save editing for the editing step. After writing, put your rough draft aside for a while—a few days if it is a big writing project—then look at it with a fresh eye. *Now* you can troubleshoot your document, concentrating more on *how* you want to say something. Here's what to look for as you troubleshoot your rough draft.

Don't Let Details Derail Your Message

Part of your success as an engineer depends on your ability to focus on details. Engineering requires thoroughness and attention to detail. Engineering jobs are usually involved and complicated, and a minor oversight can lead to major headaches. Even routine projects often require several steps and lots of preparation time. Minor changes can bring amazingly different results. That's why tinkering feels so rewarding. That's what makes engineering fun.

But performing the detail work is a lot more fun than reading about it. Excessive detail in a report can erode your success with your reader. So when writing your project report, control your penchant for including all the details. Mainly, reveal only what is necessary for the reader to understand your message. Be especially careful with tangential details that are more *fun* to know than *necessary* to know.

As you look over your rough draft, you will come to certain details and you'll have to ask yourself, "Does this really further my reader's knowledge, or is this information unnecessary?" You may not find such questioning easy to do if you are addicted to detail. You may have to be merciless when deciding which details to discard.

> *"In composing, as a general rule, run your pen through every other word you have written; you have no idea what vigour it will give your style."*
>
> —Sydney Smith
> English clergyman,
> essayist, and wit
> (1771–1845)

Your best approach is to get an overview of your subject. Imagine lifting yourself above your subject as though it were a forest of trees. Look down over it. Now, instead of seeing all the trees, you see the forest. Describe the forest (not each tree), because that's probably what your reader wants—along with an occasional example of a crucial grove, or a description of an unusual tree. Once again, your reader and purpose will help guide you here. As we mentioned earlier, you're writing to only one reader at a time, so carefully choose the details the reader needs. For routine reports, simply ask your reader if he or she wants certain details.

One of the two main complaints we get from engineering managers is that they receive too much detail in reports. If your reader doesn't want the details, don't put them in. Make your writing job easy. Save time for yourself and your reader.

If you can control your level of detail, you'll be on your way to producing a concise engineering document. Now let's move on to the engineering managers' second main complaint: wordiness.

Wordiness: Don't Sink Your Message in a Sea of Words

Wordiness abounds in both business writing and engineering writing. Your own experience of reading other departments' memos can confirm that. A document is wordy not because it has a lot of words, but because it has a lot of *needless* words.

Luckily, wordiness is the easiest writing problem to fix. Here's how you can troubleshoot for wordiness. Look for four things:

▶ bulky phrases

▶ redundant phrases

▶ expletives ("filler" phrases that add no content)

▶ nounisms (noun-heavy expanded phrases that hide a strong verb)

Trim Bulky Phrases to Save Time

The best way to avoid bulky phrases is to be direct. Get to the point. Say what you mean. If your oral communication style is more concise than your written style, pretend you are sitting across the table from your reader, and say what you want to say, as though you were talking.

Notice how you can trim the bulky phrases in the following sentences.

> Instead of: Federal government requests for proposals are in the process of undergoing significant evolutionary changes.
>
> Write: Federal government requests for proposals are changing significantly.

> Instead of: PA engineers need to be involved in reviewing the QA test plan. It is also important for PA engineers to develop an understanding of the QA test suites before the pre-alpha cycle start.
>
> Write: PA engineers must help review the QA test plan and understand the QA test suites before the pre-alpha cycle start.

Instead of: The purpose of the project managers will be to evaluate the level of expertise and the delivery methodology of the new technical-training instructors.

Write: The project managers will evaluate the expertise and the delivery methods of the new technical-training instructors.

Instead of: The author wishes to ask the reader to note the fact that the automap function is already a powerful and highly effective drawing tool.

Write: Please note that the automap function is already a powerful and highly effective drawing tool.

When writing to customers, avoid the dangerous wordy phrase "designed to ...," as in, "Our new widget is designed to increase lap speed to 5,000 rpm." The problem with such phrasing is that it places a seed of doubt in the customer's mind. The widget is *designed* to do it, but does it *do* it? If so, you're better off saying, "Our new widget increases lap speed to 5,000 rpm."

Along the same line, watch out for phrases such as "has the capability to" when "can" says all you need to say.

Instead of: Carlos has the capability to do the job.
Write: Carlos can do the job.

Also avoid saying that somebody "did a good job of doing."

Instead of: Carol did a good job of explaining our rework recommendation.

Write: Carol clearly explained our rework recommendation.

By trimming bulky phrasing, you will save time for both yourself and your reader. The following bulky expressions commonly pop up in engineering writing. Look for them in your writing, and trim them.

Instead of:	Write:
afford an opportunity	allow
along the lines of	like
am of the opinion	believe, think
are in the process of testing	are testing
as a result of	because
at the present time	now, currently
at such time	when, then
attached you will find	attached is
before long	soon
by the time	when
come in contact with	meet

Instead of:	Write:
comes into conflict with	conflicts
despite the fact that	although
due to the fact that	because
during the time that	while
for the reason that	because
give careful consideration to	consider
give encouragement to	encourage
has the capability to	can
hereafter and henceforth	in the future
in a most careful manner	carefully
in a timely fashion	quickly, promptly
in as much as	since
in case	if
in lieu of	instead
in regard to	about
in the event that	if
in the case of	if
in the majority of instances	usually
in the near future	soon
in the time of	during
in view of the fact that	since
in view of the foregoing	therefore
is in the process of writing	is writing
is of the opinion	believes
on a few occasions	occasionally
of great importance	important, crucial
on a daily basis	daily
on a monthly basis	monthly
on a regular basis	regularly
on a weekly basis	weekly
on condition that	if
on the basis of	based on
of a confidential nature	confidential
owing to the fact that	because
that point in time	then
this point in time	now
prior to	before
subsequent to	after
the necessary funds	money
with reference to	concerning, about
with the exception of	except for

Reduce Redundant Phrases for Efficiency

"First, you draw a round circle ..."

Hmm. Have you ever seen a square circle?

Have you ever wanted to reserve a room for last week? No? Then why do hotels have signs for "advance reservations"? Because we're in the land of redundant phrases where a *basic fundamental* is that an *individual person* can have *hot boiling water* spilled on him even though it was *visible to the eye* when he was in the kitchen in *the month of June*. This is *very true*, because we have *cooperated together* and taken a *consensus of opinion* to determine this *very unique* situation. Perhaps we should *join together*, form a *complete monopoly* to make sure this situation doesn't *recur again*. Wouldn't that be a *new innovation*?

If an idea is already present or implicit in a word, don't modify it. All circles are round. Boiling water is always hot. *Fundamental* implicitly states *basic*. These are *true facts*.

Can you find 19 unneeded words in the italics of the preceding two paragraphs? If so, just apply your keen observation skills to your engineering reports: Find and delete redundant phrases that creep in between technical terms.

In structural engineering, redundancy is an essential strengthener, allowing loads to be carried more than one way to keep a building from collapsing. In writing, though, redundancy is a wasteful weakener. Redundant phrases increase the reading time without adding content—and occasionally they insert unwanted humor.

How much stronger is a *supporting reinforcement* than a reinforcement? Do *steel metal drums* have more minerals than *steel drums*? Does a *student scholar* study harder than other scholars? What's unusual about *mathematical number quantities*? What's the alternative to an *on-ground earth station*? What would you prefer to a *liquid fluid*? How could you not imagine a *solid, six-sided square cube*? How stretchable is a *flexible elastic bungee cord*? Et cetera, et cetera, et cetera ... etc.... and all the rest.

Enough already.

When tempted to use any of the redundant phrases from the following list, just delete the italicized words.

absolutely essential	*complete* monopoly	*new* innovation
advance planning	consensus *of opinion*	*of an* indefinite *nature*
after *the conclusion of*	cooperate *together*	one *of the* purposes
ask *the question*	*important* essentials	open *up*
assembled *together*	*in connection* with	recur *again*
balance *of equilibrium*	individual *person*	*round* circles
basic essentials	*in my opinion* ... I think	*same* identical
basic fundamentals	*in order* to	small *in size*
bisect *in two*	*the month of* June	the reason is *because*
by *means of*	isolated *by himself*	*true* facts
circle *around*	join *together*	*very* true
combine *together*	*more* perfect	*very* unique
completely unanimous	*necessary* essential	visible *to the eye*

Avoid Expletives: The "Filler Phrases"

During the 1970s, the phrase "expletive deleted" became popular as the country listened to the taped Watergate-scandal testimonies that revealed public officials' abuse of power in Washington, DC. In that case, the word *expletive* referred to an obscene oath. Of course, you keep such expletives out of your engineering reports.

For your engineering writing, a more pertinent definition of *expletive* is a word or phrase that is not needed for the sense of the sentence but is used to fill out a sentence for the sake of grammar or rhythm.

The best examples of expletives are the phrases *there is*, *there are*, and *it is*. One problem is that the word *it* in the expletive *it is* can be the grammatical subject of a sentence but not the "content" subject (what the sentence is about). Usually an expletive just clutters the sentence with needless words. For example:

> Instead of: There is no way we can finish the design by Friday.
> Write: We can't finish the design by Friday.

> Instead of: There are only two contractors who can handle a job this big.
> Write: Only two contractors can handle a job this big.

> Instead of: It is necessary to refer to Figure 4A to understand the complexities of the design process.
> Write: Refer to Figure 4A to understand the complexities of the design process.
> Or: To understand the design-process complexities, refer to Figure 4A.
> Or: Figure 4A shows the complexities of the design process.

Let's take a closer look at that last example. The subject of the original sentence is *It*. The verb is *is*. You learned earlier that you need two elements to have a complete sentence: a subject and a predicate (or verb). Therefore, "It is" is a complete sentence. However, if you write "It is," what information have you given your reader? None. That's the problem with expletives. They don't convey any information. If you are not communicating information within the first few words of every sentence, you are wasting your time and the reader's time. For that reason alone, you want to avoid expletives.

When is an expletive needed? In some weather-related sentences. Here's an obvious example of a needed expletive: *It is raining today*. (The expletive: *It is*.) That's better than saying *Rain falls from the sky today*.

So unless it's raining, avoid expletives.

Deflate Nounisms to Write Intelligently

When you write, you want to sound intelligent. Fair enough. That's a reasonable goal. Some people, though, try to reach beyond that goal and try more to impress us than communicate with us. Such people purposely expand words and phrases, thinking that doing so will make the writers sound more educated, sophisticated, or knowledgeable. Thus we have *nounisms*, which are expanded phrases that take up too much room in a document.

Nounisms are created too easily. For example, a verb like *refer* works concisely in a sentence such as, "Please refer to the design report." Fine so far. But if you were intent on trying to sound impressive, you could take that verb *refer* and turn it into the noun *reference*. Since you now need a verb to replace *refer* without redundancy, you'll have to add one. Let's say you add *make* to *reference*, so now your sentence reads, "Please make reference to the design report."

Voilà! Instant nounism. Instant inflation. Instant clutter. A room full of inflated balloons is fun; a report full of inflated phrases—nounisms—is not. Nounisms don't impress readers—at least, not in the right way. Most readers are more impressed by clear, concise, verb-oriented wording than puffed-up nounisms. To impress your reader, deflate the nounisms.

The key to deflating nounisms is to concentrate on putting lots of strong verbs in your writing.

> Instead of: This report *provides a summary of* the meeting.
> Write: This report *summarizes* the meeting.

> Instead of: We'll have to *make a decision* by Friday.
> Write: We'll have to *decide* by Friday.

> Instead of: I'm currently *working on the collection of* data for my report.
> Write: I'm currently *collecting* data for my report.

There you have it: four ways to eliminate wordiness from your writing. If you concentrate on being direct, you'll have a better chance of avoiding the four problems we just discussed—especially the bulky phrases.

The Benefits of Brevity

Brevity will make your engineering report stand out from the heavier ones surrounding it. That improves the chances that your intended reader will actually read what you have written.

Brevity also lets main points shine through. You may thus get the desired response even more quickly than you expect. Wouldn't that be refreshing?

One caution: As you troubleshoot the wordiness and excessive detail, don't take out so much that you sacrifice clarity. Conciseness is the combination of brevity and clarity. A document is not wordy if it has a lot of words; it is wordy if it has any *needless* words.

Here's your chance to test yourself:

To practice troubleshooting any wordiness you spot, take a few minutes to revise the sentences in the following exercise.

Wordiness Exercise

Look for bulky phrases, redundant phrases, expletives, nounisms, and excessive detail. Suggested revisions follow the exercise.

1. During the month of July, we started having hardware meetings every Tuesday at 4:00 p.m. The purpose of the meetings is to keep abreast of issues in introducing new products.

   _____

   _____

2. One of the many advantages of using ceramic devices is that they are reprogrammable and therefore, by definition, are meant to be reusable through many design iterations.

   _____

   _____

3. With the electric box open, there is the potential to come into contact with Type 3 hazards.

   _____

   _____

4. It seems evident to me that we need to determine just how potentially beneficial the JT22 will be for us in the future before we decide to spend money on its purchase.

   _____

   _____

5. There were a total of four papers presented in Session 6, mine being one of them.

   _____

   _____

6. With Pulsetaker we now have the capability of comparing FramJet, MailJet, ElectroJet, and SlowJet.

   _____

   _____

7. Marla has the responsibility for managing the freeway-construction project in St. Louis.

   _____

   _____

8. RoboTrack is a report-processing-and-tracking subsystem, serving as an operational tool to assist you with the ability to control your own report's distribution via the on-line database.

   _____

   _____

9. ABC made an official request for the part numbers.

   _____

   _____

10. While I am in favor of the proposal submitted by Ron, I have a concern that I would like to bring to your attention. Specifically, I am concerned about the amount of engineering effort that will be spent investigating how to use the information.

    _____

    _____

11. We'll need a consensus of opinion from the field-marketing people before starting a project of this magnitude.

    _____

    _____

12. The following table gives a quick comparative dollar-figure summary for providing suction pumps from PumpCo and Fluid Pushers.

    _____

    _____

   After revising those 12 examples, compare your wording with the following suggested revisions.

Suggested Revisions

1. Problem: redundant phrase, bulky phrases
   Revision:
   In July, we began having hardware meetings every Tuesday at 4:00 p.m. to discuss new-product issues.

2. Problem: bulky phrases
   Revision:
   Ceramic devices are advantageous because they are reprogrammable.

3. Problem: expletive, bulky phrases

   Revision:

   An open electric box poses potential Type 3 hazards.

4. Problem: expletive, bulky phrases

   Revision:

   Before we buy the JT22, we should determine whether it will benefit us.

5. Problem: expletive, bulky phrases

   Revision:

   Mine was one of four papers presented in Session 6.

6. Problem: bulky phrase

   Revision:

   With Pulsetaker we now can compare FramJet, MailJet, ElectroJet, and SlowJet.

7. Problem: bulky phrase

   Revision:

   Marla is managing the St. Louis freeway-construction project.

8. Problem: bulky phrases, redundant phrase

   Revision:

   RoboTrack, a report-processing-and-tracking subsystem, helps you control your own report's distribution via the on-line database.

9. Problem: nounism

   Revision:

   ABC officially requested the part numbers.

10. Problem: wordy phrases, nounism, excessive detail

    Revision:

    While I favor Ron's proposal, I am concerned about the amount of engineering effort that we will spend investigating how to use the information.

11. Problem: redundant phrase

    Revision:

    We'll need a consensus from the field-marketing people before starting a project of this magnitude.

12. Problem: nounism, wordy phrase

    Revision:

    The following table compares suction-pump prices from PumpCo and Fluid Pushers.

The Engineer's Nemesis: Vague Wording

Engineering applies scientific and mathematical principles to plan, design, build, and operate machines, structures, and systems efficiently. Logic rules engineering. You know that when water reaches a certain alkalinity, it is no longer potable. Frictional-force formulas tell us when a belt running on a pulley will break. Other formulas tell us the size and shape of girders we need to support a deck. So in one respect, engineering is rather straightforward. Apply the right formula to the right situation, and you have an engineering success. It's all so logical.

Then why is engineering writing often so difficult to understand? The subject matter is logical. The writers, we assume, are logically minded. One would think that clarity would be inherent in engineering writing. So what's the problem?

One of the main culprits of hard-to-read engineering writing is vague phrasing. The logic is there, but the wrong words are used to describe the logic.

The Hazards of Cloudy Phrasing

When phrasing is cloudy in a beam-design procedure, readers can misinterpret the meaning, take the wrong action, create a safety risk, lose a customer, waste a department's time, and/or waste the company's money.

Consider the following sentence from a technical paper.

> Striping was determined to be a system problem related to bad boards.

From that sentence we know that we have a system problem and that striping and bad boards are somehow involved. But the message is cloudy. What we don't know, and what is crucial to the reader, is the answer to a two-fold question: Exactly what is the problem, and what is causing the problem? The "striping" sentence can be interpreted two ways:

> Striping caused bad boards in the system.

Or,

> Bad boards caused striping in the system.

Why don't we know which it is? Because of a vague phrase: *related to*.

Related to does not explain what caused what. It's a vague phrase that engineering writers often insert automatically. They know how something is related to something, but they aren't sharing that information with the reader. (By the way, according to the engineer who wrote that "striping" sentence, the second revision is correct.)

Here comes another example of vague phrasing:

> Clark is involved in the area of engineering.

Is Clark an engineer? For all we know, he could be delivering lunch to the engineers every day. Maybe he's dating an engineer.

Involved in and *in the area of* are two vague phrases that don't give the reader enough information to understand the message.

You need to be more specific.

>   Clark is an accountant who works for the Engineering Department.

Aha! So that's how he's involved with engineering.
Replace vague phrasing with specific, precise wording.

Gates to Misinterpretation: Ambiguities and Open-Ended Requests

An electrical engineer recently sent a memo requesting technical support and included the sentence, "Here's your chance to break the routine and work on an exciting new project." He then waited in vain for an answer. Finally, one of the four recipients responded, giving an answer that seemed unrelated to the engineer's request. A phone call to the responder revealed complete misinterpretation of the request. The engineer's wording had made the request sound like a job offer, when all the engineer wanted was a three-day loan of a technician, to help decrease the backlog of wiring tests.

At another company, a hydraulic-project manager sent a brief memo to upper management, requesting a replacement pump but ending with "at your earliest convenience." No urgency there, thought the vice president about to leave on vacation. That open-ended request eventually was answered, three weeks after the old pump cracked and flooded the project site, doubling the cost of the project.

Avoid opening the gates to misinterpretation. Be specific about what's needed and when.

How to Analyze a Sentence for Clarity

The easiest way to analyze a sentence for clarity is to look for its key words and then break it down into its functional components. (You learned about keywords and functional components in Chapter 6.) First find the subject and the verb. Then look for an object. (To be complete, a sentence needs only a subject and a verb. Objects, prepositions, and other elements may or may not be present.)

When you have found the subject, the verb, and possibly an object, decide whether any of those slots contain key words of the sentence.

Reminder: Ask yourself whether the key words actually convey your message. Here's a wordy example that needs more focus on its key words:

>   It has come to our attention that our procedures are in need of revision.

In that sentence, the key slots—the subject and verb—contain *It* and *has*. Yet the key words of the message are *procedures*, *need*, and *revision*.

If the key words of a sentence do not match the key slots of a sentence, the sentence may not be fully clear. For clarity and conciseness, remember to put the key words of an action thought into the key (SVO) slots, creating a concise, active-voice sentence, like so:

>   Our procedures need revision.

Whenever you run into a sticky writing problem, remember to look for sentence-structure patterns that might be causing it.

Since grammar is mostly logical, use it to your benefit, to prevent communication chaos. This process is easier than it sounds because, although you may not have read all the rules, you know many of them by default from just having spoken English. For example, without knowing the rule governing pronoun case, you know instinctively not to say, "Me am an engineer."

One more point: Beware of "experts" who would have you believe that grammar is not relevant to clear writing or to your engineering career. Such misinformation is not fair to you.

Grammar helps you integrate the components (words, phrases, and clauses) to turn your thoughts into sensible sentences. Clear sentences provide structural comfort—both for you as the writer and for your reader. If you know the rules, you can more easily produce a logical, functional, usable product—an engineering report.

Jargon: To Use or Not to Use

Similar to vague phrasing is jargon. Jargon is made-up language familiar to only an elite group. Within that group, jargon can be a fast way to communicate. However, used outside that group, jargon becomes a hindrance—not an aid—to communication.

We once presented a writing workshop for a group of product-marketing engineers who were all from the same department within a large high-tech company. During the workshop, we heard several engineers use a technical word that was unfamiliar to us. When discussing jargon, we asked what the technical word meant. A fellow on the left defined the word, and immediately a woman on the right said, "No. That's not what it means." When she defined the word for the group, another person in the back said, "You're both wrong. It means ..."

We thanked all three people for helping us make our main point about jargon:

Although you can usually use jargon acceptably within your small technical group, *avoid* using it outside your group, and definitely don't use it outside your company.

Final Editing and Polishing Without Pain

If you're like most engineers, here's where your passion for detail cools down. Details are fun until they're the ones that frustrated you in school: fine-tuning the words, their order, their meaning, their spelling, and the intervening punctuation.

If you've written a perfect first draft, you have no editing to do. Ah, if only life were that easy! Nobody writes a perfect first draft, so you will have to edit. On the bright side, though, when you reach this stage, you probably are about 90 percent finished. Here's why:

You took time to prepare a planning sheet before writing your first draft, didn't you? If so, your draft should already be close to what you'd proudly release. By preparing the planning sheet, you have dramatically reduced your needed editing time.

Yet, if you don't invest that remaining 10 percent of your report-writing time, the other 90 percent may look more like a 30-percent effort. Without the final tweaking, your brilliant ideas may miss their mark. After all your work, wouldn't that be a senseless waste of your 90-percent effort so far? Glad you agree. Here, then, is how to approach the editing job painlessly.

"Blot out, correct, insert, refine,
Enlarge, diminish interline;
Be mindful, when invention fails,
To scratch your head, and bite
your nails."

—Jonathan Swift
English writer/satirist
(1667–1745)

The ABCs of Editing

As you edit your engineering report, aim for the ABCs: accuracy, brevity, and clarity. Keep your mind's eye on those targets, and you will troubleshoot the final details more expertly. Here are a few reminders:

- for accuracy: Check spelling, facts, and numbers.
- for brevity: Delete wordiness and excessive detail.
- for clarity: Avoid ambiguities, vague phrasing, unclear requests, and jargon.

Why Mechanical Errors Mask Your Intelligence

True, some engineering geniuses can't spell well. Yet many readers equate mechanical errors with low intelligence. So if you're a "spelling-challenged" or "punctuation-shy" genius, invest extra editing time to maintain your credibility.

Careful proofreading shows respect for your reader and for your own work. A carefully edited page reflects your professionalism and pride in your own written work. A few minutes of proofreading may pay off in the form of a published technical article, a new contract, or the project leadership you've been wanting.

The Four Editing Steps

For the most efficient editing, take these four steps, preferably in the order shown:

1. Delete excess information.

   Delete first, to save time in the next three steps. By deleting unneeded words, sentences, or paragraphs, you avoid wasting time looking up the spelling or usage of words that you won't need.

   What should you delete? The two main problems that we discussed early in this chapter: the excessive detail and the wordiness. Remember not to delete *needed* information.

2. Rearrange what's left.

   Make sure your document has the following:
   - a clear orientation
   - an obvious key point
   - just enough supporting detail

- no irrelevant sentences
- a logical sequence of ideas
- logical word order within a sentence
- a controlled paragraph length
- clear, smooth transitions to direct the reader
- a strong concluding statement

Note: If you prepared a good planning sheet and numbered your main points before writing your rough draft, you should not have much to rearrange.

3. Rewrite for clarity, completeness, smoothness, and tone.
- Clarify any vague, ambiguous, or confusing sentences.
- Close up any gaps in information.
- Check for subject-verb agreement and noun-pronoun agreement.
- Revise awkward, complicated, or choppy phrasing.
- In series and lists, use parallel phrasing.
- Use lists to replace bulky paragraphs of details or steps.
- Even when reporting negative beta-test results, try for a positive tone. (What new opportunity did the tests reveal, or what higher percentage of the test suite showed positive results?)

4. Correct mechanical errors.
- Correct the spelling. Proofread to catch a phrase that says, "The software is not ready for release" when you meant to say, "The software is now ready for release." Big difference.
- Repair typographical errors, such as duplicated or missing words, crowded or inconsistent margins, and mixed-up ranks of subheadings.
- Correct the punctuation to avoid fragments, run-on sentences, and missing marks.

   These four punctuation marks are commonly abused or ignored:
   - comma   (the shortest pause)
   - semicolon (a weak period)
   - hyphen   (the clarifier in technical phrases containing a multiple-word describer before a noun)
      Examples:
         state-of-the-art technology
         filtering-system discharge
   - apostrophe ('s for singular possessive; s' for plural possessives; no apostrophe for straight plurals; contractions such as *it's* for *it is*)

   (For detailed guidelines in using those and other punctuation marks, see *The Gregg Reference Manual* by William A. Sabin. Publisher: Glencoe/McGraw-Hill, New York, NY, 1992.)

"Cut out all those exclamation marks. An exclamation mark is like laughing at your own joke."

—F. Scott Fitzgerald
American novelist
(1896–1940)

Computer-Based Editing Tools: Tips and Cautions

Use your spelling checker, but don't rely on it. It may not catch sound-alike words or misused words that are spelled right. Take time to proofread one more time after using the spelling checker.

Use your grammar checker, too. It monitors sentence length, active versus passive voice, subject-verb agreement, and other sentence subtleties. Now that you have read this far in the book, you'll get much more out of your grammar checker than you might have before reading these chapters.

Check your word-processing system for other tools, such as outline-format templates, report templates, and graphics resources. Such tools can reduce your report-setup time.

Generally, high technology has simplified your writing and editing jobs over the decades. Movable text, bold and italic type, font (typeface) choices, and other devices all save time for you and your fellow engineers as you strive to squeeze more productivity out of each workday while communicating the results of your work.

Become familiar with the writing and editing tools already in your own computer. The shortcuts you find could allow you more time for your main engineering job.

Summary of This Chapter's Main Points

▶ Save major editing for the third step in the writing process.

▶ Rid your document of excessive details by taking an overview of your subject and making sure the overview isn't cluttered.

▶ Troubleshoot wordiness by looking for and correcting four problems:
  — bulky phrases
  — redundant phrases
  — expletives (filler phrases)
  — nounisms (expanded phrases that hide a strong verb)

▶ Replace vague phrasing with specific, precise wording.

▶ Analyze sentences for clarity by looking for key words in key slots.

▶ Avoid jargon except in small-group situations in which you are *sure* that your audience understands the jargon.

▶ Don't risk turning your reader away from a well-written document because of spelling and mechanical errors that you could easily correct.

▶ Use the editing checklist that follows.

An Editing Checklist for Engineers

DELETE:

▶ extra words
  — redundancies
  — vague phrases
  — strings of prepositional phrases

▶ extra sentences
  — unneeded details

▶ extra paragraphs
  — cumbersome data better in lists or columns

REARRANGE:

▶ overall organization
  — content
  — unity

▶ lead (opening sentence)

▶ paragraph division
  — subtopic paragraphs
  — transitions (for coherence, especially after deletions)

▶ sentence division and order
  — sentence variety
  — word order within sentences

CORRECT (polish):

▶ spelling/typos

▶ punctuation

▶ grammar

▶ inconsistent terms, headings, or page format

▶ crowded copy
  — needed white space (wider margins; subheads)

REWRITE:

▶ awkward or cumbersome phrases

▶ unclear or confusing sentences

▶ series of details
  — bulky paragraphs that might be turned into lists for clarity and emphasis

▶ incomplete messages
  — ideas not yet transferred from planning sheet to draft

▶ disagreement in number (subject-verb; noun-pronoun)

▶ unparallel phrasing

▶ vague summary or interpretation; open-ended requests

PART THREE

Engineering Specific Writing Projects

12 Memos and Letters: Talking on Paper

Memo or Letter: What's the Difference?

Memos and letters are more alike than they are different.

Both memos and letters may contain the same type of information: welcome news, requests, a crucial decision, a product-related legal point, a supplier's technical announcement, an equipment-update offer, a guest-speaking opportunity, or a problem description.

In their best forms, both are brief—ranging from a few sentences up to a full page, but not lead-weighted multiple pages.

Some correspondence, such as thank-you or congratulatory notes, can be just a quick formality—a courteous convention helping to build a respectful or comfortable rapport between sender and receiver. That's good. In a high-pressure technical environment, courtesy is so rushed some days that a "pat on the back" letter or note of appreciation provides a pleasant, welcome change of pace.

So how does a memo differ from a letter? The main difference is that a memo's primary reader is usually *inside* the sender's company or organization, and a letter's primary reader is usually *outside* the sender's company.

The memo's primary inside reader may be your technical peer, employee, immediate supervisor, marketing manager, engineering vice president, or president—or someone in another department (such as an internal customer). Usually, an inside reader doesn't need as much introduction to you, your topic, the product, or your terminology as an outside reader does.

The letter's primary outside reader may be an external customer, a prospect, a supplier, a regulatory agency, a recently graduated job applicant, a consultant, an industry-standards contact, a technical-conference organizer, a publisher, a lawyer, a formal-study participant, or a manufacturing representative.

The letter you write represents your company, not just you. Thus, our earlier advice about keeping the reader in mind applies doubly here, because your letter may be the

> *"I have made this letter longer than usual, only because I have not had the time to make it shorter."*
>
> —Blaise Pascal
> French philosopher and
> mathematician
> (1623–1662)

reader's first or only impression of your company. Neatness, correct spelling, clear organization, and concise writing all show a professional attitude and respect for your reader.

If you're merely writing to document an action or decision in case you get questions later, you may have not an immediate reader, but a distant-future one within your company. For example, a year from now, the engineer who inherited your job when you were promoted may need to review all correspondence about a past project.

If today's memo might become evidence in a legal proceeding—as for trademark protection—the potential readers would be both internal and external.

The main definition of a *memorandum* (the full form of the word *memo*) is "a short note written as a reminder; or a written record or communication, as in a business office." *The American Heritage Dictionary of the English Language* (Anne H. Soukhanov, Exec. Ed., Houghton Mifflin Co., Boston, 1992) shows that *memorandum*, originally the Latin word *memorare*, eased into Middle English as a manuscript notation meaning "to be remembered."

If *you* want to be remembered positively by your memo readers, note one key word of that "short note" definition: short. Even *technical* memos should be short overviews, including only enough details to clarify the main point. If your reader is a fellow engineer who needs all the details, put those details into an attachment or a more flexible report format. You'll learn about report formats in a later chapter. For now, view a memo as a brief, "big picture" message that gives your reader just the *main points*, not the *details*, about your topic.

Your engineering experience can help you easily apply one expanded meaning of *memorandum* (from *Webster's New World Dictionary of American English, College Edition*, Victoria E. Neufeldt, Ed. in Chief, Simon & Schuster, Inc., New York, 1988): "a short note ... to help one remember something or remind one to do something; or ... a record of events or observations, especially ... for future use."

Doesn't that last line sound familiar? In your engineering projects, your memos record technical events (such as tests, analyses, changes, and results) and observations (findings). The "future use" of a technical memo may help produce a redesigned integrated circuit, a safer automated-manufacturing process, or a stronger spiral column.

Memo and Letter Sample Formats

A memo may be printed on plain paper, on a template (in electronic form—such as an on-line E-mail message), or on a "speed" form that leaves room for the reader to write a fast response and return the memo. Under the centered "Memo" title, the memo heading usually includes these one-line sections: *To, From, Date,* and *Subject*. The text of the memo starts three lines below the subject line and is single-spaced, with double-spaced paragraph breaks. If the body of the memo requires only a few lines, double-spaced text works well; in that case, any paragraph break would still be just double-spaced.

No signature is needed at the bottom of the memo; however, in the heading you might want to handwrite your initials beside your name (or after your job title if you add your title to your name). If you have more than a half page of data to support the main point of your memo, prefer putting the data on an attachment, to keep the memo in one-page summary form.

Here's an example of a memo format:

MEMO

(triple-space between centered title and heading)

To: Pat Reese, Senior Design Engineer
From: Terry Meridian, Manufacturing Facilities Manager
Date: April 6, xxxx
Subject: XOX555 Failure-Analysis Results

(triple-space between heading and text)

The failure analysis of our site's Redwood Creek Bridge section that is sagging has revealed riprap erosion and sand scouring under the bridge's center (#2) pier. The resulting lack of support has tilted that pier, risking collapse of the entire bridge.

Although the original design allowed for swiftly moving storm waters, this year's century-record storms far exceeded the standard safety allowances. Fortunately, the continuous design of the girders prevented the bridge from falling and limited the damage to sagging—a warning sign of an eventual collapse. You were wise to close the bridge and reroute the warehouse traffic around to the side entrance.

The attached Action Options Sheet details the four alternatives for repairing or replacing the sagging bridge deck and pier. All the alternatives will allow reopening of the bridge within five months of the starting construction/repair date.

After reviewing the alternative solutions, please call me to arrange a planning meeting.

(double-space below text)

Attachment

A letter has no such heading. Instead, a letter (printed on high-quality, corporate letterhead with matching envelope) contains a date line, an inside address (which includes the name, company name, and address of the recipient), and a salutation. Those elements may be all flush-left (all starting at the left margin), or they may be in what's called a modified-block letter style, starting the date and signature block at the same tab stop, at or to the right of center. The body of the letter is single-spaced, with double-spaced paragraph breaks.

The signature block of a letter includes a complimentary closing (such as "Sincerely," or "Cordially," depending on how formal the letter is), a four-line open space for the sender's signature, a typed line showing the sender's full name, and the sender's title on the line below.

After the signature block, double-space below the sender's title. At the left margin, place the sender's initials in all-capital letters. (If someone else, such as an assistant, prepared the letter, he or she would follow the sender's initials with a slash and his or her initials in lower case.)

If you are sending a copy to someone not named in the inside address, put "cc:" and the second reader's name and title under your initials, also flush-left.

On the following page is an example of a letter format (with spacing noted) in the modified-block style.

The text in the body of the memo and letter might be the same, depending on the reader's needs.

For other mechanical details and options about letter format, consult the current edition of William A. Sabin's *The Gregg Reference Manual* (Glencoe/McGraw-Hill, New York, NY).

Generally, the destination of the correspondence lets you know whether to use the memo style or the letter style. Before you write either, though, think about whether you need to put the message in writing at all.

To Write or Not to Write

"If you don't say anything, you won't be called on to repeat it." Those words, attributed to Calvin ("Silent Cal") Coolidge, the terse 30th President of the United States, make sense even about technical topics.

Even in the engineering world, sometimes silence is the best way to handle a situation. Sometimes not.

Remember that one way to save yourself a lot of writing time is to ask yourself whether the memo or letter you're about to write is really necessary. People get so many memos that some memos aren't read at all. What makes yours special enough to ensure reading?

Do you read all the messages that weigh down the in-basket on your desk? Or do you let the "staple rule" help you decide when—or whether—to read them? That is, if the memo has a staple in it, you know that you're in for more than one page of reading. So, especially if you're in a hurry to start an overdue engineering project, you may flip the stapled memo onto your "to read" stack, and read just the one-page messages (without staples!) as soon as you receive them.

That's not such a silly scenario. Many engineers and other readers set their incoming-mail reading priorities by using the staple rule.

Sample Letter Format

(about 2 inches, to allow for the letterhead)

June 5, xxxx   (date line)

Ms. Jane Albrecht, Senior Analyst   (inside address, 4–6 lines below date,
Application Analysis, Inc.   single-spaced)
123 Maple Street
Silverton, CA 99999

Dear Ms. Albrecht: (salutation, 2 lines below inside address; 2 lines above body)

Thank you for analyzing our two latest application ideas for the Frazbillum Widget. Your suggestions helped to focus our goals on our major market without excluding our secondary market.

When our applications engineers have completed the follow-up tests for both applications, I will send you the test results. We plan to complete the tests by July 1. If you receive our results by July 5, can you send us your reevaluation summary by July 12?

I will call you on June 9 to confirm a schedule that will work for you and help us plan our test suite. Meanwhile, congratulations for your IEEE award.

                    Cordially,   (complimentary closing,
                                          2 lines below text; lined up with date)

                                          (4 open lines for signature)

                    Terry Fassler   (sender's name)
                    Project Supervisor   (sender's title, single-spaced)
                                          (two lines open below title)
TF/ml   (sender's & typist's initials)
cc: M. Brewen, Applications Manager   (copy notation, single-spaced)

Of course, a letter is usually only one page. No staple. A fast read. The formal presentation of a first-class letter, sealed in an envelope, may also arouse a reader's curiosity enough to get read. Some letters, though (such as unsolicited ones sent to "Current Occupant"), often get buried in the stack or dropped into the circular file.

No, we are not giving you an easy excuse to avoid writing all correspondence. Just "not wanting to" isn't the wise way to decide whether to put the highlights in writing.

How, then, can you avoid taking the time to write a two-page software-change memo, a one-page customer letter, or a half-page E-mail message—only to have your correspondence set aside, ignored, or tossed out unopened? You can start by analyzing the value of what you're about to write.

Questions to Ask Before Writing

To determine whether the correspondence is worth writing, ask yourself a few questions:

▶ Why am I writing this memo or letter?

— What's my main reason for putting the message in writing?
The following reasons, for example, would justify a written message:

  ▶ You may be announcing a schedule for an upcoming technical-review meeting with too many logistical details for the reader to remember without seeing them in writing.

  ▶ You may be answering a technical question, using Boussinesq's equation to determine the soil pressure a planned beach café's load would exert through the footing of a pier to the soil below. You might include the equation or a diagram of the load to apply the equation to the planned construction.

  ▶ Your reminder memo may keep a current field-survey project on track.

  ▶ Your reader may be difficult to reach by phone or in person because of frequent travel, field tasks, or multiple meetings.

  ▶ Your manager may have asked you to put your computer-network-upgrade request in writing, even though you have already discussed the request and received spoken approval. Such an assigned memo may help your manager justify the purchase when reviewing the budget with upper management.

— What secondary reasons justify my writing time?
Here are a few examples of unspoken reasons for writing a memo or letter:

  ▶ You may want to document an idea, suggestion, or decision as your own, to avoid misinterpretation or misplaced credit later.

  ▶ Your past experience with that reader may have included a conflict that arose because of unwritten, vague agreements about technical details. In that case, a memo or letter summarizing the current agreements at each critical step can help prevent further conflict.

  ▶ If you expect to head similar projects a few months or a year from now, your memo can record this project's success (or needed changes) before you begin the next project. That way, you learn from and build on your own experience more easily, without having to recall details later from your long-term memory.

▶ What result do I expect this letter or memo to achieve?

— What do I want my reader to do, say, or believe after reading my memo or letter?

— If asking for approval or another action, when do I want it?

— If the reader need not do anything, what next step do I plan or expect?

— What benefit may result from this correspondence?

▶ What could happen if I don't write this memo or letter?

— What's the worst thing that could happen without a written version of this message?

— What professional danger might I risk for my company, my group, or myself without this correspondence?

▶ Is a memo or letter the best way to convey this message to my intended reader(s)?

— Or would a phone call or meeting be more efficient, personal, or diplomatic?

   ▶ Some messages are best not put into writing, at least as the first medium. For example, sensitive issues may require a more personal touch, such as a private, face-to-face meeting to avoid a cold, insensitive approach. Negative news, too, may meet less resistance or resentment when discussed face to face.

▶ How will my reader respond to this message?

— Is my reader a technician who may resist my main point? Or a senior researcher who might object to my investigative method? A busy analyst who may delay responding? A traveling manager who might avoid fulfilling my spending request? A former employee who may not see how the content applies to his or her current job?

   ▶ If you answer "yes" or "maybe" to such questions, you might choose to preface the message with a personal talk (by phone or in person) to involve your reader early and diplomatically. The result of that personal talk can help you decide whether to put the points in writing. Then, if you must write the letter or memo, you can open it with a reminder of a pertinent key point that you two discussed or agreed on already. Showing such respect for your reader will likely help improve his or her reaction and response.

   ▶ If you can't talk with your reader before sending a crucial memo, remember to put yourself in the reader's mind as you plan your message, to help anticipate the response.

When you decide that a letter or memo is the most appropriate medium to suit your purpose, reader, and/or content, you're ready to plan the message. Jot down the key words on your planning sheet. (You already learned how to use the planning sheet; it was explained in Chapter 3 of this book.)

Then take a few more seconds to set the stage for a successful message: Decide what tone will work best.

How the Right Tone Sends the Message Home

Now's the time to work on your "memo mindset." Even if you're swamped with other jobs awaiting your attention, the attitude you take toward the memo or letter—and toward your reader—will surface between the lines. The tone will convey not only your message but also your attitude.

Of all writing jobs, memos and letters are the most like conversation. Face-to-face conversation includes not only words but also subtle, unspoken meanings through body language that can reinforce or contradict the spoken words. In correspondence, tone is like body language, saying as much as—or more than—your words say. Don't let your tone seem like an impatient sigh, two crossed arms, or a haughty glance. Make sure that your tone matches your words.

Remember, a professional tone reflects respect for your reader. So with your professional thinking cap on, decide on an appropriate tone. Depending on the situation, you may select a tone that's formal, informal, casual, or all-out down-home friendly.

For a thank-you note to a pipeline supplier, use a positive, informal, yet professional tone:

> Your always-on-time delivery to our Mainville construction site helped our District crew complete the water-rerouting project a week before the deadline. Thank you.

For a recommendation letter to a prospective client of that same supplier, give your letter a more formal (but not stuffy) tone:

> Pipeline Transportation Corporation has delivered pipe materials to South Bay Water District for the past nine years. That supplier's consistently prompt delivery, thorough safety practices, and efficient order-monitoring system make PTC one of the District's most valued suppliers.

For a brief memo to compliment an employee for a job well done, use a casual but appreciative tone.

> You did it! You spearheaded one of our most successful design projects this year. Thanks for your excellent work and award-winning results.

You get the idea. Think about the tone you would use in a face-to-face conversation with your reader in the current situation, and just put that tone into your memo or letter. When possible, mention the *result* that the reader helped to produce.

With a positive, appropriate tone in mind, you're ready to transfer the key words of your message from your planning sheet to the letter or memo.

The Three-Part Pattern of Letters and Memos

In engineering correspondence, just as in movies and in life, the three-part pattern keeps working—in the form of a beginning, a middle, and an end.

The beginning, middle, and end of letters and memos are called the *orientation, information,* and *close.*

Part	Placement	Function
Orientation	opening sentence or paragraph	orients the reader to the topic, situation, or main point; may remind
Information	immediately after orientation	serves as main body giving needed details, facts, reasons, examples, findings, alternatives, and maybe conclusions
Close	final sentence or paragraph	sums up, recommends, requests, tells next step, gives deadline, stresses a benefit, or adds a personal note

Think of the orientation as the grabber. You want to grab your reader's attention within just a few seconds, because you may have no more than five seconds to make that reader want to keep reading. A clear orientation makes the reader want to say, "Now, here's something that applies to me. I care about this topic."

The orientation may answer some or all of the "Five W" questions: who, what, when, where, and why. Often it may answer just a *general* "what" about the topic, letting the information section fill in the "what" details.

If the memo announces a meeting, the orientation may include the what, when, where, and why; the information section of the memo may then give a brief background and tell what aspects of the topic will be covered in the meeting. The close might then request a confirmation, assign preparation duties, stress the importance of the meeting, or mention the expected outcome.

On the following page is an example of a memo announcing a technical meeting.

Now let's apply that three-part (orientation-information-close) pattern to several types of correspondence. These types categorize both letters and memos.

Types of Correspondence

Each letter or memo you write probably falls into one of these categories:

▶ news or updates

▶ requests (for products, help, money, or information)

▶ responses (yes or no)

▶ rapport builders (thanks, congratulations, recognition)

▶ recommendation letters (for colleagues, past employees, students, job seekers)

▶ sales letters (subtle ones, for overcoming potential resistance to your idea, project, products, or service)

Let's take a closer look at each type of correspondence.

Meeting Announcement Memo

MEMO

To: All Engineers on Main-Entrance Repaving Project
From: Chunka Conkreete, Project Manager
Date: 3/4/xx
Subject: Redesign of Pavement Joints

(Orientation:)

The Main-Entrance Repaving Project team will meet Tuesday, June 9, at 9:00 a.m. in the Myrtle Room, Building 6, to decide the most appropriate way to repair or replace the cracked control joints (contraction joints) of the old roadway.

(Information:)

The preliminary evaluation of the repaving site revealed uneven cracks at the control joints. The resulting load transfer between the old concrete slab sections has allowed ice damage, raising some roadway slabs and causing safety risks.

(Close:)

Please come prepared to suggest and justify an alternative to the existing joints, to relieve the tensile stresses in the new pavement yet prevent further cracking and uplift.

If a schedule conflict prevents your attending this crucial meeting, please ensure that one of your senior technical staff members attends in your place. The meeting must produce a decision. The project team will consider all suggested solutions and select the most cost-effective one.

News or Updates That People Want to Read

If you're writing a memo about a discovery, problem, solution, meeting, or contract win, you're just generally sharing information to keep your readers current with what's happening in your company or industry.

The key to a successful "news" or "update" message is to answer the Five W's: who, what, when, where, why. (There they are again.) Sometimes you add an H (how).

Don't drag it out. A half page to a page is usually enough.

Here's an example of a concise good-news memo:

Good-News Memo

MEMO

To: All Project Soar Engineers
From: Inna Know, Project Manager
Date: November 7, xxxx
Subject: Contract-Win Meeting and Dinner Dates

Congratulations! Your four months of hard work paid off. Aero Technomax accepted our Project Soar proposal as submitted. The design phase begins on November 12, with the first assembled units to be shipped on February 1. You will receive the phase-by-phase schedule on November 12 at the 8:00 a.m. start-up meeting.

Thanks for all your preliminary design work, overtime, and superhuman efforts to produce this contract win. The November 10 Win Dinner will be at Bent Bow Barbeque, at 6:00 p.m. See you there.

Requests That Turn Resistance into Results

Don't let a reader's potential resistance keep you from writing a request.

Whether you're requesting project help, an overdue payment, or a job interview, keep one point in mind: Ask for what you want. No, not necessarily in the opening sentence. Remember that you can choose between the key-point-first and key-point-last strategies (explained in an earlier chapter), depending on the situation.

Most often, though, you will probably get better results by orienting the reader first and easing into the request—using the key-point-last strategy. You may first need to persuade your reader to see things your way—or to see the value or benefit in fulfilling your request.

Either way, when asking for anything, apply the orientation-information-close pattern to your request. Here's how to approach someone who is expected to *resist* your request:

▶ In the orientation part of your request, tell what project you're working on, what that has to do with your reader, and why. If you foresee a *benefit* that the reader might gain from the project, say what that is.

▶ In the information part, tell what aspect of the project you need help with, and at what level of detail. Perhaps explain what discrepancy, conflict, or unanswered question(s) you have found in your research.

▶ In the close, *be specific*. If you put details in anywhere, put them in here. Don't be like the engineer who assumed that the old "Your cooperation on this project will be appreciated" close was direct enough, then wondered why no response came, while the reader kept waiting for more specifics about what the engineer wanted. We repeat: Be specific. Say what you want.

— If you're requesting survey findings, tell which survey, what site, which dates, and what level of detail you desire from your reader.

— If you want just the measurement data from one phase of the survey, specify that.

— If you merely want your reader's opinion, ask the question clearly, defining the conditions or environment that might affect the opinion.

On the following page is an example of a request letter that uses one paragraph for each of the three letter-body parts: Paragraph 1 is the orientation, Paragraph 2 is the information that the reader needs before deciding whether to respond, and Paragraph 3 is the close—the specific request with a benefit from the reader's point of view.

In that example, note the benefit to the inventor: The added applications for Dr. Wyse's patent implicitly should increase product sales and produce more profits for Dr. Wyse.

"Yes" Letters Are Easy

"Yes" letters are easy and usually short. Reread the letter you are answering, though, to be sure you understand the request or problem. Get to the point immediately, giving only the details needed to solve the problem or answer the question. Following the request letter sample is an example of a "Yes" letter.

"No" Letters Are Tougher but Tactful

The "No" letter poses more of a problem because it is easier to say "Yes" than it is to say "No." In the "No" letter, you want to firmly refuse a request without alienating your reader. You may want to do business with that person later. Despite the fact that you are refusing a request, try to keep a respectful, positive tone in your letter.

Reread the request—for two reasons:

▶ to make sure you understand your reader's problem or request

▶ to make sure the requester understands your product or service

For example, companies often get consumer complaints from people who are unknowingly misusing a product. In such cases, a letter that tactfully explains how to use or gain the most benefit from the product is appropriate.

In your "No" letter, show that you understand your reader's problem or request. Open with a courteous, soothing comment that shows a positive approach. Your purpose at the beginning of a "No" letter is to establish rapport, so delay your refusal until you reach a common ground with the reader.

Sample Request Letter

July 1, xxxx

Dr. U. R. Wyse, Chief Engineer
Acme Analysts, Inc.
123 Data Drive
Silicon Slope, CA 95199

Dear Dr. Wyse:

   I am an engineer helping to design an all-weather computer
(AWC) for year-round use in both Alaskan-tundra and African-
desert camps. You have inspired me to expand the practical
applications of your recent neochip patent for use in the AWC.

   Since reading your January IEEE article about silt-activated
neochips, I have launched a project to test whether the
operating temperature affects the speed and reliability of the
neochips during seasonal climate changes. My concern is the
range of temperatures under which the neochip would have to
operate. The goal is to allow the AWC to function in all three
operating-temperature ranges: commercial, industrial, and
military.

   Here's how you can help me promote multiple AWC
applications for your silt-activated neochips: Please tell me
what you envision as the minimal, ideal, and maximum
temperature ranges in which those neochips can reliably
function, and at what speeds. You, of course, will receive a full
printout of my one-year test results in both the Alaskan and
African experimental sites. Please respond before August 15 to
allow sufficient planning time before the tests begin in
September.

                    Respectfully,

                    Sandy Soyle
                    Senior Engineer

SS/st

Sample "Yes" Letter

July 10, xxxx

Mr. Sandy Soyle
Geocomp Ltd.
4321 Teckie Drive
Lost Almost, NM 87777

Dear Mr. Soyle:

Your project sounds ambitious—exactly the type of project I had in mind as I was designing the silt-activated neochip (SAN).

I have enclosed an abbreviated printout that should give you an idea of the expected temperature ranges within which the SAN can operate and at what speeds. I'd be especially interested to know what you learn when this range is extended.

Good luck with your project. Do keep in touch with me as you progress.

Sincerely,

Dr. U. R. Wyse
Chief Engineer

URW/tfo

Never talk down to the reader, and never accuse the reader. Here's where passive voice comes in handy.

Subordinate the bad news to the good news (if you have good news). Even if you have no good news to add to the bad news, explain or justify your refusal reasonably and logically. Although requesters don't like to be refused, they more readily accept refusal if they can see a logical reason for it.

Avoid giving company policy as a reason in itself. That's a lame excuse and appears as such to the reader. Using company policy as an excuse is a great way to turn off a reader. Instead, give the reason *behind* the company policy, and avoid the words *company policy*. If possible, offer a reasonable alternative or consolation. Be diplomatic.

Then end positively, perhaps with a *benefit* that your suggested alternative offers.

Here's an example that follows those "No"-letter guidelines:

Sample "No" Letter

July 10, xxxx

Mr. Sandy Soyle
Geocomp Ltd.
4321 Teckie Drive
Lost Almost, NM 87777

Dear Mr. Soyle:

Your project sounds very interesting. I'm quite eager to see how the neochips will stand up to such tests as you've mentioned.

Currently, Acme Analysts' contract with the U.S. Navy precludes our sharing the general type of information you have requested.

However, I plan to be in Santa Fe next weekend to indulge one of my hobbies, collecting Southwest Indian pottery. I'd be happy to meet you in Lost Almost on Monday. If you can give me some more specific parameters, perhaps the Navy may grant us permission to share some information with you.

Please call me at your convenience, and we can set a meeting time.

Sincerely,

Dr. Ulysses Wyse
Chief Engineer

UW/sja

Goodwill Notes Build Rapport

Although thank-you notes and similar rapport-building missives are easy to write, we don't see enough of them in the business world. So get out there and say "thank you" to your friends and colleagues. Offer congratulations when someone accomplishes a goal. Recognizing another's accomplishment makes work more enjoyable for everyone. As you know, what goes around comes around. Be sure what you send around is positive.

Here are a few quick tips to remember. If you want to say "thank you," be sure to say "thank you," not "I would like to thank you." The word "would" is conditional, so the message that comes across is "I would ..., but ..." "But what? You don't like me so you're not going to thank me. Is that what you're trying to say?" Just come straight out and say "thank you."

Also, avoid thanking in advance, as in "Thanks in advance for your help on this project." That's a turn-off. People may feel that you're trying to coerce them into doing something they normally wouldn't do. Instead, say "I will appreciate your help on this project." (Notice we said "will," not "would.") Then, as soon as the person does the favor, send a short thank-you note, mentioning how that person's help affected the outcome.

Keep rapport notes short. Here are a few examples:

▶ congratulations:

> Congratulations on writing that winning proposal. I know you put a lot of hard work into it, and it shows. I'm glad you got the win. Nice job.

▶ recognition:

> I'm pleased to announce that Carolyn Bogart, from our Market Research Department, has just won the American Engineering Society's coveted Design Award for her work on steel design and analysis.
>
> Carolyn has been with Acme Design for 10 years, joining us soon after her graduation from Cal Tech. Part of her prize money from the award comes in the form of one year's tuition at the prestigious Acier Academie in Paris. Next year, Carolyn will transfer to our Paris facility, where she will work in the Special Projects office while attending the Academie.
>
> Congratulations, Carolyn, for this well-deserved recognition.

Recommendation Letters

With the proliferation of lawyers and lawsuits, some companies are refusing to write recommendation letters, figuring that such a letter can be a legal time bomb. Therefore, before you write a letter of recommendation, you'd better check with the legal department at your company. With that disclaimer out of the way, let's continue.

Readers of recommendation letters usually want to know:

▶ how long you've known the individual

▶ your business relationship with the individual (Were you his or her manager, co-worker, peer, customer, vendor ...?)

▶ your honest evaluation of the individual's skills, with examples

On the following page is a sample recommendation letter.

Subtle Sales Correspondence (from the Engineer's Viewpoint)

No, we're not trying to turn you into a sales machine. But we're about to let you in on some techniques that make successful sales people *successful*.

Sample Recommendation Letter

October 15, xxxx

Ms. Darby Franklin
Transportation Design Resources
555 Canal Way
Whitewater, MI 48699

Dear Ms. Franklin:

   Kenneth Desmond worked under my direct supervision here at
Fantasy Bridgebuilders from May xxxx through August xxxx as a
design engineer. During those four years when our department worked
on two major projects, he proved to be a capable and creative engineer.

   On several occasions, he solved highly complex design problems on
his own and with his team. Mr. Desmond can effectively switch from a
leader's role to a support person's role, and he is easy to work with.

   I strongly recommend him for the position described in your letter.

   Sincerely,

   Ernest Fellows
   Chief Designer

EF/bl

As an engineer, you have to sell your ideas. If you don't, you'll get passed over or run over.

The key is to use subtlety and not approach your audience like a loud, orange-suited barker outside a risqué "theater," hailing all passersby to pay for a peek.

All persuasion is based on self-interest. People buy something only if they see a benefit to buying. So when you try to sell your idea, all you have to do is stress how your reader will benefit from your idea. In other words, you have to tell the reader what's in it for him or his team or his company. Explain how it will help him and his people. Most benefits finally come around to saving money one way or the other for the reader. So the sooner you can explain how your idea will save money, the better your chances of success.

Now is definitely the time to use positive words and a positive tone. Your first step in persuading someone is to get that person on your side. Positive words help you do that. Thus, the sales letters you receive in the mail emphasize words like *free* and *money*.

Remember, *you* is also a very powerful word. So use *you* with positive words to get your reader's attention.

A possible exception to maintaining a positive tone, especially an overwhelmingly positive tone, is when you are trying to sell the solution to a problem. In this case, just stating the problem and offering the solution is often your best bet. It's difficult to describe a problem in positive terms, so just state the problem. Of course, if you see an *opportunity* lying beneath the surface of a problem, you can safely use the positive approach for your problem-solution memo—so long as you clarify the opportunity and its potential benefit from the reader's point of view.

When you want to persuade, especially if you think your reader may offer some resistance to your idea, remember to use the key-point-last strategy. (The strategies were covered in Chapter 9.) To approach a person who may resist your entreaty, for example, first summarize a problem that you know your idea will solve. Second, perhaps mention all the problems that the initial problem might or will cause. Third, offer your solution (which is your key point) at the end.

If you expect no resistance to your idea, use the key-point-first approach. State your idea, explain why it's ideal, and tell what problems it will solve.

One way to practice persuasive writing is to draw three columns on a sheet of paper. Head the left column "Feature." Head the middle column "Advantage." Head the right column "Benefit." Now pick a product that you produce or work with. In the left column, list the feature(s) of that product. Now ask yourself, "So what?" List your answer(s) in the Advantage column. Ask your "So what?" question again, this time about the advantage you just listed, and list your answer(s) in the Benefit column.

For example, the feature of a new car is power steering. So what? Well, that makes the car easy to steer. That's an advantage. So what? Easy steering means that you'll get less tired and drive more safely. Those are benefits.

When you're extolling the virtues of your product or idea, answer the "So what?" question for the reader and stress the benefits.

On the following page is an example of a subtle sales memo that answers the "So what?" question.

Electronic Mail: Pros and Cons

Technology has simplified and sped up our daily communication to the point that we can call or send a message to someone anywhere on the globe in just a few seconds. That's a plus when you have to get the message there right now—or when you just want to get it done and off your desk the fastest way. Another plus: You might even get the response today; that's helpful when you have to decide the next step immediately to meet a deadline or handle an emergency.

On the minus side, though, technology has made it too easy to send a message to someone faster than you can fully develop the thought—especially on a rushed day. The resulting potential for disaster zooms to your recipient's telephone, voice-mail system, or already-full electronic mailbox, playing with fate.

Subtle Sales-Approach Memo

MEMO

To: Bill Whitcomb, Manager
From: Reese Baldwin
Date: March 2, xxxx
Subject: How to Improve Our Contract Chances

During the past six months, our group has been unable to capture three lucrative state contracts, for two reasons: lack of workforce and lack of proposal-writing expertise.

Now the situation is worsening. Our group morale is dropping. We were hoping to get more engineers in our group, but because we did not land the contracts, Corporate assigned the latest group of new college graduates to other departments. Now we feel as if we're in a downward spiral caused by a catch-22 situation: We can't get the workforce because we don't have the contracts, and we can't get the contracts because we don't have the workforce. In addition, at least three people in my group have their résumés on the street.

My people need a boost, and they need a goal to focus on. Here's what I suggest. First, I know of an excellent proposal writer at ABC who may be forced into early retirement. If so, I'm fairly sure we can get him on a contract basis to help us with our proposal writing. I'd like your permission to talk to him off the record about working for us.

Second, many of the new engineers the company has hired don't have the background our department requires. I'd like to set up our own recruiting team to visit several selected campuses this spring.

Tom Edwin (my chief engineer) and I have discussed this idea but have not said anything to our group. We know which schools we'd like to visit and how many graduates we can hire so we can bid on at least two proposals I know will be in the pipeline early next year.

Right now we may lose the people we do have. If I can tell them that we will be increasing our workforce and seeking a good proposal writer, I know they'll be motivated to help us recruit and prepare for the new bids.

Tom and I will be happy to meet with you at your convenience to discuss this problem and our proposed solution.

When would be a good time for you to meet?

Fast Memos and New Frustrations: E–Mail Cautions

Just as with mail that you drop in the mailbox outside your building, you can't call an electronic-mail (E-mail) message back if you realize you didn't mean to say what you said the way you said it. With postal mail, though, you probably take more time to make it right than you might with the more easily sent E-mail.

In a phone call (another more established application of technology), you can rephrase your message if the person you call doesn't grasp it the right way at first. Even if you must leave a voice-mail message, you can sometimes replay and revise your message before hanging up the phone. Not so with E-mail. If the E-mail recipient conscientiously keeps up with incoming messages, your message gets read today—perhaps immediately.

As you dash off your next E-mail message, you might well ask yourself, "What have I to say—and how important is the message? Is voice mail or E-mail the best way to deliver that message?" Many of the general-correspondence questions suggested earlier in this chapter, in the "To Write or Not to Write" section, also apply to E-mail.

For professional courtesy, remember, too, that E-mail is meant for short messages, not 10-page updates or 20-page reports. Don't fill up your reader's mailbox with something that would be better sent as hard copy through the post office. If you decide that E-mail is your best medium for this message, take time to say what you mean to say—and include your phone number and electronic-mailbox number—before pressing "send."

> *"I have now attained the true art of letter-writing, which we are always told is to express on paper exactly what one would say to the same person by word of mouth. I have been talking to you almost as fast as I could the whole of this letter."*
>
> —Jane Austen
> English novelist
> (1775–1817)

Fax Messages That Respect Your Reader

Most of the cautions about E-mail apply to facsimile (fax) messages, too. Don't tie up your own or someone else's fax machine with long reports or proposals.

Think of your reader's convenience, too. Hard copy through the post office is usually crisper, cleaner, easier to read—and in a more convenient page order at the receiving end— than what goes through the fax machine. So reserve the fax medium for brief or urgent messages.

Set up a standard fax-cover-sheet template to use as the first page for most of your fax messages. The cover sheet should have your letterhead or equivalent information—with, of course, your telephone and fax numbers. On the cover sheet, include labeled blank lines to fill in the recipient's name, department, company, fax number, phone number, number of pages sent, and transmittal date. That way you'll have a complete record for your own file, because your fax machine merely "borrows" the pages, which never leave your office. The fax cover sheet also helps ensure that your fax will reach the intended recipient, even if the receiving fax machine is not in your reader's immediate department.

On the cover sheet include a "Message" section for your handwritten or printed transmittal comments (such as a reminder of who requested the fax) to avoid confusion when your reader receives other faxes besides yours.

If your reader needs no cover message, you might replace a full-size cover sheet with the time-saving 3M Post-It™ fax-transmittal memo tab (about 1½" by 4") stuck onto the top or bottom corner of the first transmitted page. That little form, which has blanks for the critical names and numbers, comes in mini-tablet form.

Whatever your medium of correspondence, remember that you are talking to your reader—you're just not talking face to face.

Also remember the KISS rule: Keep It Short and Simple.

Summary of This Chapter's Main Points

▶ Use the *memo* format for readers inside your company. Use the *letter* format (with inside address, formal close, and signature line) for readers outside your company.

▶ Question whether to write the message or present it orally.

▶ Keep your tone conversational, respectful, professional, and appropriate throughout the memo or letter.

▶ Use a three-part pattern in all correspondence.
1. orientation
2. information
3. close

▶ Limit E-mail and fax messages to brief or urgent memos/letters.

▶ Keep your correspondence short. Follow the KISS rule (keep it short and simple).

13 Writing Useful Reports

> *"If you cannot— in the long run—tell every- one what you have been doing, your doing has been worthless."*
>
> —Erwin Schrödinger
> Austrian physicist
> (1887–1961)

Reporting Is More Than a Mop-Up Step

Of all the engineering documents you are called upon to write, reports are probably the most prevalent—and perhaps, up to now, the most procrastinated.

Why? Even though reports are such an integral part of your job, why might you resist writing them? Do you perhaps agree with the engineer who said that reports seem like a mop-up step—getting in the way of "real" work that's waiting to be done? Or do you suspect that many reports don't get read—and that, even when yours do get read, they glean too few grains of glory or grins of appreciation from your readers?

Even if you don't mind report writing all that much, you may still find reports challenging, because they vary a lot in length, style, types of information, and format. That variety forces you to do some thinking to know what or how much to include in each report.

Report-Writing Skills Earn Growing Respect

So much for the downside of the reporting task. The upside is that report writing *is* important work. Engineering reports inform management, technical staff, and others about events that affect the company's competitive edge and survival. Such concerns, in turn, affect your job and compensation.

Every month you can probably find at least one article in *some* engineering or educa- tion magazine or journal calling for engineers with better communication skills. According to the articles, what educators are realizing is that engineers have to be able to communicate technical information (mainly through reports) to two distinct audiences: fellow engineers and senior management. Industry has known this need for years, as have many schools. Unfortunately, not enough schools are taking this need to heart. Slowly but surely, however, more engineering schools are recognizing the importance of turning out engineers with better communication skills. The newspaper help-wanted ads for engineers increasingly include "excellent communications skills" in the job requirements.

How Reports Can Help You and Your Company

Here are a few examples of how your engineering reports (both technical and nontechnical) might help you and your company.

> *"In science, the credit goes to the [one] who convinces the world, not to the [one] to whom the idea first occurs."*
>
> —Sir William Osler
> Canadian physician/anatomist
> (1849–1919)

▶ A monthly report lets you *document the accomplishments* that justify your salary.

▶ An incident report lets you *air a problem* that may be costing your company money. You may become the hero whose solution cuts costs and boosts your company's profits. The written report may even pay off big for you when your manager rereads your report at performance-review time.

▶ A progress report tells management that you're keeping your nose to the grindstone.

▶ A good executive summary of your technical report impresses senior management with your ability to explain the business implications of technical information.

Your engineering reports can document or produce a win-win situation for the company and you. By seeing the importance, application, and benefits of your reports, you'll approach the report-writing task more willingly.

Sidestep the Engineer's Report-Writing Trap

Okay. Let's say you're ready to tackle your next engineering report. What is most important to say in that report?

Knowing what to say and what not to say is a skill that improves with experience. You can start building that skill right now, though, by avoiding a common report-writing trap that teases engineers.

Excessive detail, which we cautioned you about in Chapter 11, presents the biggest trap you face in engineering your reports. We expand on that topic here, to help you sidestep the trap in its favorite hiding place: report writing.

By definition, reports are detailed accounts of proceedings or transactions. Yet detail, like an onion, has many layers. How many layers of detail do you want to peel off for your reader?

Detail overload is one of the fastest ways to ensure that your report stays in your reader's "I'll read it someday" pile. In other words, you might unwittingly set your own trap—and kill your reader's desire to read your report. That, in turn, can kill your chances of communicating an important message to a reader who needs to know it.

Having researched all the details, you understandably may be tempted to put them all into your report. Don't. Even technical-report readers don't always want all the details.

Here's one way to save yourself time: Always question the details you're thinking of including in a report, by keeping in mind your report's purpose and your reader's needs. On the topic of details, focus more on the reader than on the purpose. The best way to avoid the details trap is to think like your reader.

How to Think Like Your Reader

From the reader's point of view, a report can be just as challenging for a manager to read as it is for an engineer to write. Often, report readers must force themselves to concentrate to get through rambling technical data that lack an interpretation, conclusion, or recommendation. Don't make your manager wade through a report that's loaded with details but lacking a clear main point. Give the overview, the big picture. Managers need to see a main point that the details support.

You naturally view your reports from the engineering writer's perspective. To weigh the importance of details, though, reverse that view. Every so often, step back from the details and look at the big picture you are trying to describe. Ask yourself whether the inclusion of certain details will add or detract from the reader's view of the big picture.

As you plan and write your current report, forget for a moment that you're the engineer who's writing that report. Imagine, instead, that you are the manager who must read it. Put yourself into your reader's mind. Learn as much as you can about your reader and his or her needs, and then write the report to fill those needs.

Are You Sure the Report Is Needed?

Sometimes, as you think about the report topic, you may even warily wonder whether the reader needs the report in writing—or at all. That's not a thought to be dismissed lightly. Many unneeded, unread reports weigh down readers' in-baskets, file folders, and forgotten stacks, just gathering dust. Ideas discussed and implemented orally are often just as effective as those agonized over in written reports.

Don't be afraid to challenge the necessity of a report. Before doing so, though, find out what justifies the report itself; consider the likely benefits of the written report and the possible consequences of no report.

In fact, some engineering reports—especially routine ones that rarely get read—can be eliminated. Others might be consolidated with other similar reports to reduce redundancy. Before eliminating any report, though, check with the people who now receive such reports and ask them whether they still want to receive them. By keeping the reader's perspective and by giving your colleagues the choice of receiving or not receiving certain reports, you can avoid the risk of having those people feel that they're being left out of the communication loop if they don't get certain reports.

If the reports are still needed, some formats might be shortened or simplified. Other reports can be reduced in frequency without closing lines of communication.

If you're thinking like the manager, you can more objectively decide whether you need a written report or just an oral summary of the topic.

The correspondence chapter (Chapter 12) of this book already gave you questions to ask before writing a letter, to help you decide whether to write it or not. Here are a few variations of those questions, as a reader would ask them:

- ▶ Why must I read this engineering report?
    - — What does the topic have to do with me or my department?
    - — Can I learn the main points faster by talking with the writer?
    - — Could I get the same information more efficiently in another way?

- ▶ What reaction, action, or decision does the writer want from me?
    - — Why must that be done in the way requested, or at all?

- ▶ How might this report benefit our department or the company?

- ▶ What could happen, either now or later, if I don't read this report?

That last question may seem irresponsible, but a manager who has many duties, employees, meetings, and events to juggle may not have time to give an engineer's report the attention it deserves. If, then, you're thinking as though you're that manager, what's the best way for you to get the key points of that report in the least amount of time?

If your answers to those questions tell you that the report is still needed, decide what level of detail you (the manager) want. Would a single-page overview answer your questions about the topic? Or does this report present vital test results that you must study to select an intelligent solution to a costly technical problem?

Why Is This Report Important?

If a report is important enough to be written, it's important enough to be read. What level of detail would make you want to read the planned report?

For example, you might merely want to know why the writer did what's reported, why the work is important, why it must be done that way, and what result or benefit can be expected. In that case, less is more: The less detail you have to read, the more you may want to read the report. On the other hand, as a reader who may need to be convinced, you might want to see expanded details about the background, situation, general testing methods, or the writer's interpretation of the data.

If taking the reader's point of view still leaves you unsure about the level of detail needed, go back to the primary and secondary readers themselves. Ask what level of detail they need, both specifically (for this current report) and generally (for the other engineering reports you routinely send them). Ask, too, how well your reports usually meet their needs. Your readers may surprise you by saying you can delete some routine reports and shorten others. You may also find out what detail adjustments your technical peers need to see in your investigative reports.

Listen to criticism and learn from it, especially if you're new to report writing. In terms of fulfilling your reader's needs, each report you write should be better than your preceding one.

What Report Length and Style Are Best?

Two of the considerations in meeting your reader's needs are the length and the style (formality) of the report.

No set length or style works for every engineering report. Report length can range from a single-page, nontechnical overview about a new quality-improvement program to a 400-page environmental-impact report required for a pipeline-construction project. Somewhere in between are reports on such topics as key-customer surveys, filtration-system changes, product-failure analyses, process improvements, project progress, and computer-hardware-interface problems. Even routine (weekly, monthly, quarterly) reports vary in length.

The purpose, content, and reader's potential questions all play roles in determining the appropriate length for a given report.

Engineering report styles work in tandem with length. Usually, long reports are also formal reports. Shorter reports lend themselves to a less formal, often conversational, style—as one engineer might talk to another.

For example, a report on thermodynamics might require 20 pages to explain how the Carnot cycle converts heat into work, step by step, in boilers, turbines, and pumps, to measure the efficiency of an engine. The detailed explanations for technical readers would naturally work best within a formal, structured report style. In contrast, a half-page executive overview on the same topic may use a less formal style to report that the technical team, using the Carnot cycle, determined an engine's maximum efficiency within the company's operating environment.

To decide the appropriate length and style for your current report, just keep the reader's perspective. What seems most natural for the content, purpose, and reader's needed level of detail?

Flexible Formats Improve Communication

Engineering-report formats vary from company to company and from department to department. One company may prefer one format for all types of engineering reports. This is a bad-news policy, because no single format suits all reports. Trying to write a report in an ill-suited format is an exercise in frustration and just lengthens the writing time.

The other extreme is the company with no report-format policy. While flexibility is an asset, lack of direction can also lengthen writing time.

Find out what report format(s) your company or department prefers (if any). Don't assume that a certain format is based on company policy just because most of the other engineers' reports seem to use that format. Tradition is often comforting—but it is not always the best guide for the engineering report you're working on this week.

Here's a nontechnical story about tradition:

One weekend, a young engineer was about to bake a ham. Before putting the ham into a baking dish, he cut a small slice off the end of the ham. When his friend asked why, he answered, "I don't know. That's what my mother always did." Curious himself, he called his mother and asked the reason for slicing the end off the unbaked ham. Mother replied, "That's what I always saw *my* mother do. Let's ask Grandma why, since we're following her lead." When asked, Grandma just chuckled, "I didn't have a big enough baking dish to hold the large ham we needed to feed our big family, so I *had* to cut one end off the ham to get it to fit into the dish!"

The old saying "I don't know why, but we've always done it that way" often applies to reports, too. How many engineers in your group merely checked the files for old reports and then copied the format—not because it suited their current report, but because the engineers assumed that what was in the files must have been right? After all, managers approved those reports, so the format must be the wisest to use, right? Maybe; maybe not.

The point is: Ask.

Talk with your manager. If the format you see most often at your company seems ill-suited to your writing project, challenge the format. Ask how much flexibility you're allowed. If the old format is getting in the way of function, find a better one. Yes, solid structure helps to ensure a successful report; but select a structure suited to your report's expected length, its level of formality, your reader, and your purpose. Don't be afraid to go beyond the box of tradition, especially if you need a more efficient format.

The best policy is to vary the format to fit each report. Such a combination of flexibility and direction gets you into the writing job faster.

The longer the engineering report, the more involved the format. As report length shortens, fewer portions of the longer format may be used. To get the overview of the report formats and their sections, though, let's first look at the format of the full-blown, five-pound formal report, and then work our way toward the short, informal report.

Four Engineering-Report Formats

Use the following formats as you see fit. Adapt them to your needs. Don't feel bound by tradition. The long-report format often forces padding into a report of several pages, making it weighty and cumbersome, not easily read.

"'Tis a vanity common to all writers, to overvalue their own productions."

—John Dryden
English poet
(1631–1700)

Long, Formal Reports

Long, formal reports can be technical or nontechnical. They usually include adaptable sections as shown on the next page.

Depending on company or reader preference, the conclusions and recommendations may precede (rather than follow) the discussion of facts.

Nontechnical Report	Technical Report
Cover (heavy stock)	Cover (or Cover Sheet)
Cover Letter or Memo	Letter of Transmittal or Memo
Title Page	Title Page
Acknowledgments	Preface or Acknowledgments
Summary (Executive Summary)	Abstract (within 200 words)
Table of Contents	Table of Contents
List of Illustrations (or Figures)	List of Illustrations (or Figures)
	Glossary of Terms
Introduction (with background information, if needed)	Purpose (or Introduction) Background (in Introduction or alone)
Main Body (Discussion) with subheadings for subtopics, such as: ▶ Facts/Problem ▶ Cause(s) of Problem ▶ Examples/Other Findings ▶ Consequences	Discussion of Data (main body) ▶ Problem ▶ Methods and Materials (tests, measurements) ▶ Observations/Findings ▶ Examples ▶ Analysis/Interpretation of Data
Conclusions	Conclusions
Recommendations	Recommendations
Attachments ▶ Forms, Sample Survey ▶ Illustrations (charts, curves, graphs, tables, photos, maps, diagrams)	Appendix ▶ Illustrations (charts, curves, graphs, tables, photos, maps, diagrams) ▶ Supplementary Data
	Footnotes (Endnotes)
References or Bibliography	References or Bibliography

Those two formats—or slight variations of them—should work for most of your formal engineering reports. Just delete whatever sections seem superfluous to the report you're writing.

Medium-Length Reports

A medium-length report might include only the following sections:

Cover Letter (with authorization for the report)

Statement of the Problem

Summary of Findings

Introduction

Body (facts and interpretation)

Conclusions and Recommendations

Appendix

Less Formal Reports

A less formal report may just include:

Introduction (stating problem, procedure, and results)

Conclusions

Recommendations

Facts (to support recommendations)

Appendix

Report Sections: What to Include Where

You may not need all these sections in your report. However, they are in a typical order, for quick reference. After deciding which sections to include in your report, check the following guidelines to decide what to put in each section.

Cover or Cover Sheet

For nontechnical reports, include only the report title, author's name, company name, and submission date. For technical reports, include the report title, author's name, department, company name, submission date, and report number (if any).

Try to choose a title that clarifies the subject in no more than six words. If the title needs two lines, group the words into logical thought groups, such as:

The Joys of
Widget Technology
    instead of:
The Joys of Widget
Technology

For the title on the cover, prefer a boldface type, between 14 and 24 points, depending on the length of the title. (Any larger might look like a scream.) For the company name, use a type size that is two or more points smaller than that of the title. Use bold type for the report title and company name. The other items on the cover might look best in 12- to 14-point type; just make them smaller than the title and company name.

Cover Letter, Cover Memo, or Letter of Transmittal

If your company prefers a cover letter for the report instead of or in addition to the more formal abstract, include just what you might say face-to-face when delivering the report, to help your reader better understand the report.

For a cover letter or a letter of transmittal (which is often just a more formal or slightly more detailed cover letter), use your corporate letterhead and a standard business-letter format. Include the transmittal date, an inside address, a salutation, concise content, a close (such as "Sincerely"), your neatly written signature, your typed name, and the word "enclosure." For a cover memo, intended only for internal readers, use your company's standard memo format with complete headings.

To give your reader the clearest orientation to your report, either clip the letter to the title page inside the cover, or clip or staple it to the outside of a cover sheet.

Limit the letter to one page, including a brief synopsis of the main points. You may also do some (but usually not all) of the following:

▶ Remind readers of how the report applies to them or their earlier work on part of the project.

▶ Mention the purpose and scope of the report. Perhaps add suggested uses for the report as well.

▶ Briefly summarize the results.

▶ Acknowledge special help (if using no acknowledgments section).

▶ Explain an unusual organization or approach you may have used in your report. Perhaps also mention your background experience that can build your credibility.

▶ Mention relevant sidelights, helpful facts not in the report, or an unusual procedure or experience.

▶ State the main conclusions and recommendations with a few supporting reasons (only if you have no conclusions or recommendations section in the report).

▶ Mention any limitations or problems in preparing the report, along with steps taken to overcome them (not to make excuses, but to show that you were thorough and used available time and materials well).

For a letter of transmittal, you might also do the following:

▶ Say who or what company authorized or requested the report, for what reason.

▶ Summarize financial implications.

▶ List previous or future reports about the same topic.

Set up the letter as you would for mailing, as shown in Chapter 12. Do not put a report page number at the bottom of the cover letter or memo.

Title Page

Include title; company; writer; any authorizations, approvals, or report numbers; and the place and date issued. Use all-capital, bold letters for the report title and company name. For the title page, you might use the same or slightly smaller type sizes than for the cover.

Preface (Foreword) or Acknowledgments

Such sections are optional, even for formal reports. If one of these seems appropriate for your formal report, fine; but prefer using only one, not a combination.

A preface (used for a more general readership than a letter of transmittal has) may include acknowledgments, suggested uses for the report, the author's reasons for writing the report, background experience that adds credibility to the author, or any special personal comments that would be too informal to place in the report itself. If your letter of transmittal already includes such items, the use of a preface would be redundant.

A foreword is written by someone other than the author. That someone, perhaps a well-known authority in the field, usually extols the author's worth and "impartially" endorses the report. A foreword is used more commonly for books than for reports.

A separate acknowledgments section is appropriate when you want to acknowledge other people's help but have not already done so in the cover letter (or letter of transmittal).

Summary

If your main reader wants only the big-picture overview, consider writing a stand-alone summary. That is, view the summary as having two possible uses: either as the part that gets the most attention when part of a long report, or as a separate (and perhaps only) presentation of the situation, problem, solution, and expected result. By including a summary, you ensure that your reader won't miss your message.

A clear summary saves time for both you and your reader. The clearer the summary, the fewer follow-up questions you'll receive, and the faster your manager can decide an action based on your report. Soon, your manager may want just summaries, not formal reports, for many routine engineering reports. Think of how much time you could then save for your other job priorities.

The following types of summaries are used for engineering and other reports. Select the type that best suits the length and style of your report.

Epitome

This is the shortest possible summary, stating just the main point of the report and the general conclusions the facts support. The epitome may be contained in the cover letter, or it may begin or end an introductory summary. For a short report, it suffices as the summary itself. An epitome might be as brief as one or two sentences:

> This HVAC conversion will probably occur in the next two months.
> Here's how we can ensure a smooth transition.

Or,

> Our investigation confirmed dramatic improvement during the filtration
> trials. This report offers the resulting conclusion and recommendation.

Synopsis

The synopsis may be part of a cover letter. If not, however, this one-page overview of a business report or informal engineering report usually contains only main points leading to a recommendation. Results, conclusions, and recommendation(s) are emphasized in a synopsis more than in a straight, longer summary. Tell the reader what he or she should do, based on what, why, and how you know.

Introductory Summary

This opening summary includes the problem, scope, results, conclusions, and recommendations. An introductory summary precedes the introduction and formal conclusions/recommendations sections, if those are separate sections preceding the data.

Although the introductory summary is often called "Executive Summary," prefer calling it just "Summary," to prevent even a remote possibility that a manager, thinking it is meant specifically for him or her, might separate the summary from the report body before sharing the report with his or her employees. Nonmanagerial employees, too, can benefit from the overview presented in the introductory summary.

Summary of Evidence

Instead of writing a separate summary, you may summarize pertinent facts you have just discussed, before going on to the conclusions and recommendations sections.

Terminal Summary

Like other summaries, the terminal summary includes major points that justify the conclusions and recommendations. This summary, though, *follows* the discussion of the data, so the body of the report must build to the terminal summary and fully support it. The terminal summary tells what the facts mean, tying everything together.

If you need no conclusions or recommendations section, the terminal summary may be titled "Conclusions" or "Conclusions and Recommendations."

If your report is technical, you might add a terminal summary (just calling it "Summary") to reinforce what you introduced in the abstract that probably started your report. To learn how an abstract differs from a general summary, read on.

Abstract (a Technical Summary)

An *abstract* is actually a formal summary used mostly for technical and scientific reports, but it is also placed at the beginning of technical articles, academic-degree theses, and conference papers. The abstract usually follows a cover letter (and the preliminary, nontext pages), but it occasionally precedes or replaces the letter. For most technical reports, prefer the order we suggested in the "Four Engineering-Report Formats" section of this chapter. That order generally appeals to technical readers' logic.

Limit the abstract to one paragraph, using fewer than 200 words. That is standard format for an abstract.

Although you can choose between two types of abstracts (descriptive and informative), prefer the informative type for your technical reports. A *descriptive abstract* usually tells the scope but not the main points of a report. The more common—and reader-preferred—*informative abstract* tells not only what the report is about but also what new ideas or information the report contains.

You can build an abstract from the headings and subheadings of your outline, and you might include your conclusions and any recommendations. Work as much key-point content into the abstract as possible within the 200-word limit.

Edit the abstract mercilessly, to present concisely the essence of your technical report. Use complete sentences, though, for easy reading.

Libraries have publications of abstracts; you may want to check a publication in your engineering field to see what has already been done on your topic.

Remember, whatever form your summary or abstract takes, it must be concise and specific, condensing all *essential* information into words a layman can understand. If the summary is a separate section, it may be circulated without the report and must be complete enough to stand alone.

If you can condense volumes of written material into a concise, usable summary, you are valuable to your company.

Table of Contents

A report of fewer than 10 pages needs no table of contents. A long report needs a detailed one. If you need a table of contents, base it on your planning sheet or outline, and add page numbers at the right margin after each heading.

Include tables, charts, or graphs in the table of contents only if you have fewer than five such illustrations. Otherwise, list them separately on the page that follows the table of contents, and divide the list into sections for the various types of illustrations.

The table of contents must show the logic and organization of your report, so keep your headings clear and concise—just specific enough to tell what a section is about. Headings may be key phrases or short sentences—no more than one line each.

▶ Use precisely the same headings and page numbers in the table of contents as in the text. Usually put just two levels of headings in the table of contents—with roman numerals and capital letters, if you use the outline style.

▶ Check related headings for consistency in logic and phrasing. For example, if your report title is "Improved Gas Mileage for the Guzzlers," your headings might read:

    I.   How Car Companies Remodeled Their Heavy Cars
       A. General Motors Shortened the Cadillac Bumper
       B. Ford Reduced the Continental Ashtray by Four Pounds
       C. Chrysler Eliminated the New Yorker Trunk

List of Illustrations (or Figures)

This list will be a separate section if you have five or more tables, charts, graphs, drawings, or other illustrations. Divide the list into types of illustrations. For example, list all the tables first, then list the charts, then list the graphs, and so on. Include the page number for each illustration, for your reader's easy reference.

Glossary of Terms

If you must use technical terms that some of your intended readers may not already know, include a glossary of terms. Give concise, clear definitions in layman's terms. That way, even management readers outside your field of engineering will understand what you're talking about.

Besides (or instead of) including a glossary, you can help readers by briefly defining a technical term, within the text, the first time you use the term.

Likewise, when using an abbreviation for the first time, put it in parentheses immediately after the full term. For example, "This report describes the purpose of installing a chlorine gas scrubber system (CGSS)." After that, you can use just the abbreviation in that report. If the report has several subsections, you may need to use the whole phrase at or near the beginning of each section, and then use the abbreviation after that in the rest of the section. The section-by-section reminder saves readers from having to look back at the report opening to remember the exact meaning of the abbreviation.

Introduction

As the first page of the engineering report proper, the introduction prepares the reader generally for the more specific discussion to come. Include the following:

- the purpose of the report (the problem to be solved)
- the scope of the problem and/or research (what your report covers—and doesn't cover—and why)
- a brief background, if applicable
- the methods used to collect the data for the report
- any limitations in preparing the report (not excuses) and steps taken to overcome them
- a glossary of terms the reader may not know (unless you have a long list that should be placed in the appendix)
- the organization of your report (if you have used an unusual approach)

If you also include a cover letter with the report, be careful not to duplicate information in the letter and the introduction to the body. In the same way, don't repeat in the introduction what you said in the summary or abstract.

Purpose

Use this briefer form of introduction to replace the more general, multipoint introduction if you want to state only the purpose and perhaps the scope of the report. Using this section also frees you to add a separate, more detailed background section, if needed.

Background

This section can replace a general introduction if the historical or technological background of your report topic requires fuller discussion than a general introduction would allow. Just don't get carried away with details. Remember, the background isn't the report's main body—just a lead-in to help your reader put your report into perspective and understand your upcoming discussion.

Main Body (Discussion of Data)

State your observations or findings in logical sequence. Tell why you did something, but emphasize what you *found out*, not what you *did*. Include only the facts relevant to solving the problem. Use specifics to support all general statements. Let your facts show that you checked everything thoroughly. Notice the difference between these two examples:

> Vague: I checked the number of competing filtration systems in several companies throughout the area.

> Specific: To estimate the number of competing filtration systems being marketed locally, I informally surveyed the chief chemical engineers at four Silicon Valley companies on May 1, 19xx.

Specifics such as those in the second example above help to inspire a reader's confidence in the report writer's work.

Use subheadings in the discussion section to break up otherwise long blocks of text. Subheadings may include key words about these subtopics:

Nontechnical Report Subtopics

▶ *Facts/Problem:* telling what's happening in what situation

▶ *Cause(s) of Problem:* saying why the problem occurred

▶ *Examples/Findings:* describing incidents or detailing specifics

▶ *Consequences:* reporting the effects or predicting potential risks

Technical Report Subtopics

▶ *Problem:* telling what's happening in what situation

▶ *Methods and Materials:* saying what tests, measurements, or other methods you used to find the cause of the problem

▶ *Observations/Findings:* explaining what you observed during the research; telling what cause or other key facts you found

▶ *Examples:* describing specific events, incidents in the affected workplace, a machine or a victim of the problem—to help readers grasp the concept

▶ *Analysis/Interpretation of Data:* summarizing what the test results indicate, what pattern the measurements reveal, what trend your observations show, or what deeper problem the research unearthed

Your interpretation of the situation or data helps your reader understand the meaning and importance of the facts or numbers you're presenting. That interpretation forms the basis for—and easily leads into—your conclusions and recommendations.

The two key sections of an engineering report are the conclusions and recommendations sections. As the writer, you're the expert on your topic. You investigated the problem, you ran the tests, and you evaluated the results. Nobody knows more about this special topic than you do. Yet the details can't stand alone; you must tell what they mean. Make sure that you state the conclusions and recommendations clearly, basing them on the findings you have detailed.

> *"Knowledge is the foundation and source of good writing."*
>
> —Horace
> Roman poet and satirist
> (65–8 BC)

Conclusions

The conclusions section may be placed before or after the introduction, or after the body, depending on the nature of your report and the preference of your reader or company. Include only the conclusions that can be fully supported by your facts, and include *all* logical conclusions, both positive and negative. Be objective. When placing a conclusions section before the body, provide more explanation of why you reached each conclusion, as your reader has not yet seen the supporting facts. Give the major supporting data, saving the details for the body.

When placing conclusions after the body, do not repeat points you just discussed in the body. If you need to refer to a point, use key words to remind your reader of that point. You may analyze and interpret what has been discussed, such as good and bad features.

Here are four variations for organizing the conclusions:

▶ same order that each topic was discussed in body

▶ most important results first (reverse order of climax)

▶ positive results first, negative next

▶ negative results first, positive next

Recommendations

Aim the recommendations at your report's purpose, and base them on the conclusions you have presented.

You may combine recommendations with conclusions; yet, because your reader may agree with your conclusions but not your recommendations, prefer using separate sections. Like the conclusions section, the recommendations section may come before or after the introduction, or—most commonly—after the body (discussion).

Include what is to be done, as well as when, where, how, and by whom. If you recommend taking no action, do so clearly and decisively. Your reader wants to know what you think should be done. However, you are to suggest and recommend, not demand or command that your reader do something.

Whether your recommendations are for application of an idea or a product, for additional study, for a proposed program, or for a future action—include reasons for your decisions based on the conclusions and remember: Be objective.

You may want to include alternate courses of action or other sources to check as well. Most managers want to know their alternatives, especially when a report recommends spending any money. The easiest way to present alternatives is in a columnar format, with variable headings for the columns. For example, the following three-column list of alternatives helps to highlight the recommended alternative.

Alternatives	Advantages	Disadvantages
A: Repair the inlet valve.	Least expense now. Postpone new system.	Possible recurrent breakdown. Higher long-term cost (price rises). This and other system parts may fail.
B: Replace the inlet valve.	Longer-lasting fix. Postpone new system.	Other parts of old system may fail. Higher long-term cost (price rises).
C: Replace entire system.	Surest solution. System discount. Lowest long-term cost. Faster system than old. Higher efficiency.	Highest short-term cost.

Notice that Alternative C (the recommended one) has the most advantages and the fewest disadvantages, to support the recommendation.

A side point about consistency: Although the columns' limited space may force you to sacrifice some parallel phrasing in the list, the key-word items do clarify the specifics concisely. Just be sure to make the alternatives in the first column parallel by starting each alternative with a verb. That's the imperative mood at work. If space allows, word all the advantages and disadvantages in noun phrases (things) or all in short, full sentences. For example, in our list of advantages, the unparallel "Postpone new system" would become "Postponement of new system." The two full sentences in the "Disadvantages" column could instead start out as "Possible failure of ..."

Attachments

For a nontechnical report, you may want to include a sample form, outline, sample survey, survey-results tally, photograph, expense sheet, questionnaire, or illustrations. Such items, though, can get in the way of the main report if they interrupt the flow of ideas. Separate the supplementary items from the main report, especially if they require more than a page or must be approved or filled in and returned to you.

Appendix/Appendices

An appendix replaces the attachments section (especially for technical reports) and is usually more extensive. If you have more than one appendix, precede the set with a title page saying "Appendices."

Include in an appendix any necessary illustrations that would interrupt easy reading of the body of the report: long charts, curves, graphs, tables, photographs, maps, lists, forms, questionnaires, related past reports or related summaries, flowcharts, or sets of diagrams. If you want to add data not considered as illustrations, you may want two subsections of your appendix: "Illustrations" and "Supplementary Data." Order the items according to the order their topics appear in the text.

Include only what you have discussed in the text. Select appendix items with care. Don't just pad your report with them; they won't help a poorly written report. If carefully selected, though, they support a well-written one.

References/Footnotes (Endnotes)

If your engineering report includes quotes from other publications, you can cite the sources either in *footnotes* at the bottom of the page where the footnote number appears in text, or in *endnotes* at the end of the report. Footnotes give immediate source information. Endnotes avoid distractions during the main report reading and keep all references together, with endnote numbers in the order quoted. If you prefer the endnotes method, use the heading "References," as some readers may not understand the term "Endnotes" to mean the references you cited.

For a nontechnical report, you won't usually need separate references and bibliography sections.

Bibliography

If included, a bibliography goes at the end of the report, after the appendix. You may include sources cited in the text, ones that gave you important information, or all those that you relied on heavily—whether or not you quoted the sources in the endnote section.

Adaptable Formats for Miscellaneous Reports

A few report types often have their own formats.

Activity Report: Advertising Your Worth

If you write weekly, monthly, or quarterly reports to your immediate manager, you're usually telling what you have done to earn your salary in that time period. You might also have to report on each phase of a project as you complete that phase, or show what progress you and your team have made. Here's your chance to prove that your company can't do without you.

Try to limit the report to one page. Be concise. Your manager will then better see your overall contributions more easily. That improves your chances when your manager reviews all your current year's reports before writing your performance review.

Adapt the following format to your needs, using subheadings and bulleted lists:

Key Accomplishments (also called Summary or Highlights)

Completed Projects/Completed Phases of Project X

Ongoing Projects/Status of Phase X

Planned Projects/Next Phase

Training/Other Accomplishments

Problems/Limitations/Requests

Plans for Next Reporting Period

Incident Report

Do management and yourself a favor. To report an incident or problem, consider a half-page to one-page summary report of these subheading points, in memo form:

Situation/Circumstance/Environment in Which Problem Occurred

Problem

Cause of Problem

Solution (temporary or permanent)/Recommended Solution

Results/Expected Results

Managers tell us they would rather have those points covered, even in a paragraph or two, than to have them omitted or buried in a 10-page report of details. Remember that even technical managers often need just the overview. If they want more details, they usually ask.

Failure Analysis Report

This engineering report, more technical and detailed than the incident report, should be informative enough to help management weigh the significance of the problem and to prevent recurrence of the failure. Don't risk a costly wrong decision by management because of a buried detail, an incomplete test cycle, or an omission about the number of units you tested.

Although the formal technical-report format already described may work fine for some failure analyses, you may need the more specific format subheadings below:

Description of Failure

Circumstance/Situation (in which the part, equipment, or system failed)

Frequency of Failure/Number of Failed Units

Acceptable Level of Failure (expected failure rate, out of total units in operation)

Tests/Measurements/Interviews/Other Methods Used (to confirm failure, diagnose cause, predict recurrence)

Number of Units Tested
>This test-count information is crucial to a well-informed management decision about the importance of the problem and the most cost-effective solution.

Cause(s) of Failure

Attempted Solutions and Their Results

Conclusion

If your manager expects you to suggest a solution, add these three points as subheadings:

Solution (to prevent recurrence)

Alternative Solutions (and reasons for rejecting those alternatives)

Expected Outcome (cost vs. benefits, both short-term and long-term)

Informal Recommendation Report

If your manager has requested a brief review of a situation or problem, you probably need no formal headings and subheadings of the long-report format. Instead, use a memo format, briefly summarizing thcsc points:

Overview of the situation (in a few sentences)

Your recommended solution(s), reasons, benefits

Alternative solutions considered (in a column format, to compare advantages, disadvantages, cost vs. benefit, and comments)
>Include the recommended action in this alternatives list, giving your recommendation first or last. Naturally, show your objectivity by ensuring that your recommendation has the longest advantages list and the shortest disadvantages list.

A comments paragraph about your recommendation
>Perhaps mention the expected side benefits to other departments, your suggestions for overcoming possible objections, expected payback time, required/available resources, or ways to implement the recommended actions.

Feasibility Report

If you are wondering whether a different equipment arrangement might make your office more efficient, you're doing an informal feasibility study. You usually wouldn't need a report for something that simple. If, though, the rearrangement might affect other people in your group, at least discuss the idea with them first. If the move would involve the whole department, give your manager an oral or memo-style feasibility report. If your company has asked you to find out whether to move Pump Station #4, your investigation—and your feasibility report—would be more extensive.

Before you launch an expensive project, the cost consideration makes it worth your time to ensure that the project is feasible—meaning whether it is possible to accomplish successfully (profitably). Forethought is essential to avoid unwarranted, unwise, and unprofitable projects.

A feasibility report can be a summary paragraph or a 100-page report, depending on the size and complexity of the considered action. The feasibility-report format, which is quite flexible, usually includes some or all of the following sections, with or without headings, depending on the length of the report:

Title Page

Summary or Abstract (telling proposed action, problem that led to it, scope of project, and expected outcome)

Contents Page (for long reports)

List of Illustrations (if applicable)

Glossary of Terms (if too numerous to define within the text)

Introduction (telling purpose and scope of the investigation and of the report, plus possibly a brief background, study limitations, acknowledgments). Include this only if you include no separate summary section.

Main Body (study methods, resources, people involved, etc.)

Conclusions (based on your research, test results, knowledge, and experience)

Recommendations (suggested action or inaction—based on your conclusions—specifying the Five W's and One H: *who* should do or not do *what, when, where,* and *how*; add expected outcome, which tells *why* to do what you're recommending)

References

Attachments/Appendix/Appendices

Trip Report

If you visit customers, potential customers, or technical staff in the field, your trip reports tell your manager whether the cost of your travel is paying off for the company. Briefly summarize these points:

Purpose of trip

Names of all team members taking the trip (if you didn't go alone)

Beginning and ending dates of the trip

Companies, departments, people visited (and their titles)

Date of each visit

Project(s)/problems/opportunities discussed at each visit

Outcome of each visit (observations, conclusion, decisions, new orders, future-order potential, needed process changes)

Stick to specifics in a trip report. For example, if you are reporting on a seminar or trade show you attended, don't waste your manager's (reader's) time by repeating how wonderful the conference was. If you do, your report comes across as a weak justification for the three days you spent away from the job. Instead, explain what you learned and how you will apply what you learned. That gets a manager's attention.

Form Report

Some routine reports work more efficiently as forms, especially if all the readers know the technical background and implications of the fill-in sections on the form.

For example, you might save a half-hour each day for every employee on a shift by letting a one-page form report replace a from-scratch end-of-shift report that takes time away from the production line. Any daily routine that requires a report might benefit from a column-format report form, which varies according to the product, equipment, check-off items, or incidents.

A High-Tech Resource: Handy Formatting Software

To give you even more ideas for formatting your reports, consider an already-available supplemental resource: computer software with report-format templates. Check out the most recent programs to see which ones might work for you.

Too numerous and fast-changing to name here, such software programs can save hours or days of work on your next report. Just be sure you study and select or adapt the formats carefully to suit your purpose, your reader, and your message. The study time you invest will help you decide whether the software will smoothly expedite or slow down your report writing.

Don't Let Form Overshadow Function

When you have the option to write an informal, memo-style report instead of a detailed, formal-format one, do so. Remember, a one-page report has a much better chance of being read than a formal report that could double as a doorstop.

Whatever engineering-report format you choose, let function, not form, be your guide. Of course, the form (format) should support the function. By tailoring the engineering-report format to your purpose and reader—and by stressing your key points, without excessive detail—you can write readable reports that clearly document your worth to your company.

"The only impeccable writers are those who never wrote."

—William Hazlitt
English essayist
(1778–1830)

Summary of This Chapter's Main Points

▶ View reporting not as a mop-up step, but as important work that helps you document your hard work.

▶ Use your reports to help keep your firm's costs down and profits up.

▶ Sidestep the engineer's report-writing trap: excessive detail.

▶ Think like your report reader by putting yourself into your reader's mind.

▶ Question whether a certain report is needed.

▶ Vary the report length, style, and format to suit the purpose, content, and reader's perspective. Short reports are usually informal, even conversational; long reports are more formal.

▶ Test the tradition of using an old, cumbersome format. If the old format is hard or inappropriate to use, find a better format. Ask your manager whether and how the format can change.

▶ Choose between (and adapt) nontechnical and technical report formats.

▶ Know what to include in which report section; decide when to omit and when to combine report sections.

▶ Design the summary or abstract as a clear, concise time-saver that gives your reader the big picture. Limit an abstract to 200 words, limit most summaries to a paragraph, and limit a synopsis to one page.

▶ For efficiency, give special reports their own format.

▶ For readability in short, informal reports, let function rule the form.

14 Producing Persuasive Proposals

> *"We will build a machine that will fly."*
>
> —Joseph Michael Montgolfier
> French inventor/aeronaut
> who invented the first air balloon
> (1740–1810)

At the simplest level, a proposal might be just an oral offer to organize a company bowling league. In its most complex form, a proposal can be a 500-page (or longer) formal offer to revamp a federal agency's electronic-mail system.

Generally, a proposal is a company's offer to supply a certain service or product to a prospective buyer, within a certain time, for a set fee.

Look at a proposal as a company's major sales tool. *Sales* is not a dirty word. If someone didn't sell your company's product or service, the doors would close and you, with your fellow engineers, would be out of a job. Luckily, through proposal writing, the engineer's usual negative view of sales takes on a more positive, sophisticated aura. Proposals give you a chance to help your company survive, prosper, and grow. Your engineering expertise helps your proposal team show your company's technical superiority and sound ideas, to win contracts that keep you employed.

Two Types of Proposals

The two main types of proposals are commercial sales proposals and government proposals.

Sales Proposals

Styles of *sales proposals* vary, but all must stress the benefits of the proposed solution. So before submitting the proposal, be sure you know the customer's requirements and/or have identified a definite problem. Learn as much as you can about the customer's business and the current need, to avoid sending a "boilerplate proposal" that looks like an extended form letter.

Government Proposals

The *government proposal* (or *procurement proposal*) is often submitted in response to an agency's rigid *Invitation for Bids (IFB,* also called a *Solicitation for Bids)* or a flexible *Request for Proposals (RFP)*. The success of your proposal depends on how well your company responds to the specifically stated problem.

Even if you think a product or service other than the one requested would better solve the problem, you must mold your proposal to the requested product or service. You must also match all the numerical and precise time limits set by the requester; otherwise, you will be considered "nonresponsive" and will be rejected.

Team discussion is crucial to helping the technical staff, management, and accountants decide whether the required weeks and expense will produce a feasible, cost-effective proposal. If your company decides to submit the proposal, tailor every part of the proposal to the IFB or RFP.

If you received no request, find out the agency's needs as you would for a sales proposal.

The Key to a Successful Proposal

A successful proposal is one that outshines competitors' proposals and convinces the receiver that its authors offer not only the best solution to a stated problem but also the highest potential to get the proposed job done.

A proposal—a close cousin of a report—must stress what the receiver wants to hear: benefits. The key is *persuasion*. No matter how technically masterful your plan, its success depends on persuasive points you use to sell your proposed idea to the buyer—whether that's the cafeteria's ice cream buyer, your manager, or a huge government agency. How persuasively you present your approach and its benefits—from the buyer's point of view—helps determine whether you or your competitor will walk away with the contract.

Feature, Advantage, or Benefit?

If you're writing a technical proposal to get project funding, or a customer presentation to make a sale, here's some background information that is crucial to understand. You have probably heard that if you are trying to sell anything—a product, service, or idea—you must explain the *benefits* to your prospect. Here's an easy way to determine whether you are really describing a benefit to the listener.

Imagine a fairly common product such as an automobile. You could have a lot of reasons to choose one car over another. Obviously, price and quality are foremost. Once you determine your price range, you seek a car that will give you good service with reasonable maintenance for a reasonable number of years.

Now we get to what is going to make you choose one car over another: It has power steering. It's a van that has a fold-down table in the back.

Power steering and the fold-down table are *features*. Let's ask a "So what?" question. So what if it has power steering? So what if it has a fold-down table?

Well, the *advantages* are that power steering makes the van easier to steer, and a fold-down table in the van lets your kids play games in the back.

"So what?"

Well, if the car is easier to steer, you'll be less tired on long trips and it will be a safer car to drive. If your kids can keep occupied playing a game, they won't bug you, and you'll go through a long trip with less stress.

That's why you're going to buy this van. Now let's find the benefits that convinced you to buy.

All products have features that the sales people have to turn into benefits. They do it by asking "So what?" as we did above. If you ask "So what?" enough times, you'll eventually find the benefit of a product, service, or idea. Usually, the "So what?" goes through two iterations so that you end up with:

Feature: power steering
"So what?"

Advantage: easier to steer
"So what?"

Benefit: less tiring; safer

Feature: fold-down table
"So what?"

Advantage: kids are occupied
"So what?"

Benefit: you drive with less stress

But what if you buy it because it's a red convertible? Ask Freud. That's too heavy for us.

Three Persuasive Points to Present

You Know the Problem

The first point of persuasion concerns the problem you're proposing to solve.

Sometimes the prospective buyer (such as a government agency) already knows the problem and wants suggested solutions. In that case, since the initiative came from the buyer, you don't have to spend a lot of time trying to persuade the buyer that there's a problem. Yet, you still have to show that you fully understand the problem by repeating in your proposal the same key words the buyer used to describe the problem.

Sometimes, on the other hand, you discover a problem that nobody has mentioned to you. In that case, you become the initiator of a proposed solution, and your persuasive task is harder. Suppose, for example, that you are a facilities engineer and you notice—within your own company—a situation that sends up a "red flag" in your mind: During your visit to one of your company's recently purchased fabrication plants, you learn that fewer-than-usual products are coming off the line each day and that many of the assemblers at this plant become drowsy early in their shifts.

In that case, be careful to discern whether what you observed was the problem itself—or just a symptom of a problem. The lower-than-usual productivity and drowsiness are symptoms, not the underlying problem itself. You realize that the problem may be poor ventilation.

After talking with the production manager and checking the ventilation paths, inlets, and outlets, you find no obstructions that would have prevented complete mixing of fresh and room air. You notice, though, that the inlet and outlet openings are unequal in area, and that the air outlet is lower than the air inlet. Both observed conditions hinder free circulation of air. A slight redesign of the ventilation system would solve the air-circulation problem.

You must diplomatically convince management that the problem exists and is serious enough to reduce productivity and increase the risk of accidents at the plant.

Thus, the "Problem" section of your internal proposal to management must include a specific description of the problem, its effects, and the consequences of not tackling the problem. For example, you might show how reduced productivity and safety risks could be costing the company more money than your minor redesign would cost. Be objective, though. Don't overstate the problem, effects, or consequences. Overstatement reduces credibility.

You Offer the Best Solution

The second persuasive point you must present is the solution that you want the receiver (prospect, buyer, or manager) to accept and approve.

If your reader is a government agency that knows what problem it wants solved, the agency may already know what solution (or product) it wants, needing only to find the lowest price for that precise product, such as supersonic nozzles. Your company's proposal team presents a bid for supplying the stated number of those specific nozzles within the stated time period, and you hope that your price is lower than your competitors' bids. No big solution discussion there, except for price. Your "best solution" would need to be the lowest price—if you can still make a profit at that price.

Another buyer, such as a different government agency, may present only the problem and want the proposers to suggest solutions to the problem. Here, you and your team have more flexibility in presenting your solution; but you'd better do your homework to find out whether that solution will actually work.

To be sure you know the requester's priorities, take time to play detective, searching out clues in the RFP you received. What's being stressed: quality, price, the provider's qualifications, or the time schedule? Study whatever requirements were stated, and be sure to respond specifically to those requirements, even if you do have leeway on the solution. Whatever seems to be the requester's priority, focus your proposal on that priority. Doing so can give you the competitive edge.

If, in contrast, you (not the proposal's receiver) initiate the proposal process, you don't have to respond to any specifications. That's good news. At least you don't run the risk of being "nonresponsive" in this case.

For example, going back to your internal proposal for redesigning the ventilation system, let's consider how you might present your solution persuasively. First, list all the alternative solutions that you have weighed or that you think the decider (or another engineer) might think of. (Yes, this "Solution" section of your proposal is much like the

"Recommendations" section of a formal report.) The efficient columnar format (perhaps listing alternatives, advantages, disadvantages, and costs) persuades graphically.

Be careful when writing your solution—it can get tricky. You want to show that you can solve the problem, but you don't want to lay out the specifics that the buyer could implement without hiring you. Here's where you use general words, not specific words. (See Chapter 5.)

Whether or not you are the one who initiated the proposal, state with authority *why* your solution is the best.

You Know How the Solution Will Work

The third persuasive point to present is the "how" of your solution. Tell how you plan to implement it.

▶ Describe your related experience and available resources (people, facilities, time available) to solve the problem as you propose.

▶ State specifically how you will organize each phase of the project; give a timetable for carrying out each phase.

▶ Detail the technical, managerial, and budgeting aspects of the project to show that you fully understand all that's involved to honor your commitment.

▶ Make sure that the proposed product or service does what you say it can. The customer will probably test it to ensure that it does.

You must convince your reader that you can fulfill your offer. First, though, you and your teammates may have to convince yourselves.

Be Sure You Want the Job

As you consider the "how," weigh the risk versus the rewards of presenting your proposal. First, especially for external proposals that respond to a request, decide objectively:

"If it's a job at any price, the answer is we don't want a job at all."

—Anonymous shop steward at Swan Hunter
Sydney Morning Herald, "Sayings of the Week"
12 April 1986

▶ Are you really qualified to deliver on your promise? Do you or does your company have the expertise, related experience, and resources to do the job? Or might you be overconfident about your ability to fulfill the contract if you win it?

▶ Are you playing on a level competitive field, or do the customer and one of your competitors have an established relationship that may preclude a fair comparison of proposals? (Are you sure that the request is not worded in a way that seems to favor the experience of a rival supplier while meeting the legal bidding requirements of the agency or customer?)

▶ Will the proposal be worth your time and expense? Will the payback be profitable for you?

▶ Do you have a flexible enough schedule to allot the needed time for the project? Or will time constraints force you to turn away routine contracts that bring more income than the proposed (and unguaranteed) project would?

Quality: How Your Proposal Predicts Your Work

The old saying "First impressions count" holds true for proposals. The amount of effort you invest in your proposal will be obvious to most readers. The quality of the content, writing, editing, formatting, and overall presentation will affect your credibility. If the proposal looks thrown together, the perception will be that your work on the project will be, too.

One careless editing slip (such as leaving another customer's name in a proposal that is partly duplicated from an earlier similar proposal) can result in a fast rejection.

Formats for Successful Proposals

Some proposal sections are similar to formal-report sections. The general format of a sales or government proposal usually includes most of the following sections.

Cover and/or Title Page

Avoid bright colors in proposal covers, especially for conservative customers. For simple presentation you may prefer using only one of these sheets, rather than giving the impression of padding. The information is identical for both sheets:

Include a brief title, the name of the person or firm for whom the proposal is prepared, the request it answers (if applicable), the company submitting the proposal, the submittal date, any important numbers (such as the RFP number or proposal number), and any proprietary or national security notices. Keep the page as brief and as attractive as possible.

Cover Letter

If you use both a cover and title page, the cover letter may go between those two pages. If you use just one or the other, the cover letter can be clipped to the front page.

Foreword

If you include a foreword, include the name of the equipment or service and any other important information not included in the title page. You may also include any pertinent personal comments. If you omit the foreword (for the same perceived-padding reason), you can add the equipment/service name to the title page information if the addition doesn't clutter the title page.

Table of Contents

Only a long or complex proposal needs a table of contents. Even then, headings from the proposal body may suffice. Include just enough detail to help your reader find information fast.

Summary

Include the main points from the proposal: the problem, how your product or service solves the problem, and your firm's qualifications to do the job. You may also mention your readiness to do the work, but don't go overboard. Ensure a concise, appealing summary that makes the reader want to read the proposal body.

Sometimes a "grabber" lead (a dramatic opening sentence) works well, depending on the audience. Here are two examples:

> We can halve our fabrication costs by automating our manufacturing process.
>
> The time is right to cash in on the industry's latest trend: Write-Only Memories.

Before using a grabber lead, though, think about how it will affect your main reader. If such an opening might be viewed as frivolous, don't risk it. On the other hand, this *is* a *proposal*—a marketing tool to help sell your technical wizardry. Just weigh your options.

The point is, write a summary that captures your reader's attention, whether gently or dramatically. For example:

> To streamline your current inventory process, we recommend the FIFO Facilitator software package for two reasons:
>
> 1. It will solve the two major problems stated in your RFP.
>
> 2. The Facilitator's Security Parcel will eliminate the theft problem that you mentioned at our meeting.

Product or Service Description

This may be a sales brochure about your product or service. Include the benefits of any features mentioned.

Glossary of Terms

If you have too many technical terms to define where you use them in the text, add a glossary section to your proposal. Beware, though, of forcing the reader to flip back and forth between the glossary and your proposal text as you introduce each term. Prefer layman's terms when you can, especially in the nontechnical parts of your report.

Illustrations

Selectively include charts, graphs, photographs, or drawings showing how your customer will benefit by using your product or service. Depending on the customer's priorities, the benefits might be lower costs, higher productivity, or improved safety.

Management Qualifications

Include your company's reputation, longevity, organization (preferably on an organization chart), profit and growth numbers, special qualifications to do the particular job, and résumés of the program managers who would be assigned to the project. (Don't include a well-known name of a colleague if that person won't be part of the project team. Such a tactic easily backfires.)

Technical Plan

Show that you understand the customer's problem, and describe your approach to solving it. Include brief additional illustrations that clearly show your approach.

Facilities and Related Experience

Describe the facilities and equipment to be used for the project, and tell when they will be available. Include the scope, numbers, and procuring agency/customer of any similar work you have done.

Cost Analysis

Calculate the dollar figure that your proposal, if accepted, will cost the prospective customer. Include any training and support costs, and explain what the proposed training and support will encompass.

Appendix or Attachments

Add any other supporting information that does not fit elsewhere in the proposal or that would interrupt easy reading of the preceding proposal sections. Remember that if anything looks like padding or expensive presentation, the resulting impression of wastefulness can cost you the contract. You want a balanced image of professionalism and cost-awareness.

Other Possible Proposal Sections

Formal proposals may use some or all of the preceding section titles. You may even combine some of those headings with carefully selected items, as warranted, from the following list if indicated by your company's special expertise or your customer's RFP:

Background about the problem or your earlier association with the reader's company

Subject, purpose, and scope (perhaps in an introduction)

Need for and feasibility of solution

Proposed schedule (including total number of days or weeks)

Proposed methods, with team-member task breakdown

Probability of success and expected resulting products

Quality-assurance guidelines

Cost breakdown and method of payment

Collateral but pertinent literature about your company

References (names and phone numbers or testimonial letters)

Requested next step or diplomatic call to action

Simplified Format for Informal or Internal Proposals

Even if you're proposing an internal technical project to top management, you're writing a type of sales proposal. In this instance, though, the internal style is usually less formal— in a memo format. Such a proposal might simply include the following sideheadings.

Subject

Place the proposal title in the subject line of a memo, or on the reference line of an external proposal in letter form.

Introduction

Although this section is optional, in it you may give the purpose, scope, and possible background commentary. (Alternatively, instead of using a separate introduction section, you may include these points in the summary.)

Summary

Briefly describe the problem, solution, alternatives, implementation/resources, and expected outcome of the proposed project or product.

Conclusion

Emphasize—in nontechnical terms—why your proposed solution is best, what next step you plan or expect, or your appreciation for the opportunity to present the proposal.

Attachments

In this optional section, include only any attachments that will help your reader grasp your proposal quickly. Examples are charts, graphs, or forms that are pertinent to the proposal.

If you are simply presenting a proposal by yourself to another person, let the function determine the form (as with reports). For simple proposals, oral presentation may be enough. For brief external proposals, a letter format may work best. Be efficient and be objective.

May these guidelines help you create successful proposals.

Summary of This Chapter's Main Points

▶ Remember that a proposal is a firm's offer to supply a certain service or product to a prospective buyer, within a certain time, for a set fee.

▶ Decide whether to submit a proposal, by weighing risks versus rewards. Know your competitive odds.

▶ Submit proposals that give you (and your fellow engineers) a chance to help your company survive, prosper, and grow.

▶ In a sales proposal, stress *benefits*.

▶ In a government proposal, respond specifically to the rigid Invitation for Bids or the more flexible Request for Proposals.

▶ Use your engineering expertise to show your company's technical superiority and sound ideas—to win contracts and keep your job.

▶ Show that you know the problem, you offer the best solution, and you can make the solution work.

▶ Remember that your proposal quality predicts your work quality.

▶ Select a format that projects professionalism, efficiency, and cost-awareness. Don't pad the proposal.

15 Procedure Writing: Tell Your Reader Where to Go and What to Do

"What we have to learn to do, we learn by doing."

—Aristotle
Greek philosopher and scientist
(384–322 BC)

In his wonderful science fiction novel *Dune*, Frank Herbert imagined a "spice" that enabled a certain sect of people to possess all the knowledge of their forebears. If we had such a spice today, so that new employees could immediately know our standard processes, we would not need to write procedures. But until we get that spice, we're stuck with procedure writing.

Procedures (including instructions and manuals) are critical documents in any engineering company, because the demand for them is high. The procedure takes the place of a teacher who would have to work alongside an individual, constantly explaining what to do next. A well-written procedure frees the more experienced engineers from that training duty. On the other hand, a poorly written procedure, which generates more questions than answers, makes standing beside the trainee seem like a good idea.

This chapter presents principles you can use to write any type of instructions, procedures, or manuals. If you have to tell people how to perform a task, this chapter is for you.

First, though, a word about procedure nomenclature. Despite probably being around since cave dwellers used pictographs to explain how to fell a mammoth, procedures still lack classification. To date, no group has classified the various types of procedures we have in the engineering world. So after interviewing some technical writers, university professors, and engineers who attended our technical-writing workshops, we narrowed the classification down to five types of procedures. You or your company may have different names or use some of the names interchangeably. What you call them is your business. What we're concerned about is the quality of writing that goes into them.

Five Types of Procedure Guides: Something for Everyone

When you have to document how to do something, you're writing one of the five types of procedure guides:

▶ Instruction Sheet

▶ Standard Operating Procedure

▶ Operations Manual

▶ Tutorial

▶ Reference Manual

In common, they explain how to perform a task. They differ in the level of detail they provide, and their readers differ in level of skill.

Instruction Sheet

The reader here is probably an experienced person but could just as easily be a beginner. Instruction sheets usually explain how to repair or install a part or how to assemble a consumer product. Instruction sheets are usually short documents—at least, they should be.

Standard Operating Procedure

The reader here is a beginner. The standard operating procedure (SOP) explains how to perform an on-the-job task such as sorting the mail or entering data into a computer. Let's say that you are planning a three-month sabbatical and your manager wants you to document your daily work routine for your temporary replacement. An SOP is what you would write.

Operations Manual

The reader of the operations manual (OM) may be a beginner, but more than likely is advanced in his or her subject knowledge. The OM provides a comprehensive overview with all the details and is usually organized by topic, either alphabetically or chronologically. An OM, for example, can describe how to run sophisticated equipment or how to run a factory.

Tutorial

The tutorial (a prelude to the reference manual) is usually for beginners. It is a complete but not detailed overview of a task and includes sample exercises to build the reader's skill and confidence.

The term *tutorial* is also used for scientific and engineering society publications that are technical updates of current issues.

Reference Manual

The reference manual (RM) is what you use after you've mastered the tutorial. The skill level is moderate to advanced. The RM is a comprehensive overview with all the details. This is the manual so often maligned, because it so often is loaded with useless technical detail and lacking in specific how-to information. (Since manuals are usually written by a team, we will discuss them separately in this chapter.)

What you may have noticed as missing is the user's guide. The user's guide seems to be used interchangeably with all the above. Go figure.

The Four Steps of Procedure Writing

What all those types of documents have in common is that they adhere to the same procedure-writing principles. The purpose of any procedure is to explain to the reader how to perform a task.

Divide your procedure-writing project into four logical steps:

▶ Step 1: Collect the data.

▶ Step 2: Organize your procedure.

▶ Step 3: Write clear instructions.

▶ Step 4: Test your procedure.

Step 1: Collect the Data

Before you can write, you need information. Essentially, you'll get your information from the following sources.

Start with your own notes and experience. Next, review other documents and previous procedures. Depending on the project, you may also want to interview other technical experts. But don't stop there. Talk to managers to find out what procedure expectations they have. Talk, also, to the *users* to learn their needs; ask the users what shortcomings they see in any of the old procedures. Ask new employees what they would like to see in the procedure. In other words, get to know your reader(s). Now you should be well-enough armed with information to start organizing.

Step 2: Organize Your Procedure

As with any major writing job, start with a planning sheet as explained in Chapter 3. First plan the overall project and outline it, and then use a planning sheet for each section. The key phrase to keep in mind as you plan your procedure is "logical order."

Mentally walk yourself through the steps, realizing you're probably going to omit a step. Don't sweat it. That's why you have Step 4: testing.

Organize your procedure hierarchically (a word that is as hard to type as it is to say!). Group the related steps in sections. Use key-word headings and subheads to guide the reader. Explain the steps in the order the reader must perform them.

Headings also help your reader to go back and easily find important sections. This hierarchical organization is especially useful in complex procedures that involve several readers or departments.

Identify each reader by title or job function, using subheads. Separate any shared steps (the steps taken by different people) into different sections. Let your page format simplify the explanation.

Plan an Easy-to-Use Format

If two groups' (readers') steps intertwine throughout the procedure, use a two-column format, identifying the *person responsible* for each action and then telling what *action* that person performs. One way to do so is by the sequence in which the actions must be performed, not by job-function groupings. For example:

Person Responsible	Action (in the following sequence)
equipment manager	Monitor the inventory review.
warehouse manager	When fewer than 500 units are in stock, tell the equipment manager your current count.
equipment manager	Tell the buyer what supplies not to reorder, and why, by completing a "Discontinue" form.
buyer	Acknowledge the "Discontinue" order by initialing the "Discontinue" form and returning the yellow copy of the form to the equipment manager.

A similar (and excellent) procedure format is the two-column page that lists *actions* in the left column and *results* of the actions in the right column. This a good format for two reasons.

First, the two-column format is easy to read and follow, especially if the reader is trying to focus on the instructions and perform the action at the same time.

Second, the two-column format is more conducive to writing imperative sentences and therefore makes your writing job easier. Remember our discussion of imperative and indicative sentences in Chapter 7? Imperative sentences give a command. Indicative sentences state a fact. Procedures have essentially two types of information: actions and background information. Use imperative sentences for actions and indicative sentences for background information. The left-hand "Action" column has imperative sentences; the right-hand "Results" column has indicative sentences.

The columnar format is also handy for a troubleshooting procedure. Here's an example showing three problem-analysis columns. On the left you list the *symptom(s)*, in the middle the *possible cause(s)*, and on the right the possible *remedy (remedies)*. In this case, the symptoms and causes can be a list of phrases, while the remedies are imperative sentences.

Symptom	Possible Cause	Possible Remedy
partial refrigeration	burner thermal valve	Check to see that valve opens during burning lighting.
	hi-temp safety valve	Check to see that valve has not failed in closed position.

If for some reason you can't or don't want to use the columnar format, at least *physically separate* the actions from background information for your reader. You can indent background information, or put it into a different type style or typeface. Whatever pleases you. Just be sure to separate the two, for easier writing and easier reading.

Numbering the steps also helps readers to keep their place while following the procedure. We prefer avoiding roman numerals; they take up too much space. However, if you have an elaborate procedure, your best bet may be to *start* with roman numerals. Following is the classic outline format that most style books recommend:

I. Begin the ...
II. Next, access ...
   A. Now start ...
   B. After starting ...
      1. Be sure to ...
      2. Watch the ...
         a) Include only ...
           (1) Fasers
           (2) Lasers
              (a) Medical
              (b) Industrial
                  i) Scientific
                  ii) Agricultural
         b) Other choices ...
           (1) Filters
           (2) etc.

A combination of arabic numerals (1, 2, 3) and letters (A, B, C) often works well. For example:

   1.
   2.
      2A.
      2B.
   3.

Another example:

   1.
   2.
      A.
         1)
         2)
            a)
            b)
      B.

The decimal numbering system you probably learned in engineering classes is good for highly technical documents in which you have to explain several levels of detail and you have to number the details. Unfortunately, this system becomes more difficult when you add more levels of details. It is too distracting for most engineering documents. If you have more than two decimal points, you're into number abuse and reader abuse. The following combination of *numbered* steps and *unnumbered* third-level subpoints (which are in italics) works smoothly:

5. Start the engine.
   5.1 Put the key into the ignition.
   5.2 Depress the clutch.
   5.3 Turn the key and step lightly on the gas pedal, then let up on the gas.

6. Engage the transmission.
   6.1 Check your rearview mirrors and look to the side to make sure the road is clear.
   6.2 Put the gear lever into first gear, step lightly on the gas, and slowly release the clutch.

   Learning to coordinate depressing the gas pedal and releasing the clutch will take a little practice. If you release the clutch too quickly, your car will buck and may even stall. If you let the clutch out slowly but step too hard on the gas, you'll notice that the scenery on either side of you will pass by quickly. Don't get discouraged. Practice will make perfect.

Note that the action is in plain type, while the background information is in italics.

Avoid Complicated Procedures

Procedures can be complicated by conditional steps or cautions.

To avoid confusing your readers, clarify conditional steps.

Although you will write your procedure in a step-by-step order, you will sometimes have to digress and send your reader on to other steps before proceeding. Such a digression may be needed when more than one possible unexpected situation might prevent the reader from taking a required step. For example:

If the bolt appears to be rusted or frozen to the beam, go to Step 22A before proceeding.

If the power fails during these steps, immediately do the following …

Just remember to bring the reader back from any digressions by saying what post-digression step to take. For example:

Once you've released the bolt, return to Step 28.

Physically and emphatically separate the cautions and warnings from actions and other background information. (Usually a *warning* is more serious than a caution, as a warning alerts a person to a danger that can cause bodily harm or damage the equipment. A *caution* alerts a person that, for example, the equipment may not function properly.) Boxes and large-type bold print are both good ways to emphasize cautions and warnings.

For example, you can put the following warning in bold print:

********************WARNING********************
Live wires can turn human beings into toast.

* * *

Don't touch these wires unless you have pulled the
red lever on the right into the off (down) position.
****

Or you can put the warning in a framed box:

> **WARNING**
>
> **LIVE WIRES**
> **CAN TURN HUMAN BEINGS INTO TOAST.**
>
> **DON'T TOUCH THESE WIRES**
> **UNLESS YOU HAVE PULLED**
> **THE RED LEVER ON THE RIGHT**
> **INTO THE OFF (DOWN) POSITION.**

Don't put action steps into a caution or warning box. Restrict these boxes to a combination of indicative sentences (stating the danger) and negative imperative sentences (stating what *not* to do to avoid the danger).

Always place cautions and warnings immediately before, and on the same page as, the steps they refer to.

Step 3: Write Clear Instructions

Procedure Introductions That Prepare the Reader

What's the first thing you do when you get a new software program? Put it in the computer and start working with it. Do you open the manual? Not unless you get stuck. Do you ever read the introduction to the manual? Probably not. Rarely does anyone else.

So don't waste a lot of time writing the introduction. Keep it short. Say only what the reader will be able to do after reading the procedure. Use the word *you* in the introduction to grab the reader's attention and involve him or her.

This manual will show you how to operate and maintain your Flower-Power automatic seeding system. To proceed, you must be familiar with gas-powered feeding systems. If you are unfamiliar with gas-powered seeding systems, read pages 130 to 139 in the Appendix.

Here's an effective way to phrase a procedure introduction:

This *(manual, procedure, user's guide, instruction sheet)*
will help you to (or will show you how to)
(verb: maintain, operate, install, etc.)
the product.

Next, tell your reader what he needs to know to proceed and where to get that information if he doesn't.

Avoid noun-heavy phrasing in your introduction.

With this lawnmower, you are provided the capability to perform the grass-cutting function at an increased level of speed.

Prefer the direct approach:

With this lawnmower, you can cut the grass faster.

Most readers are probably like you. They want to start using the product or performing the task, not start reading the documentation. Get them to the task at hand as quickly as possible by keeping your introductions short.

Why Make It Easy for the Reader?

Reading requires concentration. Reading a procedure to comprehend it requires deep concentration: a lot of brain power. If an instruction is unclear, the brain has to work out the logic of the sentence. This extra effort appropriates brain power from the concentration effort—stalling the effort and significantly hindering communication efficiency.

That brain-power stall conjures up a variation of the old television anti-drug ad that shows (1) a shell-less, uncooked egg in a cold frying pan and (2) the same egg sizzling in a hot frying pan:

(1) This is your brain. (2) This is your brain reading a procedure.

Make the procedure-reading task easy to let the reader concentrate fully on the content of each step, not on the wording. Conserve your reader's brain power.

Use Imperative Sentences for Clarity

We cannot overemphasize that the key to writing clear, concise manuals and procedures is to use imperative sentences. Nothing is more important in procedure-steps writing than using imperative sentences. You can create a stunningly readable format with fabulous four-color graphics and picturesque pull-out charts, but if your prose plods along in turgid, ponderous, passive voice, your procedure will be as useful as an umbrella in a hurricane.

Imperative sentences, always written in second person, are automatically *you*-oriented. That's why they hold the reader's attention. They involve the reader and focus attention on what to do now. They don't concern themselves with what should be done, could be done, or may be done. Imperative sentences are concerned with what's happening *right now*. Imperative sentences tell it like it is.

Don't leave your readers hanging in limbo, wondering what to do next. In no uncertain terms, tell them what to do: "Shut the door." "Take out the trash." "Live free or die!"

Remember, cookbooks are a lot easier to read than software manuals. So whenever you write any type of procedure, just pretend you are writing a cookbook. Give explicit directions to the reader on how to proceed.

By all means, avoid the word *should*. Delete the word from your procedure vocabulary. If you say something "should be done," a reader can interpret that to mean one of three things:

▶ It has already been done by, for example, the manufacturer.

▶ Previous steps the reader took have rendered it already done.

▶ It still has to be done by somebody.

But by whom? The passive-voice construction doesn't say who has to do it or who already did it.

Compare the two following sets of instructions. The first is one solid paragraph of mostly passive voice. The second uses imperative sentences for all action items and has a format that helps the reader quickly distinguish actions from background information.

Site Preparation

Areas of unstable subgrade must be corrected before processing starts. Unstable subgrade soils can generally be detected by observing their stability under the wheels of the motor grader as it shapes the area prior to soil-cement processing. When in-place soils are used, the final cross-section will be influenced by the grade at the start of construction. Therefore, before any processing is started, the roadway should be shaped to approximate crown and grade. Maintenance of crown and grade prior to soil-cement construction will permit rapid runoff of water during heavy rains and is good insurance against developing wet spots. Soil-cement street processing is facilitated by removing manhole covers and frames and covering the holes with sheet metal or planks just below the depth to be processed. After the final finishing but before the soil cement has hardened, the manhole frames and covers are replaced. Soil cement is then hand-tamped to a maximum density around the structure, or ready-mixed concrete is placed and finished to grade.

In the following suggested revision, note that the instructions are all imperative and the background-information sentences are all indicative, indented, and italicized. That clear-cut combination makes the revised procedure easier to follow than the original.

1. Correct areas of unstable subgrade before starting the processing.

   You can detect unstable subgrade soils by observing their stability under the wheels of the motor grader as it shapes the area prior to soil-cement processing. When in-place soils are used, the grade at the start of construction will influence the final cross-section.

2. Shape the roadway to approximate crown and grade before starting any processing.

   By maintaining the crown and grade prior to soil-cement construction, you will permit rapid water runoff during heavy rains and prevent wet spots.

3. Remove manhole covers and frames, and cover the holes with sheet metal or planks just below the depth to be processed.

4. Replace the manhole frames and covers after the final finishing but before the soil cement has hardened. Then hand-tamp the soil cement to a maximum density around the structure, or place ready-mixed concrete and finish it to grade.

Take Advantage of Current Technology

Some companies now have their procedure manuals on the companies' internal computer networks, so users can view various manual sections that include cross-references to other sections or other documents in the company. If your procedure will be used in this way, make sure that it fits the format of the software program used on your company's network.

Step 4: Test Your Procedure

After you've written your procedure, test it. Give it to people who are not familiar with the procedure and ask them to review it for you. Specifically ask them, "What steps did I omit?"

Why? Because you did omit some. It's one of Murphy's Laws for procedure writing. Being so close to the procedure, you have probably omitted a step that seems obvious to you. Well, it's not obvious to the reader. So don't feel bad when your reviewer comes back and says, "I think you missed a step."

Easy-to-Use Manuals

No type of engineering writing is more maligned than manual writing. But, alas, it is maligned for good reason: Too many technical manuals are trash.

The inability of some VCR manufacturers to produce a readable user's manual has become a standard joke for stand-up comics and cartoonists. Today's reader is more sophisticated than readers of a few years ago. Today's reader knows that it's not his fault that he can't program his VCR. He figures it's because the manufacturer hired a dolt to write the manual. Unfair as that perception sounds, that's what your reader will think if your manual isn't easy to follow.

Manufacturers' resistance to writing a useful manual never ceases to amaze us. Yes, it takes time to produce a good manual. Yes, it costs money to produce a good manual. So what? Any good product takes time and money to produce. That's the cost of doing business. If you write a manual that only technical experts can understand, you have severely limited the market for your product.

Writing a clear manual is an act of common courtesy. It's also smart business. Consider computer software manuals, for example.

▶ A well-written, easy-to-use manual will help sell the product to sophisticated customers who compare similar software and buy the package having the easiest-to-read manual. Since the world has a lot more nontechnical users than techies and hackers, a user-friendly manual will thus increase your market.

▶ A well-written, easy-to-use manual will reduce costly after-sale support.

▶ A well-written, easy-to-use manual will encourage customers to speak highly of the product, thereby producing the best advertising: word-of-mouth.

Writing a clear, useful manual is not that difficult to do. It takes time and effort, but it is doable. If you approach the job sensibly, writing a good manual can be a very rewarding experience.

How to Produce a Well-Written Manual

As an engineer, you can be involved in manual writing in one of two ways: As a collaborator or as the chief writer.

Most product manuals are produced by a team headed by a chief writer who gathers information from the engineers who designed, developed, birthed, nurtured, and groomed the product. The *writer* is responsible for two of the three components of a manual: writing and design. The *collaborators* are responsible for the third: information.

The collaborators will also act as reviewers of the manual, as possibly will a manager who is not necessarily a collaborator. What you now have is a committee.

Perhaps you're beginning to see why so many manuals are useless. As far as being readable, any committee-produced document has more chances of failure than success, unless the committee has a strong writer leading the project. If any of the three crucial components (writing, design, information) are bad, the manual's best use will be as a doorstop.

When You're the Chief Writer

Let's assume you are the chief writer of a manual. From the outset, you have to grasp and maintain *control* of the project.

▶ Meet with your project team and get everyone to agree about—and fully understand—the manual's purpose right from the start.

▶ Assign individual responsibilities. Who will provide technical documentation in what form and when? Who will be interviewed? Which people will review the final draft?

- ▶ Set up deadlines, and make sure your people adhere to them.
- ▶ Diplomatically ask your collaborators (and reviewers) to review the manual for *content*, not *style*. Style is the way an individual writer expresses an idea. Five people can take the same information, write about it, and each will have presented the information differently, because they each have a different style of writing. Thus, your request to review for content is very important. If all collaborators review for style, you'll end up with as many styles as there are collaborators.
- ▶ Explain that you, as the chief writer, have the last word on style.

The major problem with committee writing is that too many members think they have final *approval*, not final *review*. Approval must reside with the chief writer. Otherwise, the manual will read as though it were written by a committee. A manual that reads as though it were written by a committee is often next to useless, because most committees don't edit for content; they edit for style.

Make sure you establish at the beginning that you, as the chief writer, will have final editing authority. Collaborators approve the content, but the writer approves the writing.

Dilbert reprinted by permission of United Features Sydicate, Inc.

When You're a Collaborator

If you are a collaborator working with a chief writer, your primary responsibility is *information*. As team members, you and the writer have to focus on the same goal: to produce a manual that a reader can use. Therefore, you have to view all your information from the reader's perspective. If you can adopt a reader's-point-of-view attitude, you'll start giving quality information to the writer from the get-go.

Here's what the writer will be looking for:

▶ An overview of the product and what it does (not how it does it)

▶ What the product does better than the competition's product

▶ Why the product is significant

▶ How customers will use the product

▶ The features, advantages, and benefits of the product

For example, a new car has power steering (a feature), which allows easier driving (an advantage), which means less fatigue and increased safety (a benefit).

When you are working with the chief writer, keep in mind that the writer didn't design the product. This stuff may all be new to him or her. You're very close to the product, because you've been living with it for so long. Assume the manual writer is intelligent but not knowledgeable—just as the reader will be. Give the writer useable information. Don't throw down a bunch of specs and flowcharts and say, "Everything's in there."

Is an overview of the product in there? Are the competitive advantages interpreted and clearly pointed out in there? Are the features, advantages, and benefits clearly stated in there? That's what the writer needs, but that information is usually not included in specs.

Don't expect the writer to translate jargon into English. That's your job. Write your information for a nontechnical reader.

The writer will also need the name and function of each part and its relationship to other parts.

Furnish diagrams, charts, flowcharts and any existing literature on the product, but take the time to explain the information they hold in terms that your reader will understand.

When You're a Reviewer

As we said earlier, the writer is in charge of the writing style. Therefore, when you, as a collaborator, review a draft, review it for content, not style. You do your job and let the writer do his or hers.

And now, for your entertainment and edification, excerpts from some actual real-life procedures:

What NOT to Write in Procedures

Repeat the previous two steps until you get it right.

Ensure that the main power circuit breaker has been switched to the OFF position as indicated in the procedure referred to in the previous step prior to proceeding.

If the short condition is outside the system unit, remove it.

Type 4 to see what 4 does.

Aarrggh! (Fade.)

Yes, you can write better procedures than that.

Summary of This Chapter's Main Points

▶ Five types of procedure guides differ in their detail level and in their intended reader's knowledge level:

Type of Guide	Length	Main Type of Reader
Instruction Sheet	short	beginner-advanced
Standard Operating Procedure	medium	beginner
Operations Manual	long	knowledgeable
Tutorial	short-medium	beginner
Reference Manual	long	moderate-advanced

▶ Divide the procedure-writing project into four steps:

Step 1: Collect the data.

Step 2: Organize your procedure.

Step 3: Write clear instructions.

Step 4: Test your procedure by asking someone, "What did I omit?"

▶ As the chief manual writer, grasp and maintain control of the project.

▶ As a manual collaborator, be sure to give the chief writer readable information.

▶ As a manual reviewer, review for content, not style.

16 Designing Practical Data Sheets

The Data Sheet as a Useful Sales Tool

One of the most useful documents a company publishes is the data sheet about a technical product. Useful data sheets *bring in* money; useless ones *cost* money.

You may have already written so many data sheets that you can write them standing on your head. If so, right yourself, and use this chapter as a quick recap of how to develop and use this valuable engineering sales tool.

The data sheet is a pre-sale document, at the technical level. Its readers are engineers and other technical experts, not presidents of companies. Presidents rely on the technical staff to evaluate the technical aspects of a product. Thus, the data sheet can sometimes replace a brochure.

Salespeople, too, use data sheets to answer technical questions. Whether the product is a new, high-performance car or an HVAC application menu with auxiliary software, prospective buyers or their technical people want to see the specifications (specs) of a product. A data sheet supplies those specs.

Let's say your largest corporate customer, AOE Company, bought your company's Wonder Widget a year ago but now wants to upgrade. AOE's president asks the internal technical experts—the AOE engineers—which upgrade is best. It just so happens that the AOE engineers are on the way out the door to attend your industry's trade show. They make it a point to compare the upgrade versions at the show.

For their comparison, the AOE engineers need to know the specs of your upgraded Wonder Widget before recommending your upgrade over another. They visit your company's booth at the trade show and ask your sales representative a few detailed questions.

Here's where the data sheet comes in handy. Your sales rep, who knows generally about the product but not all the technical details, wisely offers the product's data sheet. The AOE engineers immediately turn the data sheet over and read the specifications on the back. If the data sheet is well designed, the readers can quickly compare your upgrade to the competing ones. Numbers, tables, listed features, suggested applications, and captioned photos help simplify the comparison. Over a post-show pizza, the AOE engineers agree that your upgrade beats the competition technically. They call the president and recommend purchasing the Wonder Widget upgrade. Congratulations!

Though technical, a data sheet is a quick-to-read marketing tool that carries a lot of sales weight for its compact size (often just one two-sided page) and low-key message. It highlights what a technical reader wants to know, without "hyping" the product or company. It's an engineer's dream.

What's Your Role in Data-Sheet Design?

In a small firm, you may have the jack-of-all-trades assignment of helping the sales manager write the data sheet. As the firm grows and/or as new staff members come on board, technical writers may take over writing the data sheet. These specialized people can then benefit from your data-sheet writing experience.

In your own company, the marketing group may write the single-page, two-sided data sheets, especially if the two-sider is a general sheet to accompany the detailed, small-booklet-form data sheets. If you're an applications engineer, you're more likely to write the more detailed data sheets that your fellow engineers scrutinize at trade shows.

Time–Wasting Traps to Avoid

Whether you're familiar with data-sheet writing or new to it, the better you understand the data-sheet design traps and the elements of a successful data sheet, the easier your writing task will be.

Avoid these two main data-sheet design traps:

▶ too much information crammed into one data sheet

▶ too few application pictures and captions

Let's take those traps one at a time.

The first trap, like an information overload, can short-circuit your message and extinguish your reader's glimmer of interest. Avoid redundant details and large, wordy blocks of "gray" text (big paragraphs without breaks to rest the eyes). Otherwise, you will defeat the data sheet's purpose, which is *quick reference*.

The second trap, directly related to the first, is a lack of illustrations to capture the reader's interest. If you crowd the data sheet with too much text, you use up the space needed to show the product in action. Then the page looks just like a cluttered gray blur, with no room to actually picture the applications that prove the product's usefulness.

Sections and Style of a Useful Data Sheet

What to Include

Avoid overloading a data sheet. Ask yourself, "What can I realistically put in?" The drawings and specs are more important than overly detailed descriptions. To avoid making the content "fluffy," ask yourself, "What is this product? What does it do?" Then include its key features.

Focus on the *product*, not on the company.

The front page must help market the product's features and benefits through brief paragraphs of well-controlled sentences containing concrete, what's-in-it-for-the-buyer terms. The back page, usually in tabulated-column format, includes few, if any, sentences; bold-type subheads and key-word descriptions are routine.

A data sheet—even a one-page, two-sided one—usually includes the following key elements:

▶ your company's name and logo

▶ the product name(s)

▶ product description: the product's function, features, and applications (uses)—with a low-key *marketing* orientation

▶ illustration(s): photos, diagrams, tables, charts, graphs, and/or flowcharts

▶ product specifications (product numbers, measurements, and any other numbers to let readers easily compare your product with competing products)—with an engineering orientation

▶ ordering information

As silly as this sounds, don't forget to include all the ordering information: your company's phone number, any TWX and Telex numbers, fax number, full mailing address, E-mail address (if applicable), and any part numbers or ordering-code numbers.

Yes, we have seen costly data sheets that—sadly—lack any ordering information. Proofreaders sometimes read the text carefully but forget to check what's outside the text lines. Engineers who pick up those incomplete data sheets at trade shows may not make the effort to track down the exact group that can answer questions or take orders. A small omission like that can make an otherwise-useful data sheet useless.

What Style Pleases Data-Sheet Readers

Use a concise, no-nonsense style in a readable page layout. This is no time for vague, wordy, or flowery descriptions. Keep the page uncluttered. Data sheets are compact couriers of the product's key points.

Write product descriptions that tell which product features do what for the customer, in what way. In other words, include subtle benefits—not in a glitzy way, but in a low-key, credible style. Clearly explain the product's physical features, equipment connections, and available options; include key words about the purposes of all those. To break up the "gray blocks" of production-description copy, divide long paragraphs into subtopic paragraphs, and use subheadings.

To create useful subheadings, include positive words that highlight the desirability (benefits) of the key features. For example, study these subheads that a technical writer created for a new-pump data sheet:

Reliable Performance

Selectable Flow Rates to Optimize Your Solvent Delivery Needs

Upper and Lower Pressure Limits for Safety

The Best Value in LPXX Pumps

New Customer-Service Kit

Wait. Reread those previous five lines. What positive words do you see in that sub-heads list? Underline them before you read on.

Did you find at least seven positive words in that list?

If you underlined at least *reliable, optimize, your, safety, best, value,* and *new,* good for you.

Whether you're writing or reviewing your company's data sheets, remember that you can't tell everything. Let your specs serve as the back-up data. Tell the key features, and translate the features into benefits that appeal to your technical readers.

Page-Design Tips

Two-color or four-color data sheets on heavy paper stock are the norm for a two-sided data sheet. For data sheets exceeding one two-sided page, you will probably use lighter-weight (and less costly) paper. Prefer paper that a reader can write on, for your customer's convenience.

If you have a good designer, you can do a lot with just two colors. A four-color data sheet costs more, because the printer does separate color runs (putting the sheets back through the printer after the previous ink color has dried). If the printer must wash the equipment and change ink colors between the color runs, you get charged for that extra time.

With four colors, though, you can use color-keyed icons for different modules, or you can use colored graph lines that compare and contrast details effectively. If your competitors use four-color data sheets, you may need to do the same for a competitive image.

Use bold type for main headings, subheadings, and the specs-list subtopic headings. Make the headings and subheadings slightly larger than the text that follows them. Allow enough white space to ensure an appealing, uncluttered page layout.

Leave room in the left margin for punched holes for a three-ring binder. Leave an equally wide right margin on the back side of a two-sided sheet—and on the inside-left pages of a multiple-page data sheet.

If you have specific questions about page design and layout, the best person to ask is your graphic designer.

A Flexible, Customer-Friendly Format

To ensure an easy-to-read format, just picture your customers, especially the engineers on their teams, reading the data sheet. Sure, they want to read about all the whiz-bang features, but they also want to see pictures of the Wonder Widget upgrade in action. And they want to read captions that sum up or interpret the illustrations.

Include a diagram or photo of the product being used, or add a flowchart showing the product's role in a larger system. Even simple line drawings of icons can make the point while allowing enough open space to rest the reader's eyes.

Following are the most common options for data-sheet format.

The Two-Page Format

The two-page, heavy-stock data sheet is standard but can be expanded to suit the number of features, applications, and photos needed for credibility or appeal. Many current two-page data sheets have an appealing features-and-benefits focus with graphs and charts, rather than a rigid (and some say "drier") specifications-columns format. The less rigid data sheet serves as an overview to precede or accompany a four-page or longer data sheet that includes the full specifications columns.

One marketing-communications director of a computer-software company calls her group's two-sided, four-color page a "sparkle sheet" because of its colorful design, glossy stock, and features-and-benefits focus.

This two-page format (meaning a single sheet printed on both sides) usually includes these elements:

Page l (front page):

► the company name (without address or phone number)

► the product name

► brief paragraphs about benefits (such as "saves you from manually entering design data") and functions/capabilities in various environments

► bulleted lists of technical features

► list of system requirements, if applicable

► small photo or diagram, perhaps showing the product in use; simple table or flowchart for fast reading

Page 2 (back page):

► specifications (model/part numbers, measurements, often in two or more columns for variables and selected details)

Note: The sparkle-sheet form of data sheet can include a graph or other comparative illustration instead of specifications columns.

Tip: For added objectivity, one small Silicon Valley software company also includes (with its two-page data sheet) a reprint of *InfoWorld* magazine's one-page "Report Card" that compares selected scores/specs of that company's products and competitors' products, side-by-side. A marketing-communications contact says, "The engineers love that report-card approach."

► the company name, mailing address(es), phone and fax numbers, and any other ordering information

► copyright/trademark information

(Samples of two-page data sheets are in Figures 16.1(a) through 16.1(d).)

Variation on the Two-Page Data Sheet

If your product has many appealing features that can be categorized under a few strong benefits, you might delete the benefits paragraphs and specifications, instead using the space for several subheads that tell the benefits, such as "Fast and Easy Flowcharting." Under each subhead, you can list key words of the features that achieve the benefit. An added subhead can then be "System Requirements."

Just don't forget to highlight the benefits.

Figure 16.1(a). Sample of Two-Sided (Single-Page) Data Sheet
(originally printed in four colors on glossy stock)

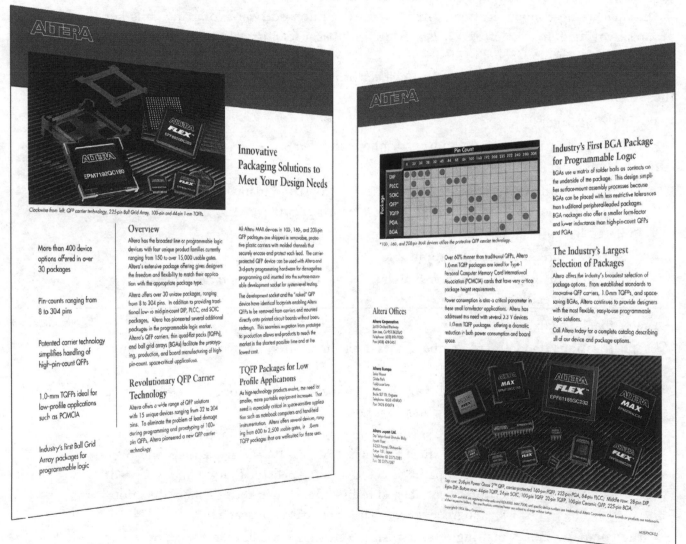

Front side of a data sheet   Back side of the same data sheet

The Four-Page Format

If your other customers are already heaping praise on your Wonder Widget upgrade, the data sheet might be expanded to four pages (four sides total). That format allows room to include descriptions and illustrations of several customers' recent applications, when available. (See Figure 16.2 for an example.)

Figure 16.1(b). Sample of Two-Sided (Single-Page) Data Sheet

(originally printed in two colors)

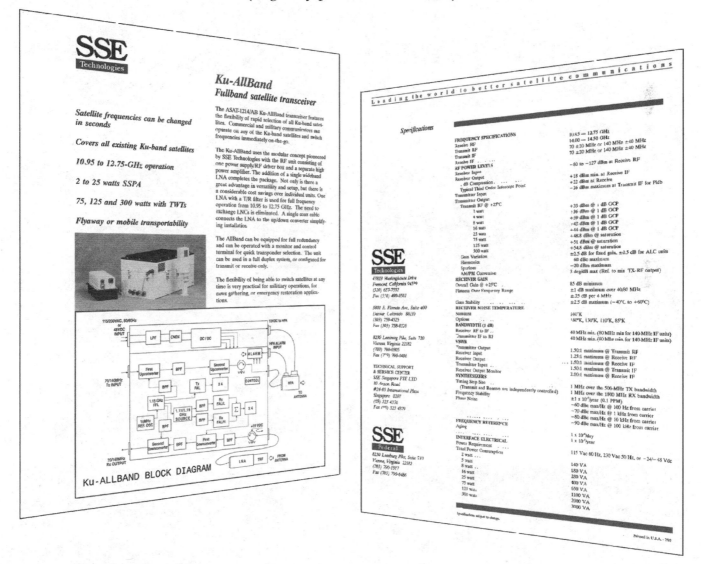

Front side of a data sheet   Back side of the same data sheet

Reprinted with permission from Penny Hill for SSE Technologies, 47823 Westinghouse Drive, Fremont, CA 94539, 1993.

When deciding what to include where, you have some flexibility on the inside pages and back page. The specs can go inside or on the back, often depending on how many offices and other ordering information you need to include on the back page. A sample list of what to put where on the four-pager appears in Figure 16.2.

Figure 16.1(c). Sample of Two-Sided (Single-Page) Data Sheet
(originally printed in four colors)

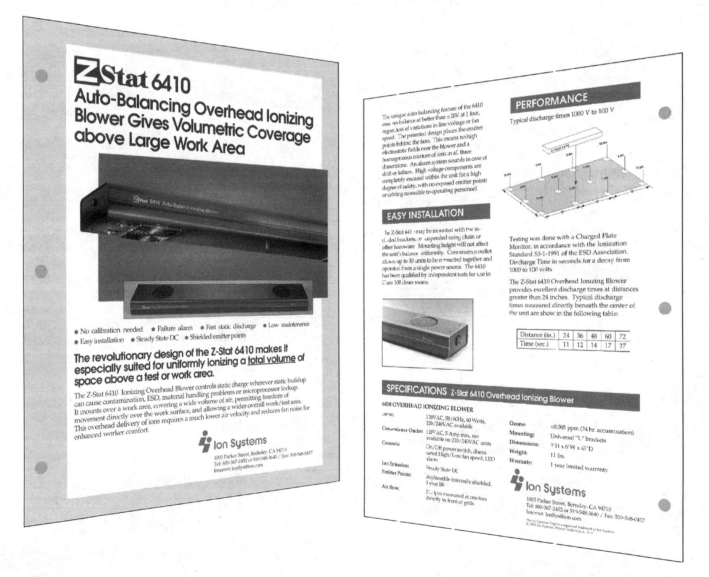

Front side of a data sheet   Back side of the same data sheet

Reprinted with permission from Ion Systems, 1005 Parker Street, Berkeley, CA 94710.

Page 1 (front cover):

▶ the company name (Wonder Widget Corporation)

▶ the product name (No-Dial Digital Widget)

▶ (optional) data-sheet publication date (month, year) and data-sheet version number

Figure 16.1(d). Sample of Two-Sided (Single-Page) Data Sheet
(originally printed in two colors)

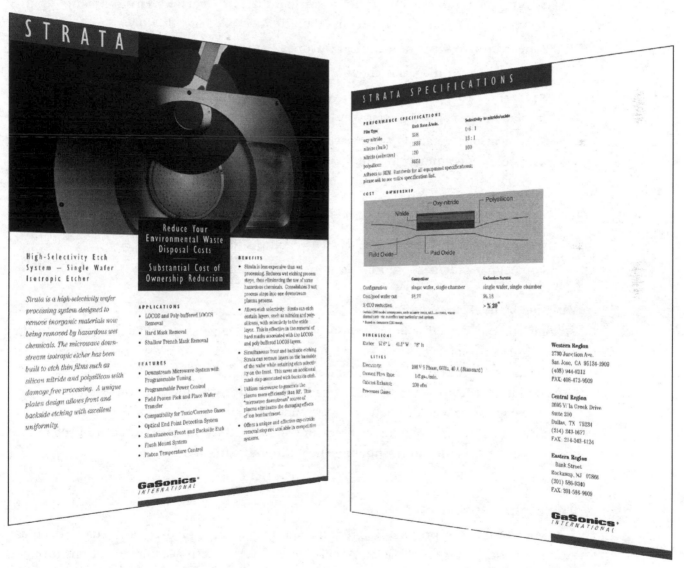

Front side of a data sheet   Back side of the same data sheet

Reprinted with permission from GaSonics International, 2730 Junction Avenue, San Jose, CA 95134–1909.

▶ a small photo or drawing of the product, preferably in a likely environment

▶ a photo caption summarizing the applications in a few key words, such as, "A low-cost widget for data, voice, and video"

▶ several brief summary paragraphs telling:
  — what the product does ("helps your team do hands-free tests")
  — a few key features ("high-security voice pads, user-friendly command prompts, and flashing recharge signal"), in bulleted-list form
  — the product's benefits ("helps your department double the speed of transmission")

Pages 2 and 3 (inside pages):

▶ subtopic sections about functions/capabilities in various environments—fuller paragraphs or more listed benefits than the two-page layout allows

▶ longer bulleted lists of technical features, with tables, charts, or graphs

▶ small photos or diagrams showing the product in use

▶ several customer applications, with results (if applicable), to help potential customers see how the product would work in their own similar environment

▶ specifications detailing the measurements, components, accessories, and variations available, in columnar format for easy comparison

Page 4 (outside back cover):

▶ the company name, mailing address, phone, fax, and other ordering information (such as sales and regional offices with addresses and phones)

▶ copyright/trademark information

Variation on the Four-Page Format

Some companies add *separate* product-applications sheets to the data sheets, instead of detailing the applications in a four-sided data sheet. The separate applications sheets may be most appropriate for sales-binder use.

The more literature your sales staff has as a resource, the fewer questions you may get from the engineers who evaluate your product for its technical and practical features. Or, if your company's more-extensive literature grabs the buying-level interest of the reader, you may get *more* questions, showing the willingness to buy.

The Eight-Page Format

If your product or product line requires more detailed explanation, the data sheet may run 8, 12, 24, 76, or more pages. According to one marketing-communications director, "The maximum depends on the product or the product family—and on how many pages your printing vendor can physically staple together."

(A sample eight-page brochure is in Figure 16.3.)

Figure 16.2. Sample of Four-Sided Data Sheet
(originally printed in one color—black—with gray shades)

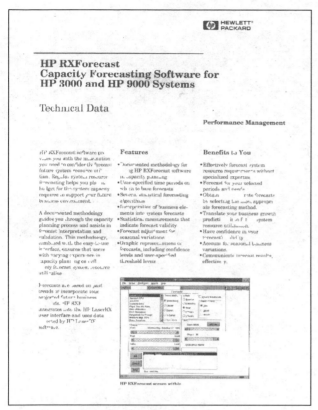

Page 1 (front cover)

Page 2 (inside left page)

Page 3 (inside right page)

Page 4 (outside back cover)

Figure 16.3.   Sample of Eight-Page Data Sheet
(originally printed as a two-color folder)

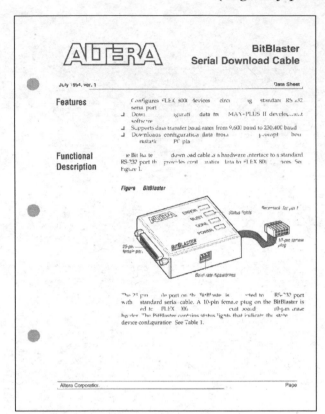

Page 1 (front cover)

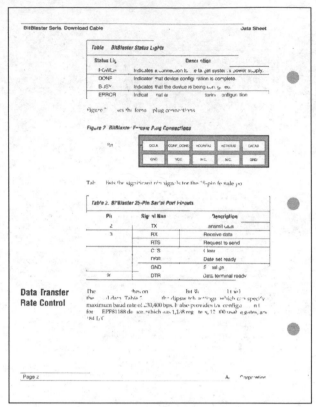

Page 2 (inside page)

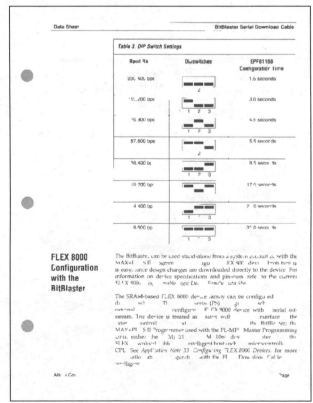

Page 3 (inside page)

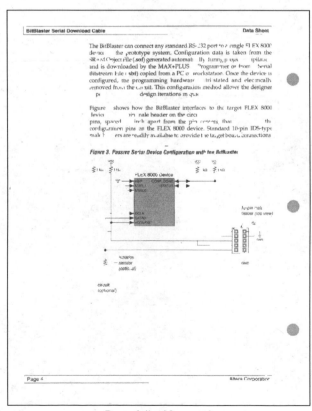

Page 4 (inside page)

Figure 16.3. Sample of Eight-Page Data Sheet
(continued)

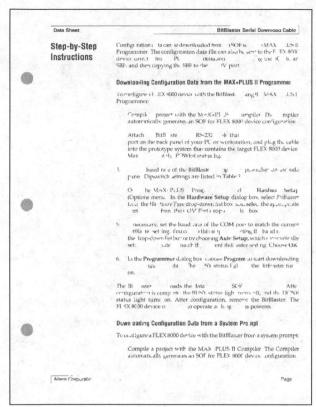

Page 5 (inside page)

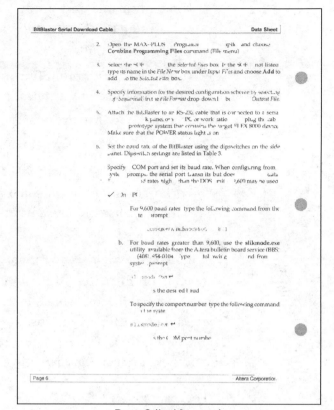

Page 6 (inside page)

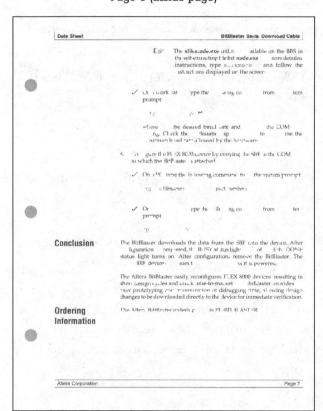

Page 7 (inside page)

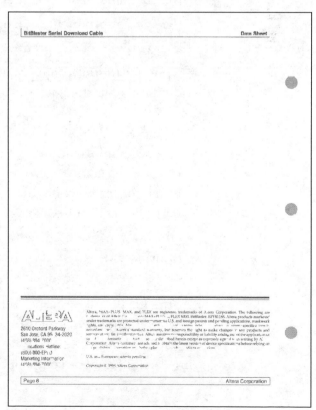

Page 8 (outside back cover)

Reprinted with permission from Altera Corporation, 2610 Orchard Parkway, San Jose, CA 95134-2020, 1994.

For now let's consider one form of the eight-page format. For a *single* product needing multiple subtopics or a variety of illustrations, the data sheet might include these sections:

▶ company name and product name, with the data-sheet publication date (month, year) and data-sheet version number

▶ features, in a bulleted list

▶ functional description (including product photo and perhaps tables and other figures introduced by subheadings, to show subsets of specs)

▶ step-by-step instructions (such as for configuring a device)

▶ conclusion (such as what happens when the configuration is complete)

▶ ordering information (such as the product's ordering code)

▶ corporate information (such as main-office and sales-office addresses, phone numbers, trademark/copyright information)

Variation on the Eight-Page Format

If your product line is a *family* of five Wonder Widget modules or components, the data sheet may become an eight-page *packet*, actually a flexible technical brochure about the product, with pull-out inserts—each insert a data sheet on a module or component of the product line. The outside pages may be a folder (the front cover and back cover) including more general marketing information about the product and the company.

For example, the front cover might include just four items:

▶ the company name (Wonder Widget Corporation)

▶ the type of product (no-dial digital widgets), with or without the product names

▶ a large photo of the product line

▶ a photo caption summarizing the applications in a few key words, such as, "No-dial digital widgets for data, voice, and video"

The back cover (page 8) might include:

▶ corporate information: your company's address, phone, trademark/copyright information, perhaps a list of sales offices and distributors, background (the product's former ordering code, the company's expertise, a brief global-service story, or other pertinent corporate items)

▶ (alternative use of page 8, for a single product:) the specifications and ordering information—especially if you want to include a lot of application stories in the center pages of the document

For the inside pages (pages 2 through 7) of the packet, you have two common options: First, you might include product information—the hard data: sections and subtopic paragraphs about the functions, features, and benefits of the product family, perhaps giving each module or component its own page.

For example, these subheadings (after a full-page photograph of the product) tell what information composes pages 3 through 7 of an eight-page data sheet for open-network satellite modems:

Features (a one-page bulleted list with lots of white space)

Function

Applications

Description (available versions; physical terms about connections to and accommodations of other equipment)

Operating Rates

Monitor and Control

Redundancy (to protect critical data paths; not redundant wording)

Most of the internal pages of the above "modems" example include a product photo or diagram; all have the company's logo in the top-right corner.

Your second option, instead of putting product information in the inside pages, is to let pages 2 and 7 be blank inside covers, with just a bottom flap to hold four data sheets (each one-page, two-sided), which your sales reps can lift out or supplement.

You can use a series of customized data sheets, showing a different application featured on each sheet, to suit the application a reader might use. (That's like the common practice of having several versions of a résumé, varying the highlighted items to suit the desired job.) This format is adaptable to various customers' needs and applications, and although it costs more initially, it may cost less in the long run.

The cost advantage is that if you change only the unseen product features, you can redo the inside data sheets without having to absorb the additional cost of redesigning the outside folder. Although such a consideration is not usually an engineer's concern, you can score points with the writer, the designer, and your manager by seeing the broader picture of designing a useful data sheet.

The Data Book: A Data–Sheet Superset for One-Stop Reading

Some companies publish a data book (not just individual data sheets) for customers. The data book, actually a "superset" of data sheets, includes not only the data sheets on all the company's products, but also the addresses and phone numbers of all the sales reps and distributors of those products. The size of the data book depends on the number of products the company makes. Standard or thinner paper stock, not the heavy card stock of single data sheets, works most compactly and cost efficiently for the book pages.

The length of a data book can run 150 to 1,000 pages.

For example, one high-tech firm that produces 10 product lines published a data book containing nearly 450 pages. Although one of the company's special products required a separate 17-page data sheet, which was duplicated in the book, most other products in the book had data sheets comprising only 2 to 6 pages. That data book is updated every two years. Between printings, the company also offers a few separate data sheets for new or special products.

How to Capitalize on Your Data-Sheet Work

If you collaborate on, review, or write the data sheets or data book at your company, you're working to improve the bottom line. Presenting technical information cost effectively is a key accomplishment.

If you know that your data-sheet work helped inspire a customer to order from your company rather than from a competitor, that's something you can capitalize on. Mention your data-sheet contribution and its results in your monthly report to your manager. That can't hurt you when your manager reviews your monthly reports later at performance-review time.

Summary of This Chapter's Main Points

▶ View the data sheet as a technical document that is also a useful marketing and sales tool.
  — Sales reps use data sheets to answer pre-sale technical questions about your company's products.
  — Engineers use the data sheet to compare competing products.

▶ Avoid the two main data-sheet design traps:
  — too much information crammed into one data sheet
  — too few application pictures and captions

▶ Include the following information in a data sheet:
  — your company's name and logo
  — the product name(s)
  — the product description(s) (function, features, and applications) in low-key marketing terms
  — illustrations
  — product specifications (part or product numbers, measurements) in engineering terms
  — ordering information

▶ Use a concise, no-nonsense style in a readable page format. Put positive words, highlighting benefits, into subheadings for key features.

▶ Keep pages uncluttered. Vary the layout (and the number of pages) to suit the product.

17 Publish and Prosper

The Rewards of Publishing

Writing for publication can be a rewarding experience, both financially and emotionally.

Publishing an article or presenting a conference paper can help you move up the corporate ladder. The corporate folk often look kindly on engineers who are willing to take the time to write an article or present a paper.

We say "take the time" because, if your company is typical, you would probably have to write articles on your own time, not on the job.

How Your Article Benefits Your Company

Many companies view articles as a necessary marketing tool and encourage their engineers to write. The companies often offer incentives: cash, products, vacation time, or some other rewards. What makes your effort attractive to the corporate troops is that you're helping to sell your company's product when you get an article published or present a conference paper. And since selling is usually not part of your job description, your corporate executives appreciate your efforts.

How Your Article Benefits You Personally

In addition to pleasing the marketing people, though, publishing also bestows personal benefits. Through an article, you acquire notoriety within your field. Suddenly, you're famous—maybe for only 15 minutes, but what the hey, it's still fame. If you know enough to write an article or present a paper, people perceive you as an expert. That's good for your ego and your image, and maybe even for your wallet.

Better yet, publishing also brings you a hidden benefit: When you publish a paper or an article, you plant a seed of knowledge outside your work cubicle. The seed blooms and produces more ideas you can harvest.

> *"I have heard that nothing gives an author so great pleasure, as to find his works respectfully quoted by other learned authors."*
>
> —Benjamin Franklin
> American public official,
> writer, printer, and scientist
> (1706–1790)

When other engineers read your article, you'll receive letters and phone calls from those who agree or disagree with you. Either way, you'll get input that furthers your knowledge and enhances your expertise. Essentially, you expand your intelligence network and make some new friends in the process.

Where to Get Ideas

Your best source of ideas is your own experience. What project are you currently working on? Why is it interesting or unique? Is it an advancement or enhancement of technology? Why? How does it solve a larger engineering problem?

Let's say you have the germ of an idea for an article. Your next step is to clarify your idea in your mind and determine whether you have a marketable idea. Use a planning sheet, as we discussed in Chapter 3, to help yourself through this preliminary "soft-thinking" stage.

How Your Lead Can Sell Your Article

Once your idea is clear to you, write the lead of your article, but no more. You're going to use this lead to sell your article. (See Chapter 4, on leads.)

The Twofold Purpose of Your Article Lead

The purpose of the lead in a magazine article differs from your routine report leads. Your lead must not only orient your magazine readers but also grab their attention. Remember, your article will compete with other articles in the magazine.

Avoid *"being*-pattern" sentences and *being* verbs. Prefer *"action*-pattern" sentences and strong *action* verbs. Remember: The subject-verb-object order produces clear, lively sentences. (See Chapter 6.) Don't say what a product *is designed to do*. Say what it *does*.

Instead of:

> Oxygen-enriched air *is* a pollutant reducer in a variety of combustion processes.

Write:

> Oxygen-enriched air *can reduce* pollution in a variety of combustion processes.

Instead of:

> California *is* well known for its abundant and diverse mineral resources.

Write:

> For more than 12,000 years, Native Californians *have been using* the area's mineral resources for their daily needs.

If possible, put a benefit into your lead.

Instead of: (acceptable sentence, but no benefit)

In today's motion control and factory automation systems, laser sensors that measure and profile distances such as depth, height, and thickness play an increasingly critical role.

(Source: Robert J. Dwulet, "Cutting Costs with Laser Triangulation," *Machine Design*, November 7, 1994, Penton Publishing, Inc., Cleveland, OH, p. 110. With permission.)

Write: (cost-cutting benefit)

By using optical triangulation, today's laser diodes have cut measurement costs from tens of thousands of dollars (for laser interferometers) to about $2,000 for a laser-diode-based sensor.

Why a Good Lead Is Crucial

Writing your lead now will help you clarify your idea and help you focus on what the reader will get out of your article. Readers flipping through a magazine will be attracted by your headline or illustration. Then they will read your opening paragraph to see what information they might get out of the article. If your first paragraph isn't informative enough to orient and interest the readers, they will keep flipping pages.

We cannot overemphasize the importance of a good lead. An effective lead does three things for you:

▶ It focuses your idea in your head.

▶ It sells the editor on your article idea.

▶ It hooks the reader of the magazine.

How to Place Your Article

Once you're happy with your lead, your next job is to find a home for your article. Before you do, though, check with your manager to see if you need corporate clearance to publish your article.

Approach #1: From Engineer Directly to Editor

Check out the publications that you think would be interested in your article. Usually, these are the same publications you read every month. Go to your corporate library and read through *at least six issues* of your chosen magazine. Here's what you're looking for:

1. Does the publication accept freelance material?

    Look for bylines on articles. If all the articles are staff-written, more than likely the publication accepts no freelance material. For example, "Pat Cohen, West Coast Editor" tells you that Pat is a staff writer. However, "Pat Cohen, Design Engineer, Fantastic Widgets Corp." tells you that the magazine accepts freelance material.

2. What kind of articles does the magazine want?

    Reading the articles in past issues will give you the gist of what the magazine likes.

3. How long are the articles?

4. Does the magazine use illustrations? What kind?

Many articles are written around one or more illustrations (charts, diagrams, etc.). Editors like graphics because graphics attract readers.

How Magazine Editors Can Help You

If you see a fit for your article, your next step is to contact the editor of the magazine by sending him or her a query letter and an outline of your article. (See the following sections for more information on outlines and query letters.) Near the front of the magazine you'll find a masthead that lists the magazine's personnel, along with addresses and phone numbers.

Although publications vary, they usually list an editor (or editor-in-chief), a managing editor, and possibly a technical editor. Contact any of these editors. If regional editors are listed, they are the staff members in the hinterlands who cover specific geographical areas. Don't contact them, because they rarely, if ever, make the decisions about freelance material.

If you are still not sure whether you have a marketable idea, ask the publication for an author's guide, which explains the magazine's editorial goals and gives you tips on how to write for that magazine.

How an Outline Can Benefit You

Unless you are an established author who has been published in the magazine before, don't send a completed article. To put a positive spin on a possibly negative outcome, let's just say that it is better to have an outline rejected than to have a completed article rejected, because the outline takes less time to write. So review your planning sheet and develop an outline.

Neatness Counts

Always send in copy that:

▶ is *double-spaced*, never single-spaced

▶ is *typewritten*, never handwritten

▶ has margins of $1\frac{1}{2}$ inches on the left, 1 inch on the right

▶ has no marginal hand-printed insertions

▶ is neat

Always include a self-addressed-stamped envelope (SASE).

Once you have prepared your outline, write a query letter.

How the Query Letter Can Help Sell Your Article

The first paragraph of your query letter must concisely explain your idea. What, then, will you use for your first paragraph of the query letter? What have you already written? That's it—your lead! The lead you wrote is the best opening sentence or paragraph to grab the editor's attention.

Editors are always looking for articles that solve problems and have two ingredients: timeliness and broad reader appeal. So here's what to include in your query letter, limited to one single-spaced page.

1. Explain your idea concisely, and then answer the following questions.
   a. Why is your subject timely?
   b. Why should your subject interest the publication's readers? (Your lead should answer questions a. and b.)
   c. Why will your subject have broad reader appeal?
   d. Why is your information practical? Your article should not be too basic or too theoretical.
   e. Why is your article immediately useful? Unproven theories or results obtained from experimental products not commercially available are usually not acceptable.

   For example, the computer industry has three types of "wares": hardware, software, and vaporware. (*Vaporware* is new hardware or software that has been announced or marketed but not yet produced.) Editors don't buy vaporware stories.

2. Explain how you propose to treat your subject. What problem does your article solve (not, What free advertising are you seeking for your product)? Editors want a *broad* view, so you can't limit your discussion to your company's product.

   You may have to do a little homework and augment your discussion with information about surrounding or similar products.

   You may also want to collaborate on an article with a fellow engineer from your company or with an engineer who is your customer or vendor. Such collaborations are wonderful win-win-win-win situations. You're happy, your collaborator is happy, the editor is happy, and the readers are happy. Such a deal.

3. Support general statements with a few specifics. Since you're still in the preliminary stages of marketing your article, don't overload the editor with details. Stick to the overview. If photos are available for the manuscript, say so, but don't enclose photos or any other artwork with the query letter.

4. Describe your general qualifications for writing the article:
   a. your previous publications
   b. your professional accomplishments (but not your résumé, because editors prefer seeing a brief summary in sentence form)
   c. your unique qualifications for writing about the subject
   (Of all the above, c. is the most important.)

5. Enclose a sample of your published work, if possible, especially if it concerns your topic.

6. Do *not* include irrelevant information such as personal comments about your family, interests, pets, or peeves.

The combination of your outline and your query letter should contain enough concrete information to give the editor a clear idea of your subject and how you plan to deal with it.

What Magazine Editors Want to See

Remember, most magazine editors want *practical* articles that will help their readers *solve a problem*. Few want articles on products only. Many will accept case histories if the cases will help their readers in a practical way. If you have solved a problem in an innovative way that would be useful to other engineers, you've got an article. Editors want articles that will give their readers guidance.

What If Your Article Is Just a Design Brief?

If your idea isn't geared toward a "full-systems" solution and doesn't seem to warrant a long article, don't worry. You can still get published. Many magazines accept short design briefs that describe a product's functions. To find such a magazine, study the publications and the author's guides.

Editors' Likes and Dislikes About Writing Styles

Here's what editors like to see in the writing itself:

- ▶ a strong lead that orients the reader
- ▶ active voice

Here's what editors sometimes receive but don't like:

- ▶ a master's thesis
- ▶ convoluted explanations that don't bring the reader far enough to an easy-to-understand, focused key point
- ▶ jargon
- ▶ an article that wanders aimlessly and does not get to the point
- ▶ an article with no logical structure

Here's what editors often have to revise:

- ▶ passive voice

So if you want to endear yourself quickly to an editor, make sure your article has a strong lead, clear explanations, reader benefits, a coherent structure, no jargon, and lots of active voice. You'll end up making some friends in the publishing business.

Remember, editors need *information* to publish their magazines. Editors are also always looking for *new authors*. Thus, they welcome anyone who has fresh information. You have that information. Don't be afraid to contact an editor directly.

Editors enjoy working with engineers. One editor who has worked on several publication types says he enjoys working with engineers the most, because "they usually don't have ego problems and are easy to work with."

Approach #2: Engineer to PR Department to Editor

To shorten your own article-placement research—and to help ensure that you qualify for any article-writing incentive your company offers—work with your on-site public relations resources.

If your company has a public relations department, take your idea there. The PR specialists can get you on the right track and get you published much faster than you can yourself. They know many of the editors and will help you deal with them. A good public relations staff can be very helpful in bringing your article idea to fruition, so heed the advice of these experts.

Depending on company size and management philosophy, the public relations function in a company can vary from very sophisticated to nonexistent. Many companies have an article-writing program built around strategic products. If your article idea involves a strategic product, you can expect the PR department to help a lot in marketing your article to the appropriate publications.

To sell your idea to your PR department, you can probably just contact someone in the department and describe your idea to get a quick "yes/no; that's a good/bad idea." Yet, you would probably be better to write something that shows your writing ability. Besides, to sell an article idea to an editor, your PR representative needs some facts. Your query letter and an outline will do that job.

How Journal Articles Differ from Magazine Articles

Everything we've discussed so far in this chapter applies to writing and publishing *magazine* articles. Although the process of getting an article published in an engineering *journal* is the same, the journal itself differs from an engineering magazine. Here's how:

Advertising Differences

Engineering journals rarely have advertising and are usually published by an association. Although some engineering magazines are published by associations, the magazines accept and solicit advertising.

Reader Differences

Journal articles, written for a very narrow readership, are usually highly technical and often esoteric. Generally, the only readers who understand journal articles are in the same narrow discipline as the writer.

In contrast, engineering-magazine articles have their targeted readers *and* peripheral readers. For example, a magazine editor wants a design engineer's article to draw the interest of systems engineers, because the solution given in the article might help the systems engineers perform their jobs better. Thus, the magazine editors purposely select articles that appeal to a broader audience. That approach sells magazines.

Editing Differences and Results

Magazine copy editors may freely edit a submitted article—rephrasing awkward sentences and cleaning up mechanical errors such as spelling, punctuation, and typographical glitches. The editing can help the writer's ideas shine more brightly.

In contrast, engineering-journal staffs rarely edit submitted articles. Granted, a journal editor might correct obvious mechanical errors. Yet even those changes can be risky if the editor doesn't fully understand the topic. Editing changes might risk inadvertent content changes in an article.

Herein lies a communication problem for journal-article writers. Overuse of passive voice, which magazine editors snip and clip, usually finds a home in technical journals. Not because it's good phrasing, but because the journal staff—wary of changing the content—resists changing even an unclear passive-voice sentence.

What does all that mean to you, the engineer wanting to share a brilliant idea with the technical world? Just this: If you submit an article to an engineering journal, you can usually expect the journal to publish what you submit, as is. That can be good news or bad news, depending on how carefully you edited your own work before submitting the article. Once it's out there in print, your article represents you. In your moment of fame, make sure that your brilliant idea isn't clouded.

An unedited journal article containing passive voice can send unclear or incomplete messages to journal readers. Left in the dark, the readers might misinterpret the meaning and erroneously misapply the statements to projects back at work. For example, if you say, "Some key timing and layout barriers are broken at the submicron level," the passive phrasing doesn't tell who or what breaks the barriers. The engineer reading the journal can interpret that sentence in several ways and may miss your main message.

Some quick editing could produce a clearer, active-voice sentence: "The new design capability breaks some key timing and layout barriers at the submicron level."

(For examples of other passive-voice versus active-voice sentences, see Chapter 7.)

You can help upgrade the writing in journals by submitting well-edited articles in mostly active voice. The resulting clarity and professional look may also make you a preferred author for a journal.

A P.S. About Understanding Your Editors

Earlier in the book, we discussed the importance of knowing your reader. We said you always have one primary reader, to whom you write, and maybe several secondary readers whom you have to keep in mind. Article writing presents your greatest challenge in determining your primary reader.

Although your primary reader is the magazine reader, the editor is a strong secondary reader. Constantly keep in mind both the editor and the magazine reader as you write.

This writing job is the only one in which you have to split your allegiance. But this splitting is not that difficult to do. Think of the editor as the reader's alter ego. More than anyone else, the editor knows what the magazine's readers like to read. He or she knows the readers' needs and desires. An editor knows the kind of articles that get read and get reactions. The editor is your best friend when it comes to explaining what your article should say and how it should say it.

Therefore, it is to your everlasting advantage to understand who editors are and where they fit in the publication organization. Magazine staffs are divided into two groups: editorial and advertising. In most magazines, the two differ like church and state.

If you suggest or imply to a good editor that if he or she prints your article you can then guarantee advertising dollars, we can guarantee that you will receive nothing but scorn and a fast escort to the exit. Although they need one another to survive, advertising and editorial don't mix. Editors take freedom of the press very seriously and seem to have a fanatic resistance to any advertising influence on the editorial pages.

Once you get the okay to write an article for publication, consider the editor to be a collaborator. You're both after the same thing: to publish an article that will get read and get reaction.

A final caution: Once you get published, you'll probably get hooked on writing articles. It will be fun to see your name in print, and you'll enjoy schmoozing with editors at trade shows and conferences.

So give article writing a try, and good luck.

> *"Work; finish; publish."*
>
> —Michael Faraday
> English chemist/physicist
> (1791–1867)

Summary of This Chapter's Main Points

▶ Article writing can benefit you and your company.

▶ Your own experience is your best source of article ideas.

▶ Use a planning sheet to clarify your idea before starting the article.

▶ Write a clear lead in the active voice, for three reasons:
 — to focus your idea
 — to sell the editor on your article idea
 — to hook the reader of the magazine

▶ Read through six issues of a chosen magazine for two purposes:
 — to see if your article would be appropriate
 — to become familiar with the magazine's needs

▶ Prepare a query letter and outline to send to the editor and/or to your public relations department.

▶ Don't mix advertising with editorial.

PART FOUR

Engineering Your Presenting Success

Introduction to Part Four

Part Four is not a stand-alone section. It builds on everything we discussed in Part One. *Oral* presentations are built on the same principles that apply to any *writing* job:

▶ Know your primary audience and primary purpose.

▶ Match your level of detail to the audience's level of understanding.

▶ Be accurate; be brief; be clear and concise.

▶ Use concrete terms that the audience can readily grasp.

▶ Determine the organizational strategies (choose key-point first or key-point last, and select the supporting strategies) that will work best to accomplish your purpose.

▶ Add the "So what?" to any technical information:
— benefits for customers and senior management
— expected outcome(s) of projects
— the next step in a project

This section of the book is based on our own experiences as professional trainers, on suggestions by fellow training presenters, and on research into the myriad of presentation-skills material published over the years.

Our purpose is *not* to load you up with every suggestion that has been made on another easy way to produce a visual or handle an incessant talker. Our purpose is to give you a thorough but concise method to prepare and execute a successful engineering presentation or meeting.

Each presentation has a life of its own. Each one is unique. Outside forces (the audience and the environment) constantly act on a presentation to give it its individuality. Just as a dropped stone can raise the level of the ocean, the addition or subtraction of one audience member can change the dynamics of a presentation.

You can adapt the information we have given you to fit any type of engineering presentation or meeting.

The basics are here. Use them as you see fit.

18 Planning Your Presentation

Speaking before a group gives you a superb opportunity to excel. A successful presentation at a crucial time can affect an important company decision, bring your company more business, or get you a promotion. Becoming skilled in oral presentations is the same as becoming skilled in math. It's a natural part of an engineer's job.

Unfortunately, most people don't view public speaking as an opportunity. Several years ago, one of those unsubstantiated statistics that are conceived in some netherworld became part of business lore. To wit, people are more afraid of public speaking than of death. Now, that's nonsense. If someone came up to you, pointed a gun at your head, and said, "Give a speech or die," what would you do? Do some fast talking, that's what you'd do.

Control: The Key to Successful Speaking

Sure, you may get anxious (in the *uneasy* sense) when having to speak publicly, but that's good. As long as you control your anxiety, you can use it to your advantage. Actually, control is the key to successful speaking. To give a good presentation, you must control five things:

- ▶ yourself
- ▶ your materials
- ▶ your equipment
- ▶ your environment
- ▶ your audience

Stated another way, the five factors of a successful presentation are:

- ▶ a knowledgeable speaker
- ▶ clear materials that reinforce the message
- ▶ easy-to-use and effective equipment

▶ a conducive presentation environment

▶ a responsive audience

> *"The theory of control in engineering, whether human or animal or mechanical, is a chapter in the theory of messages."*
>
> —Norbert Wiener
> American inventor
> and mathematician
> (1864–1964)

If you can produce and control those five things, you can become a successful speaker.

That's what you will learn in this section of the book—how *you* can become a successful speaker.

How Writing Helps Ensure Your Speaking Control

The good news is that if you have read this far in the book and have already begun applying our guidelines to your everyday *writing* tasks, you are most of the way down the road to becoming a successful *speaker*. Why? Because a good presentation is built upon a well-controlled, well-written script. An oral presentation is just a writing job taken into another dimension. The script is the starting point.

Enjoying Two-Way Communication

In an oral presentation, you build upon and go beyond the writing box. You're set free to make the written message (the script) come alive.

When you send out a written message in the form of a memo, a report, or even an E-mail message, you usually have to wait for a reply. Meanwhile, you may wonder how your reader will interpret and react to your message. In contrast, speaking allows you to have on-the-spot two-way communication.

While speaking, you get instant feedback. You can usually tell immediately whether you're connecting with your audience, by noticing the reaction clues: your listeners' attentiveness, expressions, body language, questions, comments, and other reactions. The reactions often depend on how well you have combined and controlled all the factors of your presentation.

Making the Whole Greater Than the Sum of Its Parts

We recently saw a brief documentary about how a movie scene is created, accumulatively. First, we were shown only the visual image: a pilot in the cockpit of a jet fighter in flight. Then the scene was repeated, this time with added sound effects: guns firing and hitting their targets. The scene ran a third time, this time adding the tense dialogue between the pilot and his fellow pilots on the same mission. The fourth run of the scene added the music, scored and timed precisely to accent the actions in the scene. In each of those repetitions, the addition of one more factor actually *multiplied* the dramatic effect. The whole (the finished scene) was far greater than the sum of its parts. The final dramatic product yielded a box-office hit.

Likewise, if you effectively combine and control your own presentation factors (yourself, your materials, your equipment, the environment, and your audience), the whole (the presentation itself) will be greater than the sum of its parts. You'll have your own product: a polished presentation that accomplishes its purpose.

The Persuasive Tools of a Presentation

Presenting gives you powerful tools to teach and persuade with. You have your *voice* with all its inflections, your *gestures* with all their verve, your *visual aids* with all their emphasis, and your *handouts* with all their details.

You don't think these tools are powerful? Just count up the dollars the electronic preachers take in every Sunday after giving a television sermon (presentation). They do it with voice inflection and gestures.

President Lyndon Johnson, one on one, could talk just about anybody into anything. For example, Earl Warren did not want to head the commission investigating John F. Kennedy's death. He was adamant—until Johnson talked to him face to face. In another example of persuasive power, Johnson convinced Arthur Goldberg to give up his seat on thc Supreme Court (that is a lifetime job that *nobody* can take away from an individual) to become United Nations Ambassador. Throughout his presidential term, Johnson was sure—he knew way down deep in his heart and soul—that if he could talk, face to face, with Ho Chi Minh, he could persuade him to end the Vietnam War on America's terms. Johnson and Ho Chi Minh never met face to face, and America lost the war.

Other politicians use not only their inflections and gestures: Many now pull out charts and graphs to sell an idea. Yes, engineers, we're talking about presentation power here.

The point is that by jumping from one-way written communication to two-way oral communication, you can take a quantum leap, if you use your tools effectively.

So here's how to do it.

How to Control Yourself

Obviously the most crucial element in your presentation is you, the speaker. What's your greatest fear about speaking? Probably that you might make a fool of yourself. Good! You need that fear. That fear will drive you to become what all successful speakers are: knowledgeable about their subject. *Knowing your subject* is the key to controlling yourself. Knowing your subject is your greatest confidence builder. If you don't know what you're talking about, you darn well *better* be afraid to stand up and talk. You can have stunning visuals, impressive handouts, and the latest high-tech equipment; but if you don't know what you're talking about, you're dead in the water.

As you speak, you'll be concerned about several things: the audience, the equipment, the environment, and your speech itself. By knowing your subject, you eliminate the last worry. If you are confident in your knowledge of the subject, you can more easily control the other aspects of the presentation. If you have that confidence, then faulty equipment or a rambunctious audience won't rattle you. You can deal with them.

As you know, not all presentations are limited to one speaker addressing an audience in an auditorium. You sometimes have an audience of only one or maybe a handful of people. The bulk of your engineering presentations are probably given to small groups (fewer than 20 people).

> Note: For this section of the book, we assume that you are presenting to a group of about 20 people, and we have tailored our comments to fit that model. Our reasoning is that if you can prepare for and present to a group of 20, you can handle just about any size group. Please keep this model in mind as you read through this section.

Sometimes you may not be the only speaker. Maybe you're part of a team presenting to potential customers. Maybe you're the team leader. Hmm … More responsibility. Now you're not only concerned about *your* speech and materials and equipment; now you've got to coordinate everybody else's stuff, too.

So let's get you organized before your boss throws even more responsibility at you.

How to Organize Yourself *and* Your Presentation

Let's say you've agreed or have been coerced to make a formal presentation. Now what?

Your first step is to *plan* your presentation. You have to plan your script, your materials, and your equipment. You may also have to coordinate *other* speakers. And you have to coordinate your room setup. At this point, it may seem as if you have to plan all those things at once, and in a sense you do. But to make life easier, let's take them one step at a time.

Start with a planning sheet, just as you would with any writing job. You will first determine your *audience* (instead of reader) and then your *purpose*.

Analyze Your Audience

In Chapter 2 we discussed the importance of determining who your primary reader is and what his or her needs are. For a presentation, you must analyze your *audience*. As your audience changes (or your purpose changes), your message (presentation) changes.

If you are presenting a technical proposal to senior management to gain funding for a project, find out what senior management is looking for. One thing you can count on is that senior management is always looking for *business* opportunities. Thus, explain how your project, if properly funded, will bring more business to the company.

If you are bringing fellow engineers up to date on your project, what do you think would interest them? More than likely, the same details that interest you. But if you're presenting the same update to the marketing staff, you'll have to cut back on the details and focus on the overview, explaining the marketing benefits of the project.

So how are you supposed to know what an audience wants? Ask. If you're scheduled to give a presentation to the marketing troops, do a little marketing research: Stop by the marketing department and ask those who will be attending, "What do you want to know about my topic?" Jot down key-word notes of their responses.

If your audience will be a combination of engineers and marketing people, you suddenly have two primary "readers." What do you do if you have two primary readers? Remember what we said in Chapter 2. You write two documents (the executive summary and the more technical main body) and call it one document. In the case of a presentation, you may have essentially two presentations—one aimed at marketing, one aimed at engineering.

When you begin such a presentation, orient your audience. "I've divided this morning's presentation into two parts. First I will give you an overview of the project and highlight the commercial potential we see. Then I will present the technical details to show you how the whole thing fits together."

When you finish the overview, say so and take a break, explaining that you will cover the technical details next. Very smoothly, you have satisfied the marketing people, who are now free to leave without disturbing your presentation. That is a good example of controlling your audience. (The next chapter discusses audience-controlling techniques more fully.)

If you are giving a technical presentation to a potential customer, ask your marketing people what the customer's hot buttons are. What's the customer looking for? Who's going to attend the presentation? Will there be technical people who want the details? In presentations like this, figure that engineering, top management, and marketing will all be represented, so plan your script and materials to cover all possibilities. You can always trim your presentation on the spot to fit the audience, but it's really tough to create materials and visuals on the spot.

One more point: In this section of the book, we are giving you the tools to engineer a successful presentation. Use these tools no matter who your audience is. Just because you're presenting to fellow engineers, don't slack off and produce hard-to-see, complicated visuals, assuming that your audience is smart and tenacious enough to figure them out. Smart, tenacious people are like everybody else: They don't like sloppy presentations. Remember what we said earlier in the book about having respect for your reader. The same goes for your audience.

Know Your Purpose

▶ Are you explaining an advancement in technology to other engineers at a conference?

▶ Are you extolling the virtues of a product to a potential customer, or proposing the business opportunities of your new project to management?

▶ Are you teaching employees about an advancement in technology?

In other words, are you informing, persuading, or teaching?

The Three Purposes of an Engineering Presentation

Essentially, any presentation has one of these three purposes:

- ▶ to inform
  - — technical updates
  - — conferences
  - — new-product announcements
  - — press conferences
  - — after-dinner talks
- ▶ to persuade
  - — in-house proposals to sell your ideas
  - — pep talks to your project team or to vendors/distributors
  - — customer presentations to sell or support your product/service
- ▶ to instruct
  - — training sessions
  - — one-on-one coaching
  - — new-hire orientations

Once you determine your audience and purpose, work through the rest of the planning sheet. (For planning-sheet reminders, see Chapter 3.)

When you finish your planning sheet, you'll know what you want to say, what other data you may have to collect, and which direction you are taking. Now decide what handout materials and audiovisual (AV) equipment you want to use. You have to decide on equipment and materials now, because your materials have to match your equipment. Let's talk about equipment first.

Selecting Your Audiovisual Equipment

The first rule in choosing equipment is this: Keep it simple. As an engineer, you probably love gadgets and enjoy tinkering with grown-up toys. However, don't get distracted by all the whiz-bang, high-tech multimedia equipment and software packaging that's now available. The products are good, but they don't replace *you*. You and your script are more important than the equipment you use.

Rick Gilbert, principal of Frederick Gilbert Associates, Inc., Redwood City, California, and developer of the PowerSpeaking® seminars, feels strongly about the overuse and abuse of multimedia. In his "Multimedia Madness" article in the Summer 1994 issue of his PowerSpeaking® newsletter, he says,

> Imagine a presenter entering a room with a large 30-pound suitcase. He unloads a bulky liquid-crystal display (LCD) device and spends the next 15 minutes connecting it to his laptop computer and positioning it on top of an overhead projector. The front of the room is now dominated by a large screen, an overhead projector with an LCD device balanced on it, and a tangled mess of extension cords and connector wires.

As the presentation begins, the shades are closed and the lights are turned off. The presenter sits in the dark at the keyboard of his laptop and starts typing. Bulleted sentences come in from the right, from the left, from the top. The image quality on the screen is hard to read from anywhere in the room. Eyelids droop. Heads fall as people all around the room drift off to the Land of Nod.

This communication disaster is an example of what we are lauding these days as "Multimedia!" It's new. It's hot. And it's selling briskly for all the wrong reasons.

The problem, Rick explains, is that nervous presenters (that's most of us) don't want to be the center of attention. We feel reassured that this "presentation software" will save us.

Don't hide from your audience by relying on overhyped technology that obscures your message.

The ads imply that all we have to do is create our visuals, and presto—the talk is done. We are off the hook. All the audience has to do is read the screen. If we're lucky, the people won't look at us at all.

The idea that we can use visuals to divert the audience's attention and that the presentation is nothing more than visuals is a fatally flawed idea. Like it or not, the presenter and his or her message are always more important than the visuals, no matter how fancy the visuals are. Stand-up presentations are about *human* communication—not about reading words on a screen or watching a movie. To be believed, to be persuasive, we have to show up!

For years, technical presenters have overused and hidden behind their overheads. Today we simply have a more glitzy, complex (and expensive) version of the same old problems.

As you consider your equipment, Rick says, you should first ask yourself whether you need visuals at all. If you do, keep to the simple formats like flipcharts, overheads, and handouts. "Think of multimedia last, not first."

We agree. Don't spend a lot of money on equipment just to have sentences drift onto the screen from the four compass points. You can be a very versatile presenter with a combination of flipcharts, overheads, and handouts. Most of the time you want to avoid equipment that requires a darkened room, because then people can't take notes. Darkened rooms also discourage questions and make it harder for you to respond to the questions you do get. Why? No eye contact.

But let's see what simple yet reliable equipment is available out there so that you can choose easy-to-use equipment that will fit your needs.

The overhead projector lets you face your audience and keep the lights on.

AV Choices

Overhead Projector Is Simple but Versatile

Most engineering presenters prefer overhead projectors. Most hotel and company conference rooms have overhead projectors available.

You can simultaneously work the projector and face the audience, because the image is projected *behind* you, onto a large ceiling-mounted or freestanding viewing screen. You can easily write, draw, or point out items on a transparency. *Transparencies* (also called *visuals*) are quick and easy to prepare—and easy to handle. You can show step-by-step processes by using overlays. We'll talk more about those visuals later, in the "Materials" discussion of this chapter.

The overhead's primary advantage is that you can operate it in a *lighted* room. That advantage puts it head and antlers above other equipment as a presenter's choice.

Following are four quick tips about using overhead projectors. Although these tips might seem like trivial details, they can make a difference in the quality of the projected image—and of *your* image in the eyes of your audience.

1. Overhead projectors usually come in several sizes: The full-sized models have a horizontal optical stage, or *deck* (where you lay the transparency), about 8 inches above the table or projector stand. The deck of the smallest model sits only about an inch above the table.

   Though more compact and more easily portable, the smaller models often project a fuzzier image focus than the full-size models do. Clear focus is a must for easy viewing by the audience. For better quality, prefer a full-sized (not necessarily oversized) model; and request a *recent* model to avoid getting a worn or lopsided machine with a scratched deck.

2. The full-sized and oversized models themselves vary. All have a projection arm that holds the projection head above the deck. The arm rises either from the back-right corner of the deck or from the back center of the deck. The corner arm is better because it lets you discuss the top part of a transparency and then move the transparency up to show information that's lower on the page. The back-center arm doesn't let you move the transparency copy up.

3. Always request an overhead projector with a fresh spare bulb, in case the first bulb blows during your presentation. Most models now have a quick-change switch on

the outside back of the projector to prevent interrupting or delaying a presentation. Make sure both bulbs work, and know—before your presentation—how to switch the bulb quickly and smoothly.

4. Clean the deck and projection-head glass with a damp (not wet) towel before your presentation. Smudges and dirt on the deck can distract from your message. Then recheck the focus in case you changed the tilt or moved the focus knob on the arm while cleaning the glass.

Slides Can Enlighten or Keep Audience in the Dark

Slides can be good. Slides can be impressive. A short slide show can have a strong impact on an audience. Slides also travel well. But slides require a dark room. The overall purpose of a technical presentation is to inform or teach the audience. A dark room is more conducive to sleeping than to learning. That's why slide shows are risky. (Technology may solve that problem soon.)

However, slides can be very effective as *part* of an overall presentation, if you know how to operate the projector and the remote control. Just don't base your whole presentation on a slide show.

Don't keep your audience in the dark.

Synchronized multiple-slide-projector programs (one of the original meanings of *multimedia*) can be dramatic but expensive, requiring more complex preparation and a larger setup staff. You would do best to hire professionals for such programs.

Viewing Screens with Tilt Option Work Best

When using an overhead or slide projector, you also need a viewing screen. Sometimes the meeting room has a pull-down or electronically controlled ceiling-mounted screen. That's handy but limiting, because it's not movable.

When selecting a rental screen, match the screen size to the room size and group size. You want to be able to raise the screen so the bottom of the image will be at least four feet above the floor; yet, if the room has a low ceiling, you may not be able to raise a big screen as high as you'd like. An eight-foot screen in a small room would dwarf the image and create too broad an edge around the image.

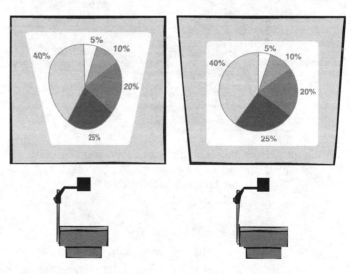

Avoid the keystoned image at left by tilting the top of the viewing screen forward (toward the projector). The resulting square image at the right shows the content accurately.

Generally, allow one foot of screen width for every six feet of viewing distance from the screen. For simplicity, though, let an AV rental company advise you about the appropriate screen size that matches your room size, group size, and purpose (transparencies or slides).

Whatever size you choose, prefer a screen that you can tilt forward at the top, to avoid the keystoned image (wide at the top, narrow at the bottom). Tripod screen bases usually have an extendable, notched anti-keystone arm that swings out over the top, to hook the screen to. Figure that the higher the screen in relation to the projector, the more exaggerated the keystone effect would be if you didn't angle the screen. So use the anti-keystone arm to tilt the screen accordingly. You want to project the image at a 90-degree angle to the screen. That produces a square image on the screen.

Boards, Flipcharts, and Posters Augment Projectors

Some trainers use these media very effectively.

▶ The *chalkboard* was probably the most prevalent writing-surface visual aid you saw from grade school through college. Luckily for business, chalkboards have been replaced by cleaner *white boards*, or *boards*. You can add, delete, or change words and diagrams, giving you real-time, two-way communication with your audience. Boards, with their special dry-marking erasable-ink pens, are an excellent medium for the spur-of-the-moment meetings that occur in every company.

Some are easel-mounted porcelain boards, for portability. Others are wall-mounted porcelain-on-steel. A board's disadvantage is the lack of a permanent record. To solve that problem, though, some freestanding electronic models have a film surface that you can advance as you write on it—then print out copies of the notes if you want.

Boards and easel-mounted flipcharts are helpful during question-and-answer periods. Posters add a professional touch to presentations.

▶ The *flipchart*, which overcomes the no-record problem, can be used instead of or with a board. (Some easels let you clamp a flipchart on top of a white board, for versatility.) The flipchart also has the advantage of letting you prepare it beforehand. Before your talk, you can lightly outline your diagrams or wording; then, when in front of a group, neatly "produce" it with the broad-tipped pen. ("Look how neatly she draws!")

You can also roll up prepared charts for easy transport. Easels, though, even the fold-up ones, can be a hassle to transport. On-site rental is an easy solution if your presentation is at a hotel. Most hotels' catering or banquet staffs can either reserve or rent such AV equipment for you. Just order the easel when you reserve the meeting room and your other needed AV equipment.

▶ *Posters*, prepared on a rigid artboard, preferably by someone with artistic talent, are a step up from flipcharts. Posters are more durable, but also bulkier, than flipcharts.

Boards and flipcharts, as adjuncts to the overhead projector, can be especially helpful during your question-and-answer period.

Microphones Vary to Suit Your Purpose

If you project your voice confidently, you probably won't need a microphone for presentations to groups of up to 50 people. For larger groups, the acoustics of the room may determine whether you need a microphone.

If you need to use a microphone, the lavaliere (usually a neck-cord type) or clip-on type is easier to use than the hand-held type. Avoid using a fixed, lectern microphone. The lectern is a barrier between you and the audience. Barriers inhibit communication.

Wireless handheld microphones are good for a large group that you may want to walk among and include in dialogue. Beware, though: We've heard some weird police calls and citizens-band radio signals interrupt an otherwise smooth wireless-microphone presentation. If you do decide to use this type, get a high-quality recent model, which may be less prone to signal interference.

Whatever type of microphone you use (if any), always have a working backup in case your first microphone goes dead.

Oh, yes. And learn how to *use* whatever type you choose.

Video Requires Professional Production

Video can be a powerful medium—so long as it is produced by professionals. With multiple monitors, you can reach thousands of people. What you can do with video is limited only by your imagination and budget. You can create text, graphics, charts, and animation, then you can morph and edit to your heart's content. Great stuff, huh?

But haven't we suddenly moved away from live presentation to video production? It's easy to lose sight, isn't it?

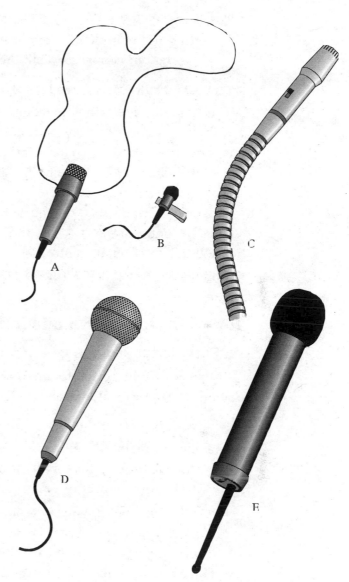

Microphone choices include A) a lavaliere (neck-cord), B) a small clip-on, C) a fixed (often goose-necked) model mounted on a lectern, D) a handheld type, and E) a wireless handheld model.

Video, like slides, can dazzle your audiences, if it's done right. As a small part of a presentation, video that emphasizes or clarifies a point can be excellent. But be aware of the disadvantages of video:

▶ It is expensive.

▶ Large-screen projection systems may produce poor image quality.

▶ Setting up multiple monitors may not be worth the trouble, just to enhance a live presentation; you must weigh the benefits.

Multimedia Quality Must Exceed the Hype

Multimedia, which now encompasses computer displays, is rapidly changing and well-hyped. Generally, though, it is expensive and often ineffective because of the poor image quality and the need for a darkened room. Remember Rick Gilbert's comments earlier in this chapter? So far, multimedia is not a good equipment choice for most professional presentations.

So now you've decided on your equipment, and you realize you will have to check it all out, to control it.

We'll talk later about controlling your materials (the visuals themselves). Chronologically, your next step is to write a script.

Your Script: The Foundation of Your Presentation

An Easy Script Structure

Your script will be the foundation of your presentation. Give your presentation an obvious beginning, middle, and end.

▶ *Orientation:* Introduce the main points to orient the audience.

▶ *Body:* Explain all your points in the same order you introduced them. For each point you cover, imagine that someone in your audience is going to think, "So what?" Answer that question for each point.

▶ *Close:* Summarize your key points, answering for your listeners any leftover "So what?" questions that are probably in their minds. If your engineering presentation's purpose is to sell something, anticipate the "So what?" questions that will force you to concentrate on the *benefits* of your product, service, or idea.

We know you've heard the following old saw before, so we even hesitate to repeat it, but it works: "Tell them what you're going to tell them. Tell them. Then tell them what you told them." Use that advice from some unsung, ancient Army sergeant to your advantage.

Writing Your Script

The entire time that you are writing your script, keep imagining yourself saying every word that you write. Visualize yourself in front of your audience.

Doing so now will keep you focused on what to say and how to say it. Some points will need more explanation than others. If you've presented some of this material before, recall the reaction of past audiences. Did you bore them with too much detail? Were they confused by a point you did not elaborate on? Put yourself in the listener's place. Is this point going to be clear to the listener? How can I say it differently? Will a visual help clarify this point?

Present your information clearly and concisely. The advantage a presentation has over a letter, proposal, or report is that you have more tools to work with: your voice, gestures, visual aids, and handouts. Those are powerful tools. Keep them in mind as you begin and work through your planning stage.

Use the visuals and handouts to *enhance* your script, not to carry the whole presentation. Since the script is the foundation of your presentation, try to write as though the script will have to stand alone without visuals or handouts. Doing so will push you to write a strong script, which in turn will give you a strong presentation.

Sometimes, of course, you may have to build a presentation around certain diagrams or charts. That's often easier to do than working only with text.

Deciding How to Present Your Script Smoothly

Now that you have completed your script, you must decide how to present it. You have three choices: You can *memorize* your paper, you can *read* your paper, or you can *speak extemporaneously*. Tough choices.

Memorizing seems as though it would hurt your brain a lot. And what happens when your mind goes blank in the middle of the speech? What are you going to do? Sing scat? We can hear it now:

"… so, as you can see, the expansion factor is a function of the specific heat ratio, k, and the ratio of the orifice to pipe diameters is—er—Shabop Bop de Bop Bop Bam Boom …"

That's probably not going to advance your career. Besides, a memorized speech always *sounds* memorized. It's lifeless and monotonous. Unless you're a professional actor, memorizing is *not* the way to go.

That leaves you with reading or speaking extemporaneously.

Of those two, reading surely *looks* a lot easier, especially if you're the nervous type. By reading, you don't have to look at your audience, you can keep your hands busy shuffling papers (so you eliminate the problem of jingling the change in your pocket), and—best of all, you may think—you have an excuse for running overtime. Of course, if you do happen to look up at your audience, you'll find that most of them have left and those who haven't left just haven't awakened yet.

Here you have a chance to strut your stuff and show what a top-rate mind you have, and you're going to *read* your paper? How insulting to your listeners! We don't mean to sound harsh here, but don't you think they're capable of reading it themselves?

Don't waste your time or the audience's time. Just hand everybody a copy of your paper and tell them to read it at their leisure. Why make everyone suffer through a mind-numbing reading?

But, you say, lots of engineers read papers at technical conferences. That's true. The next time an engineer reads a paper, look around at the audience. Many will be reading or sleeping, and those who seem to be listening are probably trying to remember where they left their calculators.

At a technical conference, copies of the papers are available. So spend your presentation time *summarizing the highlights* of your paper. Give an overview of key points, or concentrate on the main thrust of the paper, and tell the audience you'll take questions now or outside in the cafeteria after the formal presentations. Your intent here is to get people interested enough in your paper to read it *after* the presentation. If you give a good presentation, people will want to talk to you about your subject. And getting people to talk about your subject is one of the reasons you present a conference paper.

Listening to a speech that is read is worse than listening to the words of a song without hearing the music.

So you're left with *extemporaneous* speaking. Don't let the word scare you. It means "spoken without any preparation" (that's scary) or "spoken with some preparation but not written out or memorized." That second approach you can handle. Here's how.

Reducing Your Script to a Handy Key-Point Outline

Cloister yourself with your script and a mirror. Recite your presentation (the script) out loud to the mirror several times until you feel comfortable with the content.

▶ Rewrite the tongue twisters that you put in. You won't really notice the tongue twisters until you try saying them out loud.

▶ Practice enunciating. Speak slowly so you don't garble your words.

▶ After you're comfortable with your script, make a copy (save the original in case you make some radical changes that you later think are unnecessary), and reduce the copy to an *outline* of key points.

▶ Now, just using your outline as a prompt, give your speech to the mirror again. Each time you practice, you may say things a little differently. That's okay. What's important is that you become familiar with the material and that you cover all your important points.

  You will use this key-point outline, along with your visuals, to give an extemporaneous presentation. Doing so is one of the keys to giving a relaxed presentation. By reading your script several times, you will put some key phrases in your memory bank. By practicing with the outline, you will familiarize yourself with the content.

If you were to memorize your speech and try to recite it verbatim, you would get lost as soon as you forgot a line. With the key-point outline, though, you won't completely depend on your read-only memory, and you'll be more able to use your random-access memory. Each key point you see on the outline will spark phrases in your mind, but mainly they will remind you of the topics you want to cover, while leaving you free to talk about each topic more comfortably and naturally. That's why we say knowing your subject is crucial.

Have you ever noticed how a nervous speaker, who seems really uncomfortable giving his presentation, suddenly relaxes during the question period? Why? Because he is free of his script that he has been so tightly tied to. Now he is in more comfortable surroundings. It's as though he is back in his office just chewing the fat with another engineer about a typical problem.

Some presenters just say, "Well, I don't have any prepared remarks, but I'll be happy to answer any questions you have." Now that's a real cop-out, and we do not recommend that approach at all. Such a speaker is cheating the audience that came to hear him share his knowledge of the subject. He was more comfortable just answering questions. And he's lazy.

Think of listed key points you take with you to the podium as questions from the audience. They just remind you, in a comfortable way, of the topics you want to discuss.

After writing your key-point script outline, prepare some introductory remarks that will orient your audience. Getting started is always the toughest part of the presentation. By having some specific introductory remarks, you can smoothly begin your presentation with confidence.

"Good morning. My name is Edwina Engineer. For the past five years I've headed the packaging section at Sandy Silicon Suppliers. During this time I worked primarily on developing ceramic …

"Today I'll tell you all about a packaging breakthrough we've achieved."

Developing and Controlling Easy-to-Use Materials

Review your script and decide what types of materials will best help your audience understand your topic. Keep in mind your overall purpose. Create materials that will help you accomplish your purpose. You'll probably need two types of materials: visuals and handouts.

Remember, the visuals and handouts should not be the primary focus of your presentation. Your talk is the primary focus. Therefore, design materials that *support* your talk. Don't give visuals and handouts the burden of carrying the presentation. You and your talk are the most important elements.

What *Not* to Do

Picture this disturbing scene, encountered in an engineering company:

> An engineer has spent several weeks preparing an in-house presentation for his peers. He now has a stack of complex visuals for his overhead projector. He knows they are probably too complex, but he's going to explain them to the audience. He also realizes that perhaps the visuals are loaded with too much information and may be difficult to see, so he will hand out copies of them beforehand. And, since he's discussing a complex topic, he's also going to give the audience his script. In other words, he will let his materials do the work he was supposed to do: educate other engineers.

Time for the presentation. He's set and ready to go at 8:00 a.m. A few people wander in at 7:55, a few more at 8:05, and some more between 8:05 and 8:30.

Why all the tardiness? Because in this company the employees are used to getting a packet of information, hanging around for a little while during the presentation, and then leaving, figuring they will read through the materials. Besides, the presentations are always boring.

In this case, the company would have saved a lot of employee time by just having the engineers distribute information through the company mail system. Why waste time with "presentations"?

Obviously, a lot of corporate-culture dynamics have converged to make presentations in this company a lose-lose-lose situation. The presenter loses because his audience walks out on him. The audience loses because the presenter has not prepared a decent presentation. The company loses because such presentations are a big waste of employee time.

The Best Visuals: Visible, Simple, and Controllable

We highly recommend the overhead projector as your equipment of choice. It is easy to use and, as we mentioned earlier, readily available. Let's assume, then, that you will be preparing visuals for an overhead projector.

Keep your visuals visible. Keep them simple. Keep them controllable.

Visible Visuals: Light Blue Is Eye-Friendly

For text, use a 24- to 30-point Helvetica font or its equivalent. You will notice that the same size type looks smaller or larger in different fonts. Helvetica is a good choice for visuals because it is a simple, easy-to-read, sans-serif typeface. You can experiment with different fonts and sizes, but don't stray far from the look of Helvetica.

Light-blue-background transparencies are the best, especially if you are using a lot of them. Clear (uncolored) visuals let the harsh white of the screen shine through; other colors can make the lettering hard to read. Blue is more restful on the eyes. You can use other colors to emphasize a point, but do so judiciously.

Simple Visuals: The One-Six-Six Trick

You can keep visuals simple by having:

▶ one idea per visual

▶ no more than six words per line

▶ no more than six lines per visual

Preparing visuals horizontally (landscape orientation) as opposed to vertically (portrait orientation) may help you to limit the number of lines. Another advantage of the landscape orientation is that the text is at the top of the screen, where people in the back of the room can see it.

For complex topics, use overlays or break down the complex ideas hierarchically on several visuals. For example, if you were giving a presentation on combustion and had to make a point about blast-furnace gases to an audience of potential customers who knew very little about combustion, here's what you might do. First, introduce your audience to fuel types with an introductory visual that lists all the fuel types.

> **Fuel Types**
> ▶ solid fuels
> ▶ liquid fuels
> ▶ gaseous fuels

You might then say, "We have three types of fuels: solid, liquid, and gaseous. Let's examine the characteristics and advantages of each one."

Next, further break down each fuel type, and explain the necessary points that will bring your audience up to speed. For example:

> **Gaseous Fuels**
> ▶ coke-oven gas
> ▶ blast-furnace gas
> ▶ water gas
> ▶ enriched water gas
> ▶ producer gas

Give your audience some more information about gaseous fuels, and then zero in on your main point: blast-furnace gas.

> **Blast-Furnace Gas**
> ▶ discharged from blast furnaces
> ▶ 55% nitrogen
> ▶ 20% carbon monoxide

The key to developing simple visuals for complex ideas is to think in terms of orienting the reader from the *top down*. First use a visual that introduces the audience to the overall idea by showing the major components. Then show one major component at a time. If you want to explain how three out of five components have similar characteristics, put those on a single visual and show how they are related, perhaps in a simple chart. Your purpose here is to present ideas that your listeners can grasp quickly, store in their memory banks, and recall later as you introduce related ideas.

Sometimes you can also build from the *bottom up*, explaining details first, as with complicated graphs or charts. For example, you can show several levels of detail separately on visuals and then tie them together with an overview. That way, each visual carries one main idea.

Occasionally you may be stuck with a complex diagram that can't be broken down easily into separate visuals. For example, system and circuit design diagrams are often quite complex. In such cases, your best bet is to get some help, if necessary, from your graphics department to add color to your visual aids.

If you throw several ideas at your audience all at once, the audience won't remember any of them. But if you present one idea at a time (giving the audience time to digest the information) and then show how the ideas are related, you will have taught people something they didn't know. And that's a good feeling. Ask any teacher.

Controllable Visuals Travel Well

Overhead transparencies are pretty easy to work with, and they come in two weights: light and heavy. The lightweight ones are flimsy and need a frame. A framed visual does look better because it doesn't have an unfinished edge around it. Yet, framing visuals is tedious work.

More importantly, though, framed visuals weigh much more and take up significantly more room than unframed, heavyweight visuals that need no frame. Think about that when you're preparing a presentation to take on the road.

The heavyweight films are easier to handle, too. And they are available in easy-to-read light blue.

Designing and Controlling Your Handouts

We said earlier that presentations fall into three categories: informing, persuading, and instructing. The first category might require handouts; the last two definitely do.

▶ A conference-paper presentation (or, rather, conference-paper summary) is an example of an *informing* presentation. Your primary purpose is to inform your audience about a technological development or theory. People can pick up a copy of your paper in the back of the room if they so desire. This type of handout is not an active part of the presentation.

▶ A sales presentation is meant to *persuade*. A handout for this purpose has room for notes, but your presentation should be structured so that the customer doesn't *have* to take notes. The handout should emphasize the benefits you describe in your talk.

▶ If you're running a training session or presenting a customer-support orientation, you're *instructing*. Active handouts become more important. The simplest training-session handout is an outline of your topic with room for notes. The most sophisticated training-session handout is a workbook that has a lot of detailed but readable information, examples, and room for notes.

Generally, handouts do not have to be elaborate. When preparing a handout, just ask yourself what will best aid your audience's understanding of your topic.

It's always a good idea to distribute any complex illustrations (charts or diagrams) that you discuss. Be sure to identify each illustration by number for easy reference during your talk. You don't want to put yourself in the position of having to say, "No, no, not that one. It's the one that has sort of an S-curve about halfway down the page. No ... No. The one where the S-curve is kind of scrunched together. There ... there you go. Yeah. That's it."

When to Hand Out the Handout

When to hand out the handout—that is the question. It's a tricky question. If you hand out everything at the beginning, people often leaf through the handouts during the presentation and ignore you, the speaker. Some people even leave after receiving the handout. (That really hurts the ego.) On the other hand, the audience needs the handouts to understand the subject. What does a presenter do?

The best policy is to hand out materials as they are needed. Following this rule will prevent people from trying to get ahead of you and will help you to maintain control of your audience.

Essentially, you will have two types of materials to distribute:

▶ note-taking materials such as course outlines or workbooks

▶ supplementary materials such as graphs, charts, or copies of your visuals
    The supplementary materials are further divided into:
    — handouts needed during the presentation
    — handouts needed after the presentation

Distribute note-taking materials before the session starts, by placing them at participants' seats or by handing them out as participants enter.

Distribute handouts needed during the presentation as you come to those topics during the session. If you have a lot of materials to hand out, arrange them into logical subsets beforehand, then distribute each subset when you introduce its topic. For example, you don't want to hand out 50 separate sheets of paper, one at a time. Just before handing out a subset, explain its purpose. For example, say, "This next set of graphs shows us what happened during the second failure analysis."

Distributing as you go works pretty well with groups of 30 or fewer. With larger groups, ask one or more people to help you with the distribution. Just make sure to plan with your assistants what you want distributed when.

If you have summaries or other supplementary information not needed for reference during the session, save such material until the end of the session. Doing so will help avoid needless paper shuffling in the audience during your talk.

A special caution about distributing your visuals, such as overhead transparencies: Avoid distributing your whole set of visuals. Remember, visuals are meant to *support* your presentation, not carry it. Hand out only those that the participants should write notes upon.

Remember that by controlling your materials, you can control your audience.

If you are presenting a technical paper at a large conference, you may not be able to control the distribution of your paper. At such conferences, you will probably have to submit your paper a few months beforehand. Conference management will then reproduce it and make it available at the conference to whoever wants a copy. Usually conference attendees pick up technical papers at the conference-room entrance.

How Controlled Equipment and Materials Add Value

Your equipment and materials should *add* to your presentation, not detract from it. Also, remember that *you're* the center of the presentation. Your simple but well-controlled equipment and your well-organized materials are "value-added" peripherals that help you sell your ideas to your audience.

Controlling Your Environment

Your presentation environment is tough to control. Room size and configuration are not always controllable, and neither are heating and seating. These problems can range from minor annoyances to major disrupters of a presentation. If you have any say about the room you'll be using, speak up.

You want to be able to control the temperature. We always tell our seminar and workshop registrants to dress in layers, because some hotel-room temperatures are difficult to control. Often you don't have control, especially if your room is part of a hotel's ballroom and is created by dividers.

Sometimes only the hotel staff can change the temperature, and you may have to call outside the room for such help. A sharp hotel staff will check with you during your session to make sure everything is okay. Once you find a hotel that takes good care of you, give it your repeat business.

Specify on your hotel work order the type of seating configuration you want. You need space for yourself, your equipment, and your materials. You also need space for the audience. How much space depends on what equipment you are using and whether your audience will be seated at tables. Chairs and tables both vary in size. Ask your hotel contact what sizes are available.

Avoid rooms with pillars, and avoid rooms without shades on the windows. Sure, the audience may like having a bright window in the back of the room with glorious light pouring in. When you face the audience, though, you won't be able to see a thing except glorious light pouring in.

Mainly, realize that your presentation environment won't always be perfect. Get used to adapting. If a low ceiling prevents you from raising the screen high enough, position the chairs so that everyone will be able to see the lower-than-normal screen. Adapt. If you can control yourself, your materials, your equipment, and your audience, you are doing well. Believe it.

In the next chapter, we'll move on to the presentation itself and learn how to control the final factor in a good presentation—your audience.

> *"Just know your lines and don't bump into the furniture."*
>
> —Spencer Tracy
> American film actor
> (1900–1967)

Summary of This Chapter's Main Points

▶ To produce and execute a successful presentation, you must control five things: yourself, your materials, your equipment, your environment, and your audience.

▶ The whole presentation is greater than the sum of its parts.

▶ Control yourself by being a knowledgeable speaker. Once you know your subject, minor distractions will not bother you.

▶ Organize your talk by using a planning sheet.

▶ Determine your audience and its needs.

▶ Determine your purpose. Choose one of three:
— to inform
— to persuade
— to instruct

▶ Select easy-to-manage equipment, preferably what you can use in a lighted room.

▶ Write a script as the foundation of your presentation.
— Include an orientation, body, and close.
— Include benefits in proposals and sales presentations.

▶ Reduce your script to an outline and present it extemporaneously. Don't read it; don't memorize it.

▶ Practice in front of a mirror.

▶ Develop visuals that are *visible, simple,* and *controllable.*

▶ Develop useful handouts, and plan when to distribute them.

▶ When possible, control your environment.

19 Presenting: Front and Center

*"I present.
Therefore, I
panic."*

—an engineer
(any time)

This is it. Showtime!

Weeks of preparation—writing, coordinating, practicing—all of it comes down to now. You gotta show up and talk in front of a group. Let's make your first assignment really tough, so that you can experience the full speechmaking process: You're going to give a full day's training session to a group of 20 new hires. Your purpose is to teach these people how to do your job.

What Sets You Up for a Good Show

You've Already Prepared the Set

You've chosen a nearby hotel conference room away from the plant because you don't want any interruptions. You visited the room three weeks ago, so you're familiar with the room. You gave the hotel coordinator a clear and specific room-setup page showing the preferred seating arrangement and your AV equipment requirements (anything you'll need but don't plan to bring with you, such as a screen or an extension cord)

At least three days before your presentation, you gave the setup contact your guaranteed attendance count, reconfirmed the meeting-room work-order details, and got the name and phone extension of the setup assistant who will be available to let you in at the early hour you plan to *arrive* (not start). So far, so good.

Your session begins at 9:00 a.m. Now that the big day is here, how do you *start* your day, other than nervous?

Giving Yourself the Energy Edge

Actually, let's go back to last night when you were probably doing your last-minute check and getting your materials and equipment packed in your car. What did you have for supper?

We learned a two-meal energy trick years ago from a friend who runs marathons: First, load up on carbohydrates the night before a presentation. Carbos will keep your

How Group Size Affects Dynamics

The on-stage techniques given in this chapter apply generally to all your engineering presentations. Remember, though, that the model group size we gave you in the previous chapter is fewer than 20 people, and rarely more than 30.

Once you get more than 50 people in a seminar room, or more than 100 people in a convention hall, the dynamics change—weakening the energetic two-way communication you get in smaller groups. You'll still have two-way communication, but less individually. When you present a conference paper to large groups, the audiences (and potential troublemakers) are less interactive. Don't be discouraged, though. Given a question-and-answer period, true contributors will still ask questions—and will probably think the questions through before asking them in a large group.

energy up the next day. And then, on the morning of your talk, eat a good breakfast, preferably including protein. Avoid a heavy breakfast that will make you lethargic. Having just a few doughnuts will only give you a fast sugar high, from which you'll plummet in about an hour. It's very embarrassing to pass out in front of a group.

Dressing for Credibility

Dress up. Clothes make a difference—in you and in your audience. You will feel more in control, and you will *be* more in control if you are dressed well. Forget the jeans and sweatshirt; you aren't back on the old campus anymore.

Books have been written on power dressing, power suits, and power ties; and a lot of it is nonsense. But enough of it is true that it warrants your attention. A black suit with a red tie or red scarf is not a scepter that will automatically grant you sovereignty, as some books intimate; but looking good will gain you a measure of respect that you can capitalize on. Definitely. And you need every edge you can get when you stand up in front of a bunch of strangers.

If you're a man, wear a coat and tie, as in a suit (or sports coat and dress slacks)—not jeans. If your presentation is just a one-hour session in-house, at least wear a nice sweater with dress slacks. Avoid vested suits. Psychologically, the formal vest puts a barrier between you and the audience, creating the impression that you are not approachable.

If you're a woman, wear a business suit, dress, or tailored pantsuit. Choose refined accessories: a silk scarf for accent and interest; attractive but not ostentatious jewelry. Just ensure that it all works together to create a credible, confident, and professional look.

And both of you, forget the running shoes. You can buy very comfortable yet professional dress shoes these days. Looking good is half the battle. You are a professional engineer. Now you're going to be a professional speaker. If you want people to see you as a professional, dress like one. That's an added touch that makes a big difference in how you are received.

If you will do a lot of presenting for your company, especially to outside groups, visit a clothes consultant. Many major department stores employ them (sometimes called "personal shoppers"). Hiring a clothes consultant is well worth the time, money, and effort. You will be surprised at how looking good can help your career. You will also be surprised at how easy clothes shopping will become: In a brief, one-time coaching session, your clothes consultant can show you how to ignore 75 percent of the clothes on the rack and concentrate on the 25 percent that suit you.

Rechecking the Room and Equipment

Be sure to arrive about two hours before your session begins, to ensure that the room is set to your liking. More than likely, you'll have to change some things. Wrong equipment. No equipment. Too many chairs. Not enough chairs. Not enough room for you and your stuff. Tables too crowded. You name something that can go wrong, and it will at some time or another.

To remain in control, be prepared. That's why you arrived early: to take care of such problems. Immediately ask the on-site coordinator or hotel's banquet crew to help you fine-tune the setup that you had requested, so long as the reset can easily be completed before the audience arrives. Sometimes, though, you may have to adapt to a less-than-perfect room arrangement to avoid confusion at the start of your presentation.

With your key-point outline or brief notes already up front with your other materials, take a moment in the restroom for a final check of your appearance. Check your smile (no food between your teeth?). Take a few deep breaths and let them out slowly, to relax yourself, and return confidently to the presentation room.

Preparing to Start and Building Rapport

Your group starts wandering in about 8:30; since they're new hires, they're all in before 9:00 a.m. and you can start on time. As people arrive, meet them and converse briefly with them. That sets an open and friendly tone that will help establish rapport at the start of the session. During the session, you'll have to control these people, some of whom may be potential troublemakers (although even a negative person probably won't be aggressive yet when new to the company). By personally greeting someone who comes in with a scowl, you can often turn the scowl into a smile.

Try to spot the *expert*, such as someone who just joined your department after years of experience elsewhere. That's the person who knows more than you do, or thinks he does. Meeting this person early can help you disarm him if he *is* a potential troublemaker. (We'll explain how a little later.)

Then greet others—especially those who walk in alone and seem shy or hesitant. Your welcome will help both of you relax.

Of course, you don't want to get so relaxed that you forget to start on time. Don't let yourself get involved in a deep technical discussion about three-phase transformers before your talk. A few minutes before your presentation, go up to the front of the room to refocus your mind. That move will also signal that you'd like people to sit down.

Make sure you have a glass of tepid (not ice-cold) water handy up front. Put it on a side table, out of the way of your work area. Cold water constricts the throat. So don't drink cold water before you start talking, or you'll sound like a eunuch on helium. Instead, right before you start, drink something warm to open your throat. Tea with lemon is excellent; lemon juice clears the throat. In fact, put a shot of lemon juice in that glass of water, too.

You open your jacket and look at your stomach; by golly, you can't see them but you can feel them: butterflies. That's okay. Butterflies will always be with you. The trick, as a seasoned trainer once told us, is to get them to fly in formation. They're just your adrenaline fluttering. Reroute your adrenaline: Put it to work *for* you, not *against* you.

You've already started to do that with all your preparatory work. You checked out your equipment this morning. It works. You've prepared easy-to-read visuals and excellent handouts. That's under control. You've practiced your presentation. You feel pretty confident about your knowledge of your subject. You haven't even started yet, and things are going very well. How about that? Those butterflies *are* in formation.

Engineering Your Audience Control

So far we've talked about controlling yourself, your materials, your equipment, and your environment. Now it's time to gain control of your audience. You're partway there—you have dressed for speaking success. As corny as that sounds, it *will* improve your confidence, your control, *and* your audience's first impression of you. Your professional attire and confidence will command early respect from your listeners and, in some cases, intimidate the eccentrics who sometimes cause minor disruptions.

An audience may seem to be the most difficult thing to control, because the whole concept is somewhat nebulous. Dealing with people is always nebulous. It's not like dealing with an engineering problem that has seemingly logical solutions. In an engineering problem, maybe neither Solution A nor Solution B will work, but Solution C will. *People* problems usually require several attempted solutions. Solution A, B, or C, or any combination thereof, may or may not work. That's what makes people problems interesting. You can keep experimenting until you find out which solutions work most consistently over the long run.

So let's see what you have going for yourself here. You're dressed well. You know your stuff. You're definitely ahead of the game so far. The next step is to assert your authority, subtly. This is not as hard as it may seem. First of all, you're the speaker. They came here to see and hear you. That automatically puts you in a position of authority. *You* hold the power position in the room. Everyone's seat is facing you, so the audience doesn't have much choice about which way to look. It's time to start. You're on.

Lights, Camera, Action: Go for It!

Engineer, Start Your Engine

Start confidently.

Assert yourself. Look at the audience, smile, and take a deep breath to relax. Look directly at one person and speak clearly and slowly. Project your voice enough to reach the people in the back row.

Introduce yourself and your topic. Give the title of your presentation; then add a quick engineering-background comment about the company or your pertinent experience. If someone else already introduced you and covered those items, thank the introducer and go straight to the opening sentence or question about your topic.

Connect with Your Audience

Ask the audience some questions to get people involved. "What do you hope to get out of today's session?" is always a good icebreaker for a training presentation. On a technical topic, your opening question might be more specific: "How many of you have used an earlier model of our Functionopter Scanner?" That both involves your listeners and tells you something about them, to help you "connect" with them.

If you're comfortable with humor, use it. If not, don't. No rule is written that says you have to open an engineering presentation (or any presentation) with a joke. If you have a joke that's appropriate to your subject, use it, especially as an opener. But telling a joke for the sake of telling a joke is passé.

Orient the audience to the main points you will cover. Tell them what they can expect to learn today. Keep building rapport. Let the audience get comfortable with you.

Here's where you show that you have an obvious beginning, middle, and end to your well-organized presentation. Mention key-word highlights of the orientation, body, and close you structured when you wrote your script and resulting key-point outline. (To review the presentation-script tips, see Chapter 18.)

For example, if your presentation will explain a situation, problem, and solution about a recent product failure, you might just say as an orientation: "Today I'll review the lab situation in which we first discovered the circuit failure. Then I'll discuss the cause and financial consequences of the failure, and present the design-engineering team's suggested solution to prevent recurrence."

Talk for a while without using any visuals or equipment. *You* are more important than the visuals. Your unaided start shows the audience your confidence. You thus continue to strengthen your authority.

Encourage questions right from the start, especially if you're presenting to a small group. Doing so helps build rapport. If, for some reason, you don't want to be interrupted while you speak, say, "I'll be happy to answer questions after the presentation."

Make eye contact with different people. Change the object of your gaze every few seconds, especially as you make different points. For example, imagine you are in the middle of an explanation, and you are looking at the fellow in the blue sweater, about halfway back on the left, and you say:

"We can accomplish this feat in one of two ways."

Now look at the woman in the beige suit over on the right, near the back of the room.

"We can put the cart before the horse, or ..."

Now switch your eyes to the fellow in the tweed jacket up front.

"... we can put the horse before the cart."

That way the audience sees you're including everybody. Don't be tempted to concentrate on only those nice people with the wide-open eyes who sit there nodding agreement with everything you say. Look at everybody.

Move Naturally

Move around. Don't stand rigidly, legs locked like a toy soldier. Don't put a death grip on the table, lectern, or your suit jacket. In fact, if you can avoid using a lectern, so much the better.

If you want to walk a bit on stage, do so between sentences; then stop to make the point. Gestures work during sentences; walking usually doesn't.

If you walk around, be sure to pace your moves so that, as you wrap up one point, you are back to the speaker's table soon enough to glance at the next point on your outline. That way, you won't be remembered as the engineer who went silent and then sprinted back to the table to recheck her notes.

Do nothing to merely occupy your hands—at least nothing consciously. If you don't concentrate on your hands, they'll probably do just fine by themselves.

In particular, avoid the wooden use of hands to make a point. Let your gestures look natural and flowing.

If you feel comfortable putting one hand in your pocket as you talk, fine—assuming it's not a tight or high pocket. You don't want to create a distracting pull on your jacket when you're trying to show your expertise on the reliability of parallel systems versus serial systems.

Don't keep change or keys in your pocket. Lock them in your briefcase. That way you won't be tempted to jingle them absent-mindedly.

You may have some annoying mannerisms; most of us do. If you don't know what yours are, and if you're a novice presenter, have a trusted friend offer constructive criticism after this presentation. Nothing, however, can beat a first-rate public-speaking workshop for helping you spot your own presentation weaknesses and fixing them. In this book we can tell you how to prepare for a presentation, and we give you our experience-based tips on presenting. But if you will be doing a lot of presenting, enroll in a well-respected public-speaking course to give yourself that final polish.

Books are also available for improving your speech and learning how to articulate and enunciate. If you have a heavy accent, you may want to consider an accent-reduction course to ensure that your listeners can understand your words. A lot of resources are out there in the bookstores. You can also ask the more experienced presenters in your group to recommend the best consultant or other business resource for the skill you want to improve.

Don't Short-Circuit Your Audience Connection

Do not—absolutely *do not*—talk down to your audience. Nothing, not even a pitch-black room, kills a presentation faster than a pompous presenter. We all probably have memories of the stereotypical math professor who dashes off a long formula on the board and pompously sniffs, "From this, we can OBVIOUSLY assume ..." It was never obvious to us as students, and we were relieved when he finally got fired for incompetence. (True story.)

Relax. The people in your audience will not hurt you. In fact, they're probably rooting for you.

Communicate with your audience. Establish *two*-way communication. Ask, "What questions do you have?" (Avoid asking merely, "Do you have any questions?" That's not as inviting as a "What" question, according to experts in interpersonal communication.) Then, pause and look around at the people for a moment or so. That lets them know that you are sincerely interested in them.

Ask about the first visual: "Can you see this clearly in the back?" If someone says "No," move the visual up on the projector's optical stage to accommodate the person. Recheck for a clear image focus and a straight, centered placement, too.

Keep smiling. As the 17th Century Spanish writer Baltasar Gracián said in *The Art of Worldly Wisdom*, "It is very difficult to gain good will; but once you have it, it is easy to keep it."

Maintaining Your Audience Control: Equipment Tricks

Earlier, we recommended using the overhead projector for your engineering presentations, because it's the simplest machine to use in small-group presentations.

Another advantage of using an overhead projector is that it helps you control your audience. When you switch *on* the overhead, the audience looks at the *screen*. When you switch *off* the overhead, the audience looks at *you*. If you are discussing a point and you want the audience to concentrate on the screen while you talk, keep the overhead projector on. If you want the audience to focus on you, shut the projector off. Power —isn't it invigorating?

By the way, when you have no transparency on the overhead projector's optical stage, shut the projector off. Avoid having a bright blank screen distracting and annoying your audience.

Answering Questions Openly for Enhanced Credibility

When you encourage questions, everybody learns more, including you.

When someone asks a question, *listen* to the question. That may sound obvious, but we've seen presenters answer questions before the questioner finished talking, and then be embarrassed when the questioner said, "That's not what I was asking." *Don't assume.* *Listen*, and listen *intently*. Look at the person asking the question. Don't look away or shuffle through your materials. If you are presenting to a large group, repeat the question for the audience.

When you answer the question, look at the whole group. Don't carry on a dialogue with just one person. Keep your answers brief. If you over-answer, you'll discourage other people who would have asked questions.

Handling the Hard Questions

If you don't understand the question, say so: "I'm not sure I understand what you're asking."

Hypothetical questions covering a broad spectrum are difficult to answer. Your best bet here is to ask for specifics: "Can you give me an example?" If the questioner can't, you can attempt to answer what you think the question is. You can also talk to the person during a break.

Don't leave the impression with your audience that you ignored a person's question. In fact, if it appears to you that your response is not satisfying the questioner, just ask, "Did I fully answer your question?"

Sometimes with the broad-spectrum question, the questioner may say, "No, but don't worry about it. Maybe I can come up with a better example." It's a relief when the questioner realizes, without embarrassment, that he has to rethink his question to get an answer. Offer to discuss the question with that person during a break or after the program.

If you don't know the answer to a question, say so; don't try to bluff your way through it. People realize you can't know everything. However, do try to get an answer.

If you know where to find an answer, tell the questioner to try that source, or say you will check and get back to the person. If you don't know where to get the answer, ask for audience suggestions. "Have any of you ever run into a similar problem?" A fellow engineer in the audience may have just finished a project on the topic. Your openness shows respect for the experience in the audience—and enhances your credibility.

Using the Tools in Your Presentation-Power Tool Box

Letting Gestures and Voice Inflection Emphasize Your Points

Animate your talk by using appropriate gestures that match the words you're saying. Use voice inflections, not a Johnny-One-Note monotone. Think about what you're saying, and display a few theatrics to punch your points home. That keeps your audience interested. Just don't overplay, at the risk of looking insincere. *Be yourself*. Imagine that you're just telling a friend the same point, and you'll relax enough to produce a believable emphatic gesture or voice pitch.

Asking Questions to Stay Connected to Your Audience

Asking questions of the audience *during* the talk is another tool in your presentation-power tool box. Questions can help you build rapport, analyze your audience, stifle rebellion, and—most importantly—ensure that you're still connected to your audience.

You have two ways to ask a question. You can make eye contact with a person, call her name, and ask the question. Or you can ask the question and wait for a reply from someone in the audience; if no answer comes forth, call on an individual: "Pat, what do you think?"

Handling Your Visuals Smoothly

As you place, remove, and restack your visuals, keep your motions smooth—and keep the visuals in order.

To ensure the right viewing order, both now and the next time you use the same transparencies or other visuals, number each visual. Use small type at the top-right edge of the visual, where the audience won't notice the number. If you get questions later about an earlier visual, you can re-pull it and then easily replace it after the program, because the number at the top tells you precisely where that visual belongs.

Using Reference Materials as Stage Props

If you want to recommend specific reference books, software, or other resources, have a few such items with you—especially books. Hold up a book when you talk about it. Perhaps open it to a page and read a brief excerpt that supports a point you just made. Such stage props add variety to your visual aids.

What Audiences Complain About Most Often

Audiences turn off quickly to these engineering-presentation culprits:

Complaint	Your Prevention
Speakers who aren't prepared	You are well prepared.
Speakers who read their scripts	You don't. You use a key-point outline on stage.
Big hype; little or no substance	You're giving meaty content.
Speakers who mumble	You don't. You enunciate.
Speakers who don't take control	You do. You're confident.
Participants who hog attention	You disperse attention fairly.

Let's glance back at that last complaint and show you how to keep one or two participants from hogging your attention and annoying the audience.

The Challenging Participants

Occasionally you'll get some overenthusiastic engineers in your audience who, whether they mean to or not, tend to disrupt things. We hate to call them "troublemakers," because that's a rather strong term. They rarely have a nefarious agenda. They either have a sincere interest in your topic, or they just crave some attention.

What do you do with people who are sincerely interested in your subject? (Giving them a hug comes to mind. After all, you've got friends here.) If they are interested, they ask questions. So answer their questions. What about the people who crave attention? Give them some attention. Let's take a closer look at how to do so and yet stay in control.

The world is populated with all kinds of people, and eventually most kinds are going to end up at your presentations. Some are friendly, some are funny, and some are foolish. A few are hostile. So be prepared. And that's the answer to the question that may be in your mind right now: "How do I handle such people?" Be prepared.

First of all, never react harshly or hostilely. If you do, you'll lose audience support. Audiences are smart. They can spot the eccentrics. They know when somebody is about to cross the line or *has* crossed the line; but they expect *you* to handle the eccentrics. So just keep cool. You can do that; and when you do, your audience will silently support you. Keep smiling.

Here are a few tips for handling eccentric, attention-needy participants.

Taming the Talker

We have found that the most common eccentric is the talker: a friendly person who likes to ask lots of questions and loves to talk.

First of all, answer this person's questions, just as you answer everyone else's questions. This person has as much right as anyone else to ask questions.

Talkers are people who just have to release all the pent-up thoughts they have, by talking. So let them talk a bit. If you cut them off too quickly, you risk alienating them and your audience. Let them talk, and then when they take a breath, step in and say, "That's an interesting point. Thank you. Now, moving on through the problem we were discussing ..."

You want to discourage an enthusiast's questions only if the questions become frivolous. When that happens, rephrase the question and direct it back to the person. You can also state the obvious: "That's an interesting point, but I think we're straying a little too far from our topic here."

If you hear a talker making a comment (not asking a question) while you're speaking, ignore it. Just keep talking. Most talkers get the point and refrain after that—*if* you established yourself as the friendly authority at the beginning.

With a persistent talker, maintain eye contact and move close to the person. That works, too, when two or more people are talking among themselves when they should be listening to you. Sometimes all you have to do is subtly make the talkers aware of what they are doing. Your concentration on them and your close physical presence sends a signal that they may be out of line. Smile.

If a talker asks a vague question, just say, "Can you give me a specific example?" The example usually clarifies the question.

If a talker asks a rambling question, interrupt by asking, "I'm not sure I understand your main point." That usually gets the asker straight to the point. Then sincerely try to answer the question.

Handle irrelevant questions by just saying politely, "I don't know the answer to that," or "That's beyond the topic at hand," or (if true) "We'll cover that point later," whichever response is appropriate. Then get back to your agenda. Keep smiling.

We always make it a point in our writing-training workshops to talk personally, during a break, to anyone we've had to stifle during the presentation, to make sure we haven't made an enemy. What we're doing is giving the person the attention he or she craves, but without taking everyone else's time to do it. We recommend that you do the same.

Interrupting the Interrupter

The interrupters are like the talkers. Both are enthusiastic types. They may interrupt other people or even say, "I think what she means is ..."

Just say, "Well, let's let Ellen speak for herself. Go ahead, Ellen." When Ellen finishes, acknowledge the interrupter. "Is that what you were thinking, too, Alan?"

What you want to do is let people have their say, while maintaining control of the group.

Channeling the Expert

Here's the engineer who either knows more than you do or just thinks he does. Okay, so maybe he does. Use him to your advantage.

After discussing a point that you know this person is quite familiar with, ask him a question that acknowledges yet gently challenges his engineering expertise. "Fred, you've probably dealt with this situation. What can you suggest?"

With that nonthreatening approach, you have made him an ally, not an enemy. If he turns into a talker, handle him like a talker.

Sometimes, especially in a company meeting, an engineering expert feels his oats a bit more than he would in a public session. If you know he will be attending your presentation, talk to him beforehand. Tell him what you will be discussing and ask for his support. Surprising as it seems, such a ploy often works.

If the person does not agree and refuses to support your position, you have only one choice. When you get to that subtopic in your presentation, tell the audience that this person does not agree with your position and diplomatically explain why. (Make sure that you know the reason for his opposing view.) There's not much he can do now, because you have blown most of the wind out of his sails.

If you plan to present something controversial, expect some disagreement and be prepared for it. Think of objections that other engineers could raise, and be prepared with facts to overcome those objections. You can also neutralize some experts ahead of time by saying, "What I'm going to discuss now may be controversial. I understand that. All I ask is that you let me present my case. Then we can discuss the pros and cons." With that statement, you gain audience support automatically.

If an "expert" surprises you (perhaps you didn't see her in the audience), don't panic. You know your subject. Stick to your guns. If she shouts, "You're crazy. That'll never work," you might answer, "Crazy people have good ideas, too. Just give me a chance to explain, and then we can discuss the pros and cons."

Einstein's Switch

Albert Einstein was making the rounds of the speaker's circuit, giving the same speech every night to a different group of people. His chauffeur, a man who somewhat resembled Einstein in looks and manner, listened to all the speeches. One night as they were driving to yet another rubber-chicken dinner, Einstein mentioned that he was getting tired of speechmaking and was eager to get back to his laboratory work.

"I have an idea, boss," his chauffeur said. "I've heard you give this speech so many times, I'll bet I could give it for you."

Einstein laughed and said, "Why not? Let's do it."

When they arrived at the dinner, Einstein donned the chauffeur's cap and jacket and sat in the back of the room. The chauffeur gave a beautiful rendition of Einstein's speech and even answered a few questions expertly.

Then a supremely pompous professor asked an extremely esoteric question about anti-matter formation, digressing here and there to make sure that everyone in the audience would know he was nobody's fool about anti-matter formation.

Without missing a beat, the chauffeur fixed the professor with a steely stare and said, "Sir, the answer to that question is so simple that I will let my chauffeur, who is sitting in the back, answer it for me."

What you're doing is asking an impolite person to be polite. The audience knows it and so does the shouter. If she continues to interrupt, say, "It's obvious we disagree on this point, but as I said before, let me give you all the facts and then we can discuss the points of disagreement."

Again you have strengthened your audience support by appealing to the interrupter's sense of fair play, and she knows it. If that doesn't quiet her, say calmly and neutrally, "Anything's worth a try. I just know that the experimental strategy worked in all 10 of our test runs." Then go on with your presentation.

With a large group in an auditorium, you probably won't have many experts interrupting you, because the environment is not conducive to interruptions. People tend to be more intimidated in large groups.

Latecomers, Early-Leavers, and Jumpers

Sometimes you get those who come late or leave early. Some may even do both. Don't single them out for more or less attention. If someone wants to arrive late or leave early, that's his or her choice. If you could invent a magic wand that would make all people arrive on time, you could make a fortune. Until then, don't worry about something you can't control. Just start at your scheduled time, unless most of the group is late.

If the room is nearly empty at starting time and you decide to wait a few minutes, here's one way to respect and use the time of those who have already arrived: Ask them which recent, current, or upcoming projects made them decide to attend today's presentation. Their answers may even spark a few ideas to include as examples in your talk. Just don't embarrass anyone by broadcasting something that was told to you confidentially.

The main time that tardiness can cause a problem for you is when you are doing a problem-solving project as a team, perhaps after the lunch break. In this case, a latecomer is letting his team members down. However, there's little you can do at that point. *Before* the lunch break, though, you can say, "Please return promptly by 1:00 p.m., so that you can help your team solve the engineering problem you have just analyzed together."

Jumpers are the busy people with beepers who keep jumping up to answer phone calls. At the beginning of our workshops, we try to dissuade the jumpers by telling the whole group, "Please turn off all pagers and beepers. Pretend you are away on vacation or a business trip for two days. Your company won't collapse without you between breaks. Please adhere to the schedule; and refrain from going in and out of the room, because that distraction does break the group's concentration. We'll give you enough break time to prevent such interruptions. We'll also give you our full attention, and we ask the same in return—in fairness to all. Your commitment to be here full-time will be well rewarded. The time you invest in the workshop will *save* you a lot *more* time when you get back to the job."

 Ninety-nine percent of the time, that little speech will probably work for you. The other one percent will keep you on your toes.

Faders

You've prepared a solid but interesting engineering presentation, and you're not reading it, so you know you're not boring the group. Are you sure? Okay. Yet there they are: the *faders*.

You know the type we mean: One of them ate a sleep-inducing double portion of lasagna for lunch. Another has an active job that keeps her hopping, rarely allowing her to sit in one spot for very long. Two others have been working late on a pump-and-turbine problem involving the Rankine cycle with superheat and reheat. Someone else is taking a night class in ferrous metallurgy. One engineer came in before dawn this morning to finish up her status report before your session. The guy in the last row just generally gets very little rest (a party animal?). Whatever the reason, they start fading from your fantastic forensics before a break or soon after lunch.

If you sense that you're losing the attention of some in the audience (such as just before the first afternoon break), ask a question. Perhaps call first on a few people seated beside the faders. Just hearing a nearby voice respond to your question may be enough to revive a fader. Then, after that wake-up chance, call on one or two faders themselves. Giving a fair orientation comment, ask for their opinion. That usually helps them snap to attention without embarrassment.

We have now discussed most of the listener types you'll get in your engineering or customer audiences. Luckily, in the presentations you're most likely to give, you will probably not have to worry about the hecklers that frequent Las Vegas lounge shows. Be thankful for small blessings.

The Wrap-Up to a Well-Packaged Talk

You have implemented two-thirds of your on-stage presentation.

- ▶ If you followed your key-point outline, you first oriented your listeners to your *topic* and key *subpoints* at the beginning.

- ▶ Then, in the body, you covered the *explanations* or *technical details* that your audience cares most about.

- ▶ Now, in the close, bring your listeners back full-circle, to tie your *summary* points to the orientation. Stay within your time limit.

For example, let's say you are presenting a technical proposal to your top management.

- ▶ In your opening remarks to top management, you said you would present your justification, three options, and recommendation for upgrading your company's computer system.

- ▶ In the body of your presentation, you explained why your company needs the upgrade, and you compared three computer systems.

- ▶ Now, in the close (wrap-up), you summarize your justification, highlight the main thing your three-product comparison revealed, and recommend the most cost-effective system upgrade, stressing the business benefits.

If, on the other hand, you're wrapping up your training presentation for the 20 new hires who are learning how to do your engineering job, you might recap the main duties of the job, highlight the special problems you discussed, and stress the benefits of a typical solution the group analyzed. Such a training session is also an ideal setting to turn the wrap-up into an oral group quiz, based on those same three parts of your discussion.

How can your audience not love you? Or at least appreciate your well-organized, professionally presented ideas? You're a hit. Acknowledge the applause. It's for you, the engineer-turned-presenter. Congratulations.

What's left to do? Well, a few people may have some follow-up questions for you. You're relaxed and ready.

Enjoying the Question-and-Answer Period

Now that you're the recognized technical expert on the system-upgrade options, your listeners want to pick your complex brain for added hints or applications.

Enjoy the spotlight. You earned it. But *stay alert*.

- ▶ As you listen to each question, concentrate so that you can repeat it if the whole audience couldn't hear it. Then answer the question.

- ▶ Some people ask two-part or even three-part questions, so listen for the key words of the question parts. Put each set of key words into a pocket of your brain, to recall them as you answer the question parts.

- ▶ Just as you did with earlier questions, be sure you understand the question before answering it. Ask for a specific example for clarity.

- ▶ After answering a highly technical or otherwise-complex question, remember to ask, "Did I answer your question?"

- ▶ Before calling again on someone who already asked a question, call on other audience members who have *not* asked a question before. That gives everyone an equal chance to be heard.

- ▶ End on time. If you have not been given a precise time to end the Q&A session, continue answering questions so long as you have an enthusiastic audience. Be happy you captured your listeners' interest.

- ▶ When you sense that the listeners may begin to fidget in their chairs, say that you'll take one more question. After answering that last question, end the program. Offer to stay up front after the program ends, to answer remaining questions (if you have the time).

- ▶ Thank your audience for its attendance, attention, and questions. If you want the audience to do anything at the end (such as complete an evaluation of your talk), request that before you release the group.

- ▶ Read the evaluations right after your session. Enjoy the praise now. Look for constructive criticism, but don't dwell on it until you're ready to apply it to your next presentation.

The scientist and writer Arthur C. Clarke said, "Any sufficiently advanced technology is indistinguishable from magic." When you finish a successful presentation, you can rightly feel that you have applied your knowledge of advanced technology to work your speaking magic.

(Source: James Simon and Robert Parker, compilers, *A Dictionary of Business Quotations*. OUP, London, New York, 1990).

You may even offer to present a technical paper at the next engineering conference. Go for it!

Summary of This Chapter's Main Points

▶ Do all that you can to establish control before and during your talk.

▶ Review your materials, your equipment, and your environment.

▶ Prepare *yourself*. Eat carbohydrates the night before, and eat protein on presentation morning, for energy during your presentation.

▶ Dress professionally and arrive early.

▶ Greet participants at the door. You may turn a scowl into a smile.

▶ Start confidently. Smile, breathe deeply, and speak clearly and slowly. Project your voice to the back row. Involve the audience; ask questions. If you're comfortable with humor, use it.

▶ Orient your audience to key words about the beginning, middle, and end of your talk. Use eye contact, smooth movements, relaxed hands, and clear speech.

▶ Don't speak condescendingly to your audience; communicate with it. Establish two-way communication. Ask "What ..." questions. Smile.

▶ Use equipment and visuals smoothly.

▶ Encourage questions. Repeat them and briefly but carefully answer them.

▶ Keep interest high through gestures, voice inflections, and your own questions to the audience.

▶ Diplomatically maintain control; audiences will respect you.

▶ Summarize the key point(s) of your beginning (orientation), middle (body), and end (close or wrap-up). End your talk on time.

▶ Enjoy the question-and-answer period. Listen and answer thoughtfully.

▶ Thank your audience for its attendance, attention, and questions.

▶ Remind the audience of any immediate action required, such as completing and leaving an evaluation.

20 Leading Productive Meetings

What's Wrong with Meetings?

"Meetings. We can't live *with* them, and we'd like to live *without* them. Meetings take us from our work, waste our time, and don't accomplish much." Those were the weary words of a harried engineer on her way to yet another meeting.

A second engineer, heading to the same meeting, agreed. He added, "Some meetings are held just for the sake of *meeting*, not for a stated *purpose*. We just always meet on Monday morning, because that's what our division has always done."

An engineering manager walking with them said, "My concern is that each meeting costs us a lot of expensive salary time for an hour or two, without always giving the participants, our team, or the company a measurable return on the invested time. I know we need to communicate, but there must be a better way."

If that scene sounds familiar, take heart. Not all meetings are time-wasters. In fact, well-run meetings including well-focused participants can *save* time for all concerned—and save money for the company.

That brings us to the "better way."

You already have a head start toward running a productive meeting. Here's why: The presentation principles you learned in the last two chapters apply to meetings, too.

▶ Even though most meetings are more casual than a presentation, you still want a professional outcome.

▶ You need to plan, prepare, and present what you want to say. You merely run those steps on fast-forward.

▶ You want the participants (just a more-involved audience) to help you accomplish the meeting's purpose.

"Leadership ... the art of getting others to want to do something you are convinced should be done."

—Vance Packard
American writer
(b. 1914)

"Never get angry. Never make a threat. Reason with people."

—Don Corleone
fictional Mafia head
in *The Godfather*
by Mario Puzo
(b. 1920)

This chapter helps you build on the presentation principles, to ensure that nobody leaves your meeting saying it was a waste of time.

Applying the Five W's to Meeting Planning

The journalist's Five W's (*who, what, when, where,* and *why*) definitely apply to meetings.

Before scheduling a meeting, test its worth by asking yourself the following variations on the Five W's.

The *Why* Questions that Prevent Needless Meetings

To help prevent needless meetings—and meeting burnout—on your team, ask yourself these *why* questions:

▶ Why must we meet?

If the meeting is just routine and seems unwarranted, check with those who usually attend, to decide whether you have enough of an agenda to warrant a meeting.

If your team is wrestling with a technical-design problem that requires an immediate solution, your meeting is justified.

▶ Why can't we solve the problem another way: by mail, fax, or phone?

Here's an example of a topic that may *not* require a meeting:

If the agenda includes only one or two brief items, such as your report of operational-amplifier test results showing no problem, ask your manager whether a summary memo would more efficiently use the team's time than a meeting would.

If your manager agrees, write a one-page memo, saying *at the beginning* that the memo replaces the previously planned meeting. Then state the number of operational-amplifier tests you ran, their results, the pertinent summary numbers, and your *interpretation*: what the results mean. Sending that memo (perhaps by E-mail) to the whole team may take a little of your own time but only a few moments of the other engineers' time. You would probably have had to (or already did) document the tests and results, anyway.

The meeting-replacement memo saves the company a lot of salary time on routine topics.

The following topic, on the other hand, justifies a meeting:

Changes in your company have spawned rumors that your upcoming pre-construction soil-analysis project may be canceled. Your group is worried. A group meeting, with management presiding, can prevent the rumors from running wild.

When the answers to the *why* questions tell you that you still need a meeting, it's time to ask the *what* questions.

The *What* Questions That Test a Meeting's Worth

When planning your meeting, test and ensure the meeting's worth by asking these *what* questions:

▶ What must the meeting accomplish? These are common goals:

Goals	Examples
a decision	Decide go/no-go on technical projects.
	Define the best strategy for an upcoming customer-support meeting.
action	Interpret data and vote on what solution/action the team will recommend to upper management.
	Work out the logistics for an upcoming technical conference your company is sponsoring.

▶ What post-meeting action is needed?

▶ What outcome(s) will the decisions, group action, or assigned actions produce? Those outcomes could be consequences or benefits.

▶ What resistance might you meet (either to the meeting itself, or to its outcome)?

The answers to the *what* questions will lead you naturally into the *who* considerations.

The *Who* Questions That Screen the Participants

Before sending out the agenda, decide which people must attend, by asking these *who* questions:

▶ Who should attend the meeting?

   Each participant should have a valid reason for being there, away from his or her current tasks. Usually, the smaller the group, the more productive the meeting will be.

   Include the engineers who are working first-hand on the project being discussed. Together, they can give you a perspective that you might not have considered otherwise.

▶ Who else should attend?

— Who will have to contribute a report, analysis, response, or support about the topics the meeting will include? That contribution might be before, during, and/or after the meeting. Just don't overload the meeting with people having only a peripheral reason for attending.

— Who must help decide the strategy or required follow-up action? Will your meeting minutes or report be enough for the decider, or should the decider also attend?

   For example, if your manager must decide between three consultants you have interviewed, the final preselection meeting(s) should include the deciding manager.

— Who will resist, suffer, or benefit from the meeting or its outcome?

Decide which people may be affected positively or negatively by decisions the meeting produces. Not all such people are appropriate to invite to the meeting, but remember the old "taxation without representation" protest slogan of the early Colonial residents.

Similarly, consider including those whose support you will need for a successful project. You probably will ensure a smoother relationship by including such people in a meeting about the project, but not necessarily in *this* meeting.

All right. You know the *why, what,* and *who* answers. The rest is easier; just work out the logistics: the *when* and *where*.

The *When* Questions That Ensure Good Timing

▶ *When* is the best time for the meeting?

— Do you have a set meeting time, such as a weekly commitment? If not, do a little detective work before you confirm your meeting time, to avoid a scheduling conflict that might diminish your attendance.

— If the meeting is for customers, what is the best strategic timing? Are you about to announce a new product, upgrade, or service? If so, check with your public relations group. Coordinate the most advantageous timing of your meeting. By working with the PR team, you may be able to get extra "mileage" and bonus benefits from your meeting.

— When can you get a meeting room large enough (or small enough) to accommodate the expected number of participants? Reserve it as soon as you tentatively select your meeting date and time.

Even if you're lucky enough to have the same room at your disposal almost anytime, double-check to be sure that some other group hasn't already booked the room for the same time. You may have to go off-site to a hotel or conference center if your usual room isn't available or appropriate.

Plan as far in advance as you can.

▶ When will you check out the meeting room and any audiovisual or other needs to support your meeting agenda? Arrange a pre-meeting visit to any meeting room you haven't used before. If the room won't work for your purposes, early planning will let you change locations before the meeting announcement.

▶ When will you announce the meeting? Give people as much lead time as possible, to get your meeting onto their calendars early. Participants can thus plan for (and schedule around) *your* meeting.

▶ When will you expect follow-up action on the meeting decisions? Be prepared to assign deadlines to such actions.

The *Where* Questions That Technology Supports

Reserve the room *before* announcing the meeting. When you check out possible meeting rooms, consider these *where* questions:

▶ Where is the most convenient meeting site for most of the expected participants?

    If people are coming in from out of town, consider an airport hotel, both for the meeting and for the sleeping-room reservations.

    If most participants are other engineers in your department, do you want a meeting room close to your desks, for convenience, or away from your desks and phones, for fewer interruptions? We usually prefer off-site meetings several buildings or miles away from the engineers' desks. That setting lets all participants concentrate on the meeting content, not on the boss with the nose pressed against the glass partition and with the hand wildly gesturing for someone to answer a phone call.

▶ Where do you have access to technology that you will need during the meeting? For example, if you will need overhead or slide projectors, video-conference equipment, or other special equipment, where can you find it all? Never assume that every meeting room has such equipment.

▶ If you plan to serve a meal before, during, or after the meeting, where will it best be served without interrupting or distracting the participants from the meeting itself?

    If your meeting is in a hotel, the catering staff can set up meals for you. Request light lunches before an afternoon meeting, to avoid losing the group to lasagna lethargy or turkey torpor.

    By the way, when you get good service from a hotel staff, stick with that hotel (a known quantity) for later meetings, too. Your loyalty will be rewarded with peace of mind as you arrange your next meetings.

▶ If the group will convene from scattered points, where will you all meet at the outset? Try to get out-of-town people together when they arrive (perhaps for a night-before dinner or a pre-meeting breakfast) to ensure a prompt, smooth start to the main meeting.

Having answered the Five W's, you have organized your meeting.

A Time-Saving Tool for Results-Oriented Meetings

To prepare people efficiently and keep the meeting on track, consider using a meeting-agenda form that can double as a follow-up meeting summary. The form can eliminate the need for a lot of note-taking during the meeting.

The form could look like our Meeting Minder (which follows).

You can use the Meeting Minder in at least three ways:

1. At least a week before the meeting, fill in the top section and the "Topic" and "Presenter" columns. (List the topics in the logical order you plan to discuss them in the meeting.) Be realistic about how much you can cover in one meeting. Send out the form as an agenda to let people know what to bring with them.

MEETING MINDER

❏ Meeting Agenda   ❏ Meeting Minutes

For (group/committee): _____

Meeting Date: _____ Time: _____ to _____ Bldg./Rm.: _____

To: _____ From (meeting leader): _____

Distrib. Date:_____ Phone:_____ Fax/E-mail: _____

Purpose of meeting: _____

_____

Attending: ❏ _____ ❏ _____ ❏ _____

❏ _____ ❏ _____ ❏ _____ ❏ _____

❏ _____ ❏ _____ ❏ _____ ❏ _____

Absent/reason: _____

Topic	Presenter	Decision	Action Item & Person Responsible	Due Date

Preparation: ❏ Review attachments. ❏ Bring: _____

Comments: _____

Next Meeting Date: _____ Time: _____ to _____ Location: _____

2. Use the Meeting Minder as your map through the meeting.

    ▶ When you start the meeting, have extra Meeting Minder copies available for anyone who didn't bring the sent-out copy. Just having the physical list of topics will help you keep the meeting on track, to accomplish your purpose. Even the talkers (whom we discussed in the preceding chapter) will be less tempted to throw in irrelevant comments.

       If you have several topics to discuss, tell the group how much time you can allot to each topic to avoid running overtime. Then stick to that schedule.

    ▶ During the meeting, discuss the topics in the order listed. Have someone take key-word notes on the form, filling in the action, person-responsible, and due-date columns.

    ▶ Before the end of the meeting, recheck to be sure you discussed all topics and noted who is to do what by when.

3. Immediately after the meeting, fill in all the columns, using key words. The form is now in its second generation—a brief meeting summary that replaces or accompanies meeting minutes. Send it out right away to everyone who attended the meeting and to anyone else who should know the results of the meeting.

    The printed reminder of assigned actions will help reinforce the commitment to complete the assigned actions by the due date.

Your Leadership Role: The Pivot

Your pivotal role as a meeting leader is to start on time, keep the discussion to the point, and end on time. As the discussion moves around the group, you are the central control, keeping the participants' minds turning on the point at hand.

Stick to the agenda. If someone introduces a new topic, just say, "I'll add that topic to the bottom of the agenda, in case we have time to cover it at the end of the meeting." If the new topic does apply to the topic at hand, clarify for the group how it applies to the topic(s) of this meeting. Don't stray from the current topic, though.

If the newly introduced topic has no place, even later, on this agenda, stop the digression by saying diplomatically, "That's a topic for a different meeting. Our job now is to accomplish the purpose of this meeting." The other meeting participants will probably smile thankfully at your wisdom.

Defusing Conflict

Sometimes a meeting discussion can get explosive. As the leader, you're the one who must defuse the dynamite that can destroy your targeted discussion.

To keep the meeting focused on the topic or problem and not on the personalities, remind quarrelers, "We're all here to accomplish the same purpose. Keeping that goal in mind, let's list the pros and cons of this controversial point." By letting people have their say, so long as they're working toward the goal, you may get some fresh ideas for solving a problem.

Channeling the Energy

In the previous chapter, you learned how to control talkers, experts, and other enthusiasts who attend your presentations. You can apply those same tips to your meetings.

Here's an added tip for channeling the talkers and experts: Diplomatically ask them questions about the point you're discussing. After you hear their answers, ask the *group*, "Does anyone have a different perspective we should consider?" That question gives everyone a chance to participate.

Achieving a Productive Finish

Watch the time as your meeting progresses. If you had promised to end at a certain time, keep your promise.

Don't just *stop* the meeting, though. For a professional, productive *finish*, briefly summarize the group's decisions, assigned actions, and due dates. To avoid getting wordy in your oral summary, stay focused on the key words.

Add an overview point about what the group has accomplished in this meeting and what outcome you expect or hope to see. Make that overview point a positive "big picture" that the whole group can "see."

For example:

> Thank you for your focused discussion here today. Your suggestions will help us save time for the whole team on our next pipeline-construction project.

By leaving the group with the positive overview and expected outcome in mind, you help ensure follow-up cooperation.

Following Up to Fulfill Commitments

Participants who see results of their efforts in this meeting will more eagerly attend your next meeting. After all, you're a meeting leader who gets things *done*.

To live up to that reputation, though, you have one more meeting-leader's job: Follow up on the assignments listed on the meeting-summary form you sent out. Did the responsible engineers fulfill their commitment by the due date?

Ideally, *before* the due date for each assigned action, call the person responsible. You can thus check on progress and remind the person of the deadline.

If you don't follow up, you'll be setting a risky precedent that will weaken your credibility. By following up before the due dates, you show that the commitments were serious. When the next meeting rolls around, the people who commit to the next assignments will know you'll insist on fulfilling the group's expectations and the meeting's purpose.

How to Streamline a Meeting When You're Not the Leader

As a participant, you must help keep the discussion focused on the topic and the goal. Here's how:

▶ Listen carefully. Pay attention. Listen for key words that tell you the group is still on the topic at hand.

▶ Ask questions to clarify points and to bring any rambling participants back to the point.

▶ Keep the words *accurate* and *relevant* in mind. Diplomatically question any comment that doesn't seem to be either accurate or relevant.

▶ When you talk, make sure you're contributing to the group's goal. Small talk about personal matters merely delays the pertinent discussion, lengthens the meeting, and frustrates other participants.

▶ Respect the meeting leader's role, and help support that role. If the ending time is near, try to direct the discussion to a summary.

— One easy way is to jump into the discussion with a relevant point, summarizing what you hear as the group consensus to this point.

— Another way to help wrap up the discussion is to ask the leader if you're interpreting the consensus correctly. That method puts the leader back in charge.

Whether you're the leader or an equal participant, you play a key role in ensuring a *productive* meeting.

Summary of This Chapter's Main Points

▶ Apply the Five W's to your meeting planning: who, what, when, where, and why.

▶ Use the Meeting Minder:

— before the meeting, as an agenda.

— during the meeting, to keep the discussion on track.

— after the meeting, as a meeting summary to remind people of their commitments.

▶ In your pivotal role as meeting leader, start on time, keep the discussion to the point, defuse conflict as it arises, and end on time.

▶ Channel the talkers, experts, and other enthusiasts:

— Apply the presentation tips from the previous chapter to your meetings.

— Ask the talker or expert a diplomatic question about the point; after hearing the answer, ask the group for other perspectives.

▶ Ensure a productive finish to the meeting by summarizing the decisions, assigned actions, persons responsible for those actions, due dates, and expected outcome of the group's efforts.

▶ Follow up with participants to ensure fulfilled commitments.

▶ When you're not the leader, support the leader by sticking to the point.

Bibliography

Asimov, Isaac. *Asimov's Biographical Encyclopedia of Science and Technology*. Rev. ed. Garden City, NY: Doubleday & Co., 1982.

_____. *New Guide to Science*. New York: Basic Books, 1984.

Asimov, Isaac, and Jason A. Shulman, eds. *Isaac Asimov's Book of Science and Nature Quotations*. New York: Weidenfeld & Nicolson, Blue Cliff Editions, 1988.

Avallone, Eugene A., and Theodore Baumeister, III, eds. *Marks' Standard Handbook for Mechanical Engineers*. 9th ed. New York: McGraw-Hill, 1978.

Cotterill, Rodney. *The Cambridge Guide to the Material World*. New York: Cambridge University Press, 1985.

Faith, W. L., and Arthur A. Atkisson, Jr. *Air Pollution*. 2nd ed. New York: Wiley-Interscience, John Wiley & Sons, 1972.

Fadiman, Clifton., ed. *The Little, Brown Book of Anecdotes*. Boston: Little, Brown & Co., 1985.

Flaste, Richard, ed. *The New York Times Book of Science Literacy: What Everyone Needs to Know from Newton to the Knuckleball*. New York: HarperCollins, HarperPerennial, 1992.

Glasser, Lance A., and Daniel W. Dobberpuhl. *The Design and Analysis of VLSI Circuits*. Menlo Park, CA: Addison Wesley, 1985.

Havers, John A., and Frank W. Stubbs, Jr. *Handbook of Heavy Construction*. 2nd ed. New York: McGraw-Hill, 1971.

Hazen, Robert M., and James Trefil. *Science Matters*. New York: Doubleday, 1991.

Levey, Judith S., and Agness Greenhall. *The Concise Columbia Encyclopedia*. New York: Columbia University Press, The Hearst Corporation, Avon Books, 1983.

Lindeburg, Michael R., PE. *Civil Engineering Reference Manual*. 6th ed. Belmont, CA: Professional Publications, Inc., 1992.

_____. *Mechanical Engineering Reference Manual*. 8th ed. Belmont, CA: Professional Publications, Inc., 1990.

O'Hagen, John T. *High Rise/Fire and Life Safety*. New York: Dun Donnelley Publishing, 1977.

Patterson, James W. *Wastewater Treatment Technology*. Ann Arbor: Ann Arbor Science, 1975.

Peace Corps. *Water Purification, Distribution and Sewage Disposal*. Washington, 1969.

Pomeroy, Ralph S. *Speaking from Experience*. New York: Harper & Row, 1977.

Portland Cement Association. *Concrete Inspection Procedures*. New York: John Wiley & Sons, 1975.

Robinson, Randall N., PE. *Chemical Engineering Reference Manual*. 4th ed. Belmont, CA: Professional Publications, Inc., 1987.

Rowes, Barbara. *The Book of Quotes*. New York: E.P. Dutton, 1979.

Sabin, William A. *The Gregg Reference Manual*. 7th ed. New York: Macmillan/McGraw-Hill, Glencoe Div., 1992.

Schell, John, and John Stratton. *Writing on the Job: A Handbook for Business and Government*. New York and Scarborough, Ontario: New American Library, A Plume Book, 1984.

Simon, James, and Robert Parker, compilers. *A Dictionary of Business Quotations*. London and New York: OUP, 1990.

Slatkin, Elizabeth. *How to Write a Manual*. Berkeley: Ten Speed Press, 1991.

Timoshenko, Stephen. *Strength of Materials*. 3rd ed. Huntington, NY: Robert E. Krieger Publishing Co., 1976.

U.S. Department of Commerce, National Bureau of Standards. *Computer Science & Technology: Workshop on Standards for Image Pattern Recognition*. NBS Special Publication 500-8, C13.10: 500-8. Washington, 1977.

U.S. Department of the Interior. *Earth Manual: A Water Resources Technical Publication*. 2nd ed. Washington, 1974.

Vincler, James E., and Nancy H. Vincler. *Business Writing Made Easy*. Redwood City, CA: Persuasive Press, Vincler Communications, Inc., 1985.

_____. *The Vincler Writing Workbook*. Rev. ed. Redwood City, CA: Persuasive Press, Vincler Communications, Inc., 1990.

Warriner, John E. *English Composition and Grammar*. Orlando: Harcourt Brace Jovanovich, 1988.

Yarbrough, Raymond B., PE. *Electrical Engineering Reference Manual*. 5th ed. Belmont, CA: Professional Publications, Inc., 1990.

Index